D1245223

MVS Answer Book

MVS Answer Book

David J. Sacks

A Wiley–QED Publication

John Wiley & Sons, Inc.

New York • Chichester • Brisbane • Toronto • Singapore

Designations used by companies to distinguish their products are often claimed as trademarks. In all instances where John Wiley & Sons, Inc. is aware of a claim, the product names appear in initial capital or all capital letters. Readers, however, should contact the appropriate companies for more complete information regarding trademarks and registration.

This text is printed on acid-free paper.

This publication is designed to provide accurate and authoritative information in regard to the subject matter covered. It is sold with the understanding that the publisher is not engaged in rendering legal, accounting, or other professional services. If legal advice or other expert assistance is required, the services of a competent professional person should be sought. FROM A DECLARATION OF PRINCIPLES JOINTLY ADOPTED BY A COMMITTEE OF THE AMERICAN BAR ASSOCIATION AND A COMMITTEE OF PUBLISHERS.

ISBN 0 471-60821-1

Printed in the United States of America

10 9 8 7 6 5 4 3 2 1

Contents

Figures

Preface

This guide came about because I have always believed that anyone supporting or managing MVS systems, or consulting others who do, should understand and be able to communicate the major concepts, principles, and facilities of that complex operating environment. In other words, anyone doing serious work with MVS systems should have a broad level of knowledge including what the relevant products are, what problems they solve, and how the products relate to each other—knowledge that brings order to complexity and provides understanding without the details of "how it works." This is essential for effective, credible consulting and decision making.

This kind of broad knowledge can come from many existing sources, ranging from IBM manuals, to trade journals, to user groups, to personal experience. So why add yet another publication? Because it is often extremely difficult to find the appropriate level of explanation in one place for even one product, let alone for a system of related products. Even when information is found, it is often difficult to separate important principles from less important detail. And it remains true that much useful information is based largely on experience.

This guide addresses these concerns in a unique way. This is the kind of resource I wish had been available when I started working with MVS. I hope you find that true for you, too.

ACKNOWLEDGMENTS

Earlier versions of this guide have been used internally within the IBM Corporation for several years. I would like to thank the many IBM employees around the world who took the time to send me notes of thanks and encouragement.

I would especially like to acknowledge and thank the many people in IBM who have reviewed drafts of this guide, including IBM system engineers in Chicago, and members of the IBM Washington Systems Center, Large Scale Computing Division, and Storage Systems Division organizations. Their feedback and helpful comments have contributed significantly to the quality of this work.

The following terms are trademarks of the IBM Corporation in the United States and/or other countries:

- AD/Cycle (R)
- AS/400 (R)
- CICS
- CICS/ESA
- CICS/MVS
- DB2 (R)
- DFSMS
- DFSMS/MVS
- DFSMSdfp
- DFSMSdss
- DFSMShsm
- DFSMSrmm
- Enterprise Systems Architecture/370
- Enterprise Systems Architecture/390
- ES/3090
- ES/3090-9000T
- ES/4381
- ES/9000
- ES/9370
- ESA/370
- ESA/390
- ESCON
- ESCON XDF
- Hardware Configuration Definition
- Hiperbatch
- Hipersorting (R)
- Hiperspace

- IBM (R)
- IMS/ESA (R)
- KnowledgeTool (R)
- MVS/DFP
- MVS/ESA
- MVS/SP
- MVS/XA
- NetView (R)
- Processor Resource/Systems Manager
- PR/SM
- PS/2 (R)
- Remote PrintManager
- SAA
- Systems Application Architecture
- VTAM (R)
- 3090

(R) These trademarks are registered trademarks of the International Business Machines Corporation
   Other trademarks:

- (E)JES is a trademark of Phoenix Software International.
- NetWare is a trademark of Novell, Inc.

Introduction

The MVS operating system, with origins that can be traced back to the 1960s, is a highly successful operating system that is used by thousands of organizations around the world.

MVS stands for Multiple Virtual Storage, reflecting the fact that its design incorporates an addressing architecture that provides a unique address space to each job in the system. MVS, in concert with related hardware and software products, continues to evolve, allowing IBM customers to benefit from continuing advances in information technology.

In the '90s, organizations are increasingly moving from centralized computing environments to distributed computing environments based on client/server and cooperative processing principles. It might seem that an operating system like MVS, founded in a era of centralized computing, has become an anachronism. This is far from the case. While there are many applications in the world that can run on a single-user personal system, there are also many applications that require systems that manage shared resources such as data bases, and provide shared services such as automated backup of distributed files. Sometimes the shared resources and services can be managed by a small LAN server, but sometimes far greater compute power is needed. MVS supports the large-scale computing facilities and services needed by large-scale applications.

The fact is that the ultimate success of a distributed computing environment depends on the strength of each component system, so that the extensive power and capabilities of MVS are more important than ever in the new world.

This guide focuses on the MVS operating system and key related products—the functions and services, in both software and hardware, that are central to the practical aspects of managing an MVS environment.

How You Can Use this Guide

You can use this guide

- To assess your current knowledge of the MVS environment; technical strengths and weaknesses can be identified.
- To increase your understanding of large systems products and principles.
- To learn about many problems and needs common to MVS installations, and to compare the solutions adopted by your installation to those presented here. In many cases, alternative solutions to problems are discussed.
- As a reference that reviews important large-system topics and points to sources of additional information.

Prerequisites to Using this Guide

This guide assumes some background in an MVS environment and familiarity with common MVS terminology. To get the most out of this guide, most readers should perhaps have at least a year's experience or more in an MVS environment.

How this Guide Is Structured

This guide is written in a question and answer format. You could just read each question and answer together, using this guide as a specialized manual covering many large system topics. However, by using this guide as a self-assessment, you may find it more interesting and stimulating than mere description. There are no grades, and any tracking or follow-up you do is up to you.

Most questions ask for a thoughtful response, discussion, or explanation, rather than for a true/false or multiple-choice answer. The objective is to seek and promote understanding rather than rote response or the ability to correctly guess answers by, say, the process of elimination.

It is intended that the answers/discussions in this guide can stand alone in providing a basic understanding of each topic, without the necessity for outside reading. However, references are identified by numbers at the end of each question and answer. The reference numbers refer to publications listed at the end of this guide.

Product Content

MVS is a very powerful operating system. But the scope of basic function desired in MVS systems has grown so broadly over the years that no single product can reasonably attempt to "do it all." In practice, installations extend the basic MVS control program with additional program products to provide critical functions ranging from security to network management. These products may be from IBM or other software companies. This guide focuses on products marketed by IBM because that is the author's background. It must be stressed, however, that the main intent of this guide is not to promote particular products, but rather to explain and clarify concepts and principles that are important not only in the world of MVS, but also in the broader world of information technology, independent of any particular implementation.

Currency of Information

Version and release levels of major program products referenced in this guide are summarized in Appendix A.

A Note on Product Names

Some products have names that are used "conversationally," and these names may differ from the formal product names. For example, the precise name of the current level of the MVS operating system is MVS/ESA, Multiple Virtual Storage/Enterprise Systems Architecture; this operating system consists of two products: the MVS/ESA System Product and the Data Facility Storage Management Subsystem/MVS (DFSMS/MVS). In the real world, the Time Sharing Option/Extended product is generally referred to as simply TSO rather than TSO/E. Similarly, references to CICS/ESA and IMS/ESA are generally abbreviated to CICS and IMS. This guide will often use the conversational form of product names since this makes for much easier reading, but keep in mind that the names of the actual products that are required for implementation may differ.

References

Reference publications providing background and additional information have been identified by number after each question and answer. The reference numbers refer to publications listed at the end of this guide.

These publications contain the answers to the questions, or provide more detailed or related information. These are publications I found useful in writing this guide. Some discussions include my personal way of looking at things, for which references are not necessarily provided.

While references are cited at the latest available release levels, because new releases of MVS-related software products are generally a superset of the function of previous releases, most of the information in this guide and references applies to many earlier releases as well. MVS is evolving rapidly; in some cases, the guide discusses features and products that have been announced, but for which the standard forms of IBM documentation were not yet available at the time of writing. The DFSMS/MVS product naming conventions are an example of this, so that the newer names such as DFSMShsm appear in the guide, but the older name DFHSM appears in the references. On the other hand, some references cited were written prior to the availability of MVS/ESA and may not have been updated since original publication; this is particularly true of technical bulletins. However, the information they contain—certainly the information relevant here—generally continues to apply to the latest releases of MVS/ESA.

A Word of Caution

The information in this guide, while believed correct, may not be as comprehensive or complete as possible, and additional information will likely be needed in specific situations to implement solutions discussed here. For example, this guide does not attempt to identify product dependencies or to project product performance in any given environment.

This guide is not a substitute for standard sources of information such as product manuals written by the IBM development laboratories, nor is it a substitute for the normal research and analysis that is required to match solutions to requirements.

Selected portions of this guide have been reviewed by IBM development laboratories. While their comments have been incorporated into this guide, all responsibility for accuracy is the author's.

Job Management

The purpose of a computer system is to process work. In MVS, the major unit of work is a *job*, which can range from a traditional batch application to an individual TSO user. All jobs are described to MVS by Job Control Language (JCL). JCL specifies various attributes of the job such as the name of the job, programs to be run, required data sets, associated account numbers, required virtual storage, and so on.

The flow of jobs into and out of the system is managed by one of the two MVS job entry subsystems, JES2 and JES3. Generally speaking, MVS controls jobs during execution; JES2 and JES3 control jobs before and after execution through mechanisms for job submission, SYSOUT processing, and job networking.

QUESTION 1—COMPARING JES2 TO JES3

An installation is planning to move to MVS from another operating system. Part of the planning process requires the installation to select one of the two MVS job entry subsystems, JES2 and JES3. Describe the basic differences between these two job entry subsystems.

This discussion is not a recommendation for one subsystem over the other; rather, it reviews some of the many issues that need to be considered when making a choice. Let's begin with some background, reviewing the fundamental role in the scheme of things played by either JES2 or JES3.

A job is a named unit of work. A job is defined by a language called Job Control Language (JCL) that specifies the job's name, programs to be executed, data sets to be used, SYSOUT characteristics, and so forth. A job is submitted (entered) into the system by giving the JCL that defines the job to an MVS component called the *job entry subsystem.* In MVS there are two mutually exclusive subsystems: JES2 and JES3; there is no JES1. We'll use the term JES when referring to basic functions performed by either subsystem.

Years ago (and even today in a few installations), JCL was submitted to JES through reading a deck of punched cards into a card reader. Today, a job's JCL generally resides in a data set on disk and is submitted by operator commands or through JES program services called "internal readers." Often, a job-scheduling package such as OPC/ESA will be used to automate the job submission process, submitting jobs to internal readers according to installation schedules.[1]

When JES receives a job, it copies the JCL into a JES-controlled data set called a *spool.* Based on job priority and other factors, JES eventually passes the job to an MVS *initiator,* which is a facility in MVS for supporting the execution of a single job. The number of active initiators is controlled by console operators.

As a job runs, it can create one or more SYSOUT data sets. JES will maintain SYSOUT in its spool and eventually print it on printers under JES control. When a job has completed running and all its SYSOUT is printed, JES purges all information about the job from its spool.

These basic services are provided by both JES2 and JES3. Both JESs also provide remote job entry and job networking capabilities (see "Question 3—Remote Job Entry and Network Job Entry").

We've described basic job flow from JES's point of view. Let's look a

---

[1]Internal readers allow running jobs to dynamically submit other jobs. An internal reader is implemented as a SYSOUT data set with a writer name of INTRDR. In JCL this is specified as

```
// DD SYSOUT=(class,INTRDR).
```

The submitting program OPENs the data set and writes JCL statements to it. JES receives these statements since JES handles all SYSOUT processing and knows the data is really JCL because of the special writer name.

little deeper to understand some of the differences between JES2 and JES3.

Who Is in Control?

Some of the most significant differences between JES2 and JES3 are in how they manage a complex of multiple MVS images (multiple instances of the MVS operating system).

A single MVS image can be managed by either JES2 or JES3. While there are differences in this case (such as operator commands and special JES JCL statements), they tend to be of less significance than the differences in a multisystem environment, so we'll focus on that.

An installation with multiple MVS images can choose to have the JES2 spool shared by all the JES2 systems. Such a complex is called a *multiaccess spool configuration (MAS)*. Each system can *independently* submit jobs, execute jobs, and process SYSOUT. For example, if system A submits a job, either system A or system B could execute it, and its SYSOUT data sets could be printed by system A, or B, or C, or all three. It's a matter of installation policy. There are benefits to sharing in this way. Sharing spool space and printers may mean less space and printers are needed than if multiple JES2 systems ran in isolation. And there is a chance for a less busy system to run jobs submitted by a busier system. But note that this workload balancing is somewhat static. JES2 does not dynamically balance work—work is scheduled wherever there are free initiators. Operators can attempt to balance work manually by issuing commands to start and stop initiators.

In contrast, a JES3 complex provides *centralized* control: a master/slave relationship. One JES3 system, called the "global," is responsible for scheduling jobs across all systems in the complex, within constraints specified by the installation. Communication between images is via channel-to-channel adapters.

JES3 offers other job-scheduling capabilities not supported by JES2, such as deadline scheduling. See "Question 2—Automating Batch Job Scheduling" for a further comparison of job-scheduling capabilities.

JES3 can also control devices shared by the systems in a JES3 complex. For example, all tape drives are treated as a single pool and are allocated and unallocated by JES3. Since JES2 systems lack this centralized approach, operators must control which tape drives are online to which hosts so that multiple systems do not allocate the same tape drives at the same time (remember, tape drives are inherently unshareable). Some JES2 multihost complexes install non-IBM programs to provide this kind of centralized tape management.

Interactive Access

In a JES2 environment, the System Display and Search Facility (SDSF) licensed program runs under TSO/E and can be used (usually by systems programmers or operators) to monitor system activity, to display SYSOUT data sets while still in JES2 spool, and to display the MVS system log (SYSLOG) of message activity. In a JES3 environment, the E(JES) licensed program provides similar capabilities.[2]

Device Allocation

This topic is a bit more subtle and is probably the most difficult to understand, so hang in there.

In preparation for execution, the job as a whole first goes through a phase aptly called *job initiation*. As each job step executes, it first goes through *step initiation*. A major part of the initiation process is the allocation (assignment) of data sets and devices to a job according to the DD statements in its JCL.

The allocation process includes two parts. One is data set name allocation, which uses the MVS ENQ mechanism to ensure jobs can access requested data sets in either shared or exclusive mode, as specified by the DISP parameter on DD statements, for example, DISP=SHR. The second part is called device allocation. Device allocation is the way the system assigns devices to jobs. That's easy for permanently mounted DASD, because jobs can share DASD volumes. However, tape drives and many other devices are not shareable, and therefore each such device can be assigned to only one job at a time.

With that background in mind, let's look at how JES2 and JES3 differ in their handling of the data set name and device allocation processes. After that, we'll discuss some ramifications of these differences.

In either a JES2 or JES3 system, data set name allocation is performed for all DD statements in the entire job before the program named in the first job step is given control. In the case of JES2, MVS may detect a conflict such as a job requesting exclusive use of a data set that another job is currently using. If such a conflict does exist, the

---

[2]E(JES) is marketed by Phoenix Software International, an IBM Business Partner.

operator is informed and can let the new job wait or can cancel either job. On the other hand, JES3 ensures that all data sets are available to a job before it even presents the job to MVS initiation. This means that by the time the job does go through MVS initiation, there will be no data set usage conflicts to handle, allowing that part of initiation to always proceed swiftly. In this way, the operator need not get involved.

Let's move on to device allocation. An MVS/JES2 system uses the native device allocation algorithms in the MVS control program. Devices are allocated on a job step basis—as each step is initiated, it goes through the device allocation process. If a needed device is not available at that time, the operator is informed and can let the job wait or can cancel the job.[3]

An MVS/JES3 installation can elect to have JES3 device allocation algorithms override those of MVS. The JES3 function is called "setup." While there are variations on this theme, in the most extreme option JES3 setup allocates all devices needed by all steps of a job and ensures all tape mounts have been completed *before* the job is passed to an MVS initiator.

In both JES2 and JES3 systems, data set names and devices are released after the last step of a job that needs them, rather than unnecessarily being held until the job ends.

As an aside, don't confuse JES3 setup with the (less sophisticated) optional setup function that is supported by JES2 for tape devices only. JES3 setup requires no special JCL. On the other hand, JES2 setup requires specifying volume serial numbers in a special /*SETUP job statement. The operator is requested by JES2 to mount the named volumes when the job is submitted to JES2; JES2 will place the job in hold status until the operator manually releases the job (presumably after the volumes have been mounted, but nothing enforces this).

That completes the basics of how JES2 and JES3 device and data set name allocation work. The rest of this discussion will look at some ramifications of all this.

The native MVS allocation scheme used in JES2 environments, and the JES3 scheme that can optionally override it, represent differing philosophies and the intent to optimize the use of different resources. The central idea behind the JES3 scheme is to optimize use of MVS initiators and thus the processor(s), by preventing delays in allocation once the job is initiated; the idea is to move work through the system

---

[3]As of MVS/ESA SP V4, the installation can define a policy that can eliminate the need for the operator to make this decision. The policy is specified in the ALLOCxx member of SYS1.PARMLIB.

efficiently by never having an initiator wait for data sets, devices, or mounts. On the other hand, the idea behind native MVS allocation is to optimize the use of devices, keeping them allocated for as little time as possible so they are more likely available when other jobs need them.

An advantage of the native MVS scheme is that devices are only allocated to the steps that need them; this makes it more likely that the devices are available when other jobs need them. A disadvantage is that this can cause unexpected delays that may lower the effective utilization of the system—that is, lower potential productivity. Consider an example, using fictitious numbers. Assume that all MVS initiators are busy executing jobs and that the processor is 100 percent utilized; when one of the jobs has to wait for a tape drive to be allocated and a volume to be mounted, utilization may decline to 90 percent. Since all initiators are busy, no new job can be started to take advantage of the temporarily available capacity. However, at least in theory, skilled operators could start additional initiators in order to provide more work for the processor.

An advantage of the JES3 scheme is that initiators are never waiting for something like a tape mount, or for another job to free up a tape drive. Work can flow freely through the system, maximizing use of the processor resource. A disadvantage is that devices are allocated to a job even during early steps when they are not needed, making them unavailable to other jobs that might otherwise be ready to execute.

You can't win them all.

Closing Remarks

JES2 is primarily a single-system design that has been extended to support some sharing efficiencies in multisystem environments. JES3 is primarily a multisystem design. In practice, there are many more JES2 than JES3 installations. JES3 tends to be implemented more frequently in larger installations than in smaller ones.

Intense intellectual battles have been waged over which JES is better. It is interesting to note that the MVS sysplex capability is beginning to provide the JES2 world with a single-image operational capability integrated into the base MVS system (there are sysplex benefits for JES3 as well).

(References: 84, 86, 87, 97, 98, 123.)

QUESTION 2—AUTOMATING BATCH JOB SCHEDULING

Although the number of interactive applications has been constantly increasing, a significant amount of batch processing continues to exist in most data processing installations. What major facilities are available to assist MVS installations in automating batch job scheduling?

There are several facilities in MVS and associated products that assist in automating batch job scheduling; these are presented below, roughly in order of increasing function.

NetView and Automated Operations Control/MVS (AOC/MVS)

NetView alone, and NetView augmented by AOC/MVS, are systems management products that assist in automating many aspects of MVS operations. In particular, these products include facilities for automating simple time-driven events. Commands and procedures (such as starting a batch job) can be automatically initiated at a given time of day, day of the year, or repetitively at specified intervals.

JES2

JES2 offers an automatic command facility that assists with very simple scheduling tasks. Using this facility, an operator for a JES2 system can issue a JES2 command ($TA) that specifies other commands to be automatically issued at a given time of day, or repeatedly at a specified interval. For example, this facility could be used to start a job automatically at the same time every day.

JES2 also supports a priority aging feature that will periodically increase a job's priority within its class depending on the length of time the job has been in the system. Thus the longer a job waits to run, the higher its chances of being selected to run.

JES3

JES3 has a priority aging scheme similar to JES2, but JES3 increases a job's priority based not on how long the job has been in the system, but on how often the job has been passed over for selection.

JES3 provides a deadline job scheduling facility. This allows an installation to specify, via JCL and JES3 parameters, that JES3 is to periodically increase a job's priority in order to increase the probability that the job will begin execution by a given time and date.

JES3 also supports dependent job control scheduling. Through JCL, an installation can specify that a group of jobs must execute in a specified order.

Operations Planning and Control/ESA

The Operations Planning and Control/ESA (OPC/ESA) program product provides comprehensive functions to help an installation manage most facets of the batch job scheduling process. OPC/ESA can supplement either JES2 or JES3. Some major OPC/ESA facilities include the following:

- Helping installations prepare long- and short-range job schedules.
- Scheduling the work to be run while taking into account job priorities and the dependencies among jobs and different groups of jobs.
- Providing functions to automate job restart and recovery.
- Supporting online status inquiries of various batch operations.
- Allowing manual intervention as needed.
- Providing increased availability in an MVS sysplex by allowing for a hot standby copy of OPC/ESA on one MVS image to take over the duties of a "controller" copy of OPC/ESA running on another MVS image (if the controller fails or the MVS image fails).

(References: 5, 12, 86, 87, 98, 109.)

QUESTION 3—REMOTE JOB ENTRY AND NETWORK JOB ENTRY

A small company has always run a data center with only a single host system supporting locally attached hardware. The business is expanding to remote locations, and there will be a need to transmit jobs and reports to and from remote sites. The data processing manager knows that these kinds of functions are supported by system facilities called RJE (or RJP) and NJE, but doesn't understand exactly what they do or how they differ. Can you provide a basic overview of RJE and NJE?

RJE stands for Remote Job Entry,[4] and NJE stands for Network Job Entry.

RJE and NJE perform similar, but not identical, functions that allow objects related to job processing—JCL, output listings, and operator commands and messages—to be routed between remote sites.

You can think of RJE and NJE as generalized applications that use communication facilities to provide distributed *job* processing networks, just as CICS and IMS are generalized applications that use communication facilities to provide distributed *transaction* processing networks. The generalized application only provides the vehicle—it's up to the installation to provide the objects (jobs or transactions) to send from one place to another.

RJE and NJE are supported by MVS as well as by VM and VSE. In the case of MVS, these functions are available as standard facilities of JES2 and JES3.

Remote Job Entry

RJE provides the ability for remote *workstations* to submit jobs to and receive output from a host system (such as an ES/9000) attached by teleprocessing links. The output sent to a workstation can come from jobs submitted by that workstation, or from any other job; the destination of SYSOUT data sets can be specified on JCL statements.

Note that a "remote" location can vary from a department in the same building as the host system to a site in a different country. RJE allows job output to be electronically delivered to a remote location rather than manually delivered from the host site. This can greatly reduce job turnaround time; of course, someone at the remote site has to handle the operation of the workstation, including changing paper in the printer when necessary.

Here are examples of typical RJE workstations:

A 3780 combination card reader and printer designed solely as an RJE workstation. This is an older workstation type. There is no console for operator communication to the host, though it may be possible to send operator commands on punched cards as part of a submitted job. Because of its historical popularity, some products

---

[4]"RJE" is really a JES2 term. JES3 offers Remote Job Processing (RJP) to provide the same kinds of facilities. In this discussion only the term RJE will be used.

emulate the 3780 even today (i.e., send and receive the same data streams) in order to provide an RJE workstation function.

A printer attached to a 3X74 communications control unit. This is an output-only workstation. JES2 and JES3 do not directly support printers attached to a 3X74 but can do so indirectly through use of the JES/328X Print Facility program. A similar function is provided by the VTAM Printer Support System (VPS) product.[5]

A System/36, System/38, or AS/400 which, in addition to their normal data processing functions, can serve as RJE workstations. For example, some installations have used a System/36 with an attached 4245 printer as a dedicated RJE workstation. Other installations might use an AS/400 for general data processing functions as well as for occasional RJE work. These "midrange" RJE stations can use the standard console to communicate with JES on the host. Disk storage is also supported, which can be used to accept output listings for later processing (just as JES spool does on the host) and to store jobs to be sent to the host on request by an operator.

Network Job Entry

NJE allows host systems to transmit jobs and output among each other. The hosts are connected through teleprocessing links or (except for VSE) through channel-to-channel connections.

You might think of NJE as allowing mainframes to act as RJE stations to other mainframes. In contrast to RJE, where a host accepts jobs from and sends SYSOUT to remote workstations, the participants in an NJE network can both send and receive jobs and SYSOUT from each other, a so-called peer-to-peer arrangement. In fact, the origination and destination nodes of a job or output data set need not be directly connected but can be connected through intermediate NJE nodes.

NJE is a set of protocols that has evolved over time and is supported by various products. For example, MVS/JES2, MVS/JES3, VM/RSCS (Remote Spooling Communications Subsystem), and VSE/POWER can all participate in the same NJE network. Of course, jobs sent from one system to another must conform to the job control language on the target system in order to be processed correctly; output processing is not so restricted.

---

[5]This product is available from Levi, Ray & Shoup, Inc., and is marketed through the IBM Cooperative Marketing Program.

Some system facilities use NJE to implement their function. For example, the TSO/E Interactive Data Transmission Facility uses NJE to allow TSO/E users to exchange messages and data sets with users on other nodes, via TSO/E TRANSMIT and RECEIVE commands.

Here's an example of a network that uses functions of both RJE and NJE, indicating the flexibility available. See Figure 1.1. The three host systems are in different cities. JES2 is using VTAM to support communications. A job can be sent to any host for execution, and its SYSOUT can be routed to any or all of the hosts, including RJE workstations connected to any of the hosts. Thus RJE Workstation1 could submit a job to SanFran that is to be passed to the Chicago system for execution. SYSOUT could be printed at Chicago and also routed to Workstation1 and Workstation2.

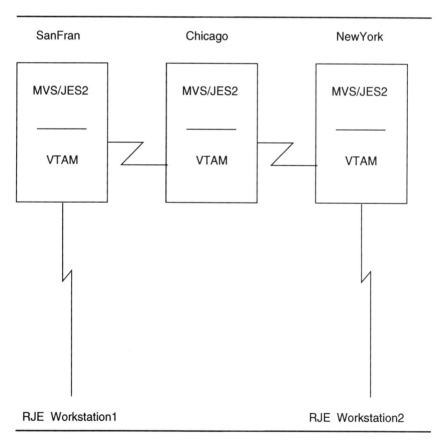

Figure 1.1.   Sample NJE/RJE network.

Closing Remarks

While the above discussion covers the basics, there is a lot more that could be said about RJE and NJE. Some additional topics to explore include different workstation types, parameters that define RJE and NJE nodes to JES, related operator commands, JCL support, and performance considerations.

(References: 39, 61, 62, 86, 87, 106, 107.)

QUESTION 4—DELIVERY OF SYSOUT DATA SETS

A manager of computer operations tells you that he is receiving an increasing number of complaints from users about the length of time it takes to deliver SYSOUT listings. In addition, listings are sometimes lost and users have to rerun their jobs to recreate them. What recommendations can you make to improve the SYSOUT delivery time and overall management of SYSOUT data sets?

Avoiding Job Reruns

Normally, after a SYSOUT data set is printed, it is immediately deleted from the JES spool. Thus, if a SYSOUT listing is lost or extra copies are requested later, jobs would need to be rerun or copies made manually.

MVS/ESA-JES2 Version 4 introduced JCL options to retain SYSOUT data sets on JES2 spool after printing so that they can be reprinted without requiring the jobs that created the SYSOUT to be rerun. This capability is most useful for reports that couldn't easily or quickly be recreated if they were lost. To prevent use of this facility from causing the DASD space used to hold SYSOUT data sets from growing uncontrollably, the MVS operator can issue a JES2 command to delete "held" (JES2's term for retained) SYSOUT data sets. For example, the JES2 $O command with the DAYS=n parameter would delete held SYSOUT created over n days ago.

Speeding SYSOUT Delivery

The more traditional solutions to improve the speed of SYSOUT delivery include additional printers, faster printers, and printers located nearer to users to reduce delivery time. Printers can be located at extended distances from the computer using several technologies.

- ESCON channel architecture extends the distance of channel-attached printers beyond the limits imposed by the older, parallel channel architecture.
- "Channel extender" technology is available in the marketplace. This technology uses special equipment to allow printers (and other devices) that are designed to only be attached to channels to actually be attached to a network. Many impact printers are designed only for direct attachment to processor channels, for example. From the points of view of MVS, the processor, and the printer, the use of a network is transparent. A typical configuration looks something like this:

```
processor ———————— C/E box ——┐
           channel            └— C/E box ——————— printer
           cable                          channel
                                          cable
```

This allows total flexibility in placement of printers that only support channel attachment and thus limited distances.
- RJE (remote job entry) printers can be connected to the host over a network, allowing essentially unlimited distances. RJE printers can include those supported directly by JES2 or JES3, or supported indirectly through the JES/328X Print Facility product or other, similar non-IBM products.
- PSF/MVS (Print Services Facility) is a licensed program that supports page mode printers such as the IBM 3820.[6] JES2/JES3 will direct SYSOUT files to PSF/MVS based on JCL specifications. The page mode printers controlled by PSF/MVS can be attached to channels, or by an ACF/VTAM SNA network allowing for unlimited distances. In one variation, PSF/MVS can route SYSOUT to a page mode printer attached to a personal computer, such as an IBM PS/2, that is running IBM's Print Services Facility/2 (PSF/2) licensed program.[7] In this configuration the PS/2 can be a print server, sharing the printer with MVS and other PCs on a local area network (LAN).

---

[6]Page mode printers are generally nonimpact printers using laser technology similar to that used in paper copiers, providing very high-quality output and potentially higher throughput than impact printers. Page mode printers are sometimes called "all points addressable" printers.

[7]PSF/2 replaces the older IBM Remote PrintManager program, which IBM withdrew from marketing in 1993.

- The LANRES/MVS licensed program supports distributed printing. MVS files to be printed can be routed to a printer on a NetWare LAN that can be any distance from the MVS host. Similarly, a file can be routed from a NetWare LAN workstation client to an MVS host to take advantage of MVS as a print server supporting shared high-speed printers. The advantage of printing a document near the user is obvious, but why send a document to a central site for printing? A good reason is that the time it takes to print large documents, or many copies of even small documents, can be dramatically reduced by printing them on a high-speed page printer like the IBM 3900, which prints multiple pages per second, compared to the many seconds per page it takes to print documents on many workstation printers.

Avoiding Paper Output

The following solutions provide ways to display SYSOUT listings interactively from a terminal, perhaps avoiding the printing of many SYSOUT data sets altogether. This can improve effective delivery time and possibly reduce costs associated with printing and manual delivery.

- In both the JES2 and JES3 environments, licensed programs are available that allow users to view SYSOUT while it is still in JES spool prior to printing. This function is provided by IBM's System Display and Search Facility (SDSF) in the JES2 environment and by (E)JES in the JES3 environment.[8] Both programs run under TSO ISPF/PDF; (E)JES runs in other environments as well, such as CICS.

    The primary purpose of SDSF and (E)JES is to provide interactive facilities of particular value to operators and systems programmers. Viewing SYSOUT data in spool is only one of these facilities. Therefore, in practice, the use of these programs may be restricted to an installation's technical support staff.
- TSO/E provides an OUTPUT command to display, save in a data set, print, or delete SYSOUT data sets. ISPF/PDF provides a user-friendly interface to this function, called the OUTLIST UTILITY. SYSOUT data sets to be displayed in this way must currently be in a "held" state, which means that JES is retaining the data sets in spool rather than printing and purging them immediately as usual.

---

[8](E)JES is marketed by Phoenix Software International, an IBM Business Partner.

Users can request that SYSOUT be held when they create the
SYSOUT data set (e.g., via a JCL parameter). The SDSF, (E)JES,
and OUTPUT techniques only display SYSOUT data sets residing
in JES spool. Installations using these techniques will have to
monitor the use of spool space since there may be a tendency for
users to let listings accumulate over time.

• A more comprehensive solution to the problem is the Report Management and Distribution System (RMDS), a program product that
maintains selected SYSOUT data sets in standard DASD data sets
outside of JES spool. SYSOUT data sets to be managed in this way
are retrieved from JES spool by RMDS based on SYSOUT class,
rather than being printed. Users of RMDS can access their reports
online through TSO/E, CICS, IMS, or an RMDS VTAM application.
The reports can be kept on DASD, or can be printed or deleted. Of
course, DASD space is required to hold the reports. DFSMShsm
could be used to manage this space efficiently; for example, reports
unreferenced for some number of days can be migrated to tape or
other DASD device in a compacted form, or even deleted automatically.

(References: 2, 18, 43, 59, 61, 63, 85, 95, 123, 129.)

2

Operations

Computing systems are machines. Like other machines, they require some amount of manual operation. Because computers can be very complex machines, especially large systems running many jobs and supporting many users, the associated operational tasks are many and may even require a crew of people. These tasks may range from powering on the processor, to starting the operating system and subsystems, to mounting and removing portable storage media, to monitoring system activity and responding to error conditions.

Broadly, system operators are responsible, on a moment-to-moment basis, for controlling the "system" and delivering service to users. At a time when users are demanding ever-higher levels of service, the MVS operations environment is becoming increasingly complex due to greater system capacity, increased workloads, larger message volumes, and larger and more complex networks. The questions below address ways to better manage MVS operations and reduce operational complexity.

QUESTION 5—CONSOLE AVAILABILITY

An installation is reviewing its hardware configuration in order to provide improved system availability before an important new application goes online. You are asked to provide recommendations for a high-availability console configuration. What recommendations would you make?

The following recommendations are based on the general principle of avoiding single points of failure, plus some special considerations for MVS operations.

At least two operator consoles should be configured; they would be defined to MVS as a master console and its alternate. The consoles should be on different paths; this means they should be attached through different control units on different channels (or, one could be the system console, discussed below). Depending on the processor model, it may also be important to place the control units only on certain channels to avoid sharing single points of failure within the channel implementation; for example, on a 4381-24 dual processor the two channels should be associated with distinct central processors, since if a central processor fails, then access to all its associated channels is lost.

In addition to standard 3270-type consoles, on selected IBM processors the system console can be defined as an MVS console. The system console is the console from which system IPL is requested; it is "hard wired" into the system rather than attached via a channel. The capability of using the system console also as an MVS console is referred to as "console integration." Because the system console is not designed to support heavy message traffic—and MVS message traffic can be very heavy in larger systems—using the system console also as an MVS console may not be practical unless sufficient automation has been implemented to minimize message traffic.

There are additional considerations due to the way MVS attempts to recover from certain error conditions such as spin loop timeouts or Hot I/O through communicating with the operator. This communication is called "synchronous" since other system activity is stopped until the message is successfully issued and an operator reply is received. (Prior to MVS/ESA SP V4, the facility that managed this communication was called the Disabled Console Communications Facility (DCCF), referring to the fact that other system activity was disabled during the communication.)

MVS goes through a somewhat complex process to select consoles eligible for synchronous communications. See reference 90 for details.

If selected consoles are sharing their control units with other terminals, or are not attached to the highest-priority control unit on their channels, then other activity (such as users pressing keys on their keyboards) may cause the communication attempt to fail. The system will then enter a restartable wait state. The operator can still recover the system but may have to alter processor storage to do so, which is rather risky.

These exposures lead to the recommendations that the control units intended by the installation to be eligible for synchronous communications be dedicated to those consoles only, and that those control units should be set by the hardware service representative to be the highest-priority control units on their respective channels.

There is another way to avoid the exposures. The optional SYNCHDEST parameter in the CONSOLxx member of SYS1.PARMLIB allows the installation to specify which consoles are eligible to receive synchronous messages. By specifying only consoles that are known to satisfy the above guidelines, which includes the system console, the exposures are avoided.

In practice, most installations follow the recommendation of having multiple consoles on multiple control units, avoiding a single point of failure. However, many, if not most, installations do not dedicate control units to a single console, but instead share control units among operator consoles and other terminals such as TSO terminals. Those installations have decided that the increased ability to recover from certain (hopefully rare) error conditions is not worth the cost of extra control units. The SYNCHDEST parameter specifying the system console may provide improved availability for these installations, without increased cost.

(References: 40, 41, 46, 90, 93.)

QUESTION 6—CHANGING CONSOLE DISPLAY MODELS

A data center manager complains that schedules were recently impacted because a new I/O configuration definition and corresponding test time were required due to upgrading operator consoles to newer models with larger screen sizes. What suggestion can you make to facilitate this process in the future?

When devices intended for use as consoles, and their control units, support the 3270 data stream and the Read Partition Query Feature, the devices can be defined to the system as a device type of 3270-X. The CONSOLxx members in SYS1.PARMLIB should correspondingly specify UNIT(3270-X).

When the specific model number is omitted in this way, MVS issues a channel command to the device when the system is initialized or the device is varied online in order to determine device characteristics such as screen size. This allows the device type to be changed without having to redefine it to MVS.

(References: 84, 90.)

QUESTION 7—VIEWING SYSLOG DATA

An installation has several 3270-type consoles and a printer that serves as a hard-copy console. In the process of diagnosing a problem with production batch jobs, the operators needed to review commands and messages issued several minutes ago. The operators went to retrieve the hard-copy output from the printer, but, unfortunately, the printer had malfunctioned and key parts of the listing were unreadable. How else could the operators review previous console activity?

Past console activity, commands and messages, can be retained within the system's JES2 or JES3 spool data set in an area called the system log (SYSLOG) until printed on command, or automatically if it grows too large. There are licensed programs available that can display SYSLOG contents within the spool data set. In JES2 environments, the System Display and Search Facility (SDSF) displays information in the JES2 spool data set, including SYSLOG, to a TSO user. In JES3 environments, the (E)JES licensed program provides a similar function.[9]

There are advantages to an interactive approach, besides not having to manage paper listings. Both SDSF and (E)JES allow users to easily scroll back and forth through SYSLOG and to search for character strings of interest. On the down side, a display screen can't be marked up with comments the way a hard-copy listing can. Note that SDSF and (E)JES also provide other facilities, such as the ability to enter operator commands and view responses, which is very useful for casual operator activity.

(References: 90, 123.)

QUESTION 8—DISPLAYING TAPE LABELS

An operator found a tape cartridge lying under some manuals in the tape library. The external label on the cartridge that would have identified the tape was unreadable. How might the operator determine the volume serial number of the tape and what data sets are on the tape?

---

[9](E)JES is marketed by Phoenix Software International, an IBM Business Partner.

The MVS program product called DITTO (Data Interfile Transfer, Testing, and Operations) is a utility that can produce a map of the contents of a tape volume. The map identifies the volume serial number from an internal label on the tape as well as the names of data sets from other internal labels on the tape.

DITTO also supports many other functions useful to operators and systems programmers. For example, with DITTO you can do the following:

Browse the contents of a tape on a display screen.

Compare the contents of two tapes.

Copy one tape to another.

Print the contents of a tape.

Display the Volume Table of Contents (VTOC) of a DASD volume.

Print disk records in dump or character format.

Search for a specific string of data within a tape or DASD data set.

(Reference: 69.)

QUESTION 9—MANAGING SCRATCH TAPES

Most MVS data centers implement tape volume management systems such as IBM's DFSMSrmm (removable media manager). These systems provide inventory management of tape volumes and help control aspects of tape processing. In particular, a major benefit of these systems is in helping to manage the process of assigning tape volumes to new data sets. How do tape volume management systems help manage this process? Why aren't there similar products for DASD?

To understand the issues, it is helpful to start by looking at how space is managed on DASD volumes.

Every DASD volume contains a VTOC—Volume Table of Contents—that identifies the *extents* (cylinder and track locations) where data sets reside. MVS creates new data sets, extends existing data sets, and deletes existing data sets by manipulating the extent information in the VTOC. MVS ensures that new and extended data sets are always placed in extents not occupied by other data sets. A DASD data set may optionally be assigned an expiration date or retention period, but that capability is used infrequently in practice. This is because once a DASD data set is created, it can only be deleted by an overt action such as specifying a JCL parameter or a DFSMS/MVS space management policy.

Tape volumes do not contain location information analogous to the extent information in a VTOC. This is because of the sequential nature of tape media. Most tape volumes only contain a single data set, written continuously from the beginning of the tape. If a tape volume contains multiple data sets, successive data sets just follow one another on the media.

How is a tape data set deleted? Specifying DELETE in JCL actually does nothing physically to the tape; at most it may remove the data set name from the catalog, but even then a job could still access the data set by specifying the tape volume serial number directly. In reality, an existing tape data set is only deleted when it is physically overwritten by a new data set (which has obvious security implications, but that's another story).

A request to place a new data set on tape generally doesn't identify a specific tape volume to be used. MVS issues a message to the operator requesting that a "scratch" or "private" tape be mounted on a tape drive.[10] What tape volume does the operator choose? All tape volumes look pretty much alike on the outside. Certainly, a brand new tape right out of the manufacturer's carton is empty. But most tapes have been used before and contain data sets created by previous jobs. If the operator selects such a tape at random, it may be that the data is no longer needed by anyone—or it may be that the data is critical input to tomorrow's payroll application. A mistake could mean a costly effort to recreate the original data, to say nothing of the untold guilt the operator would suffer. Even if all tape data sets are properly date-protected, it might seem that the operator would have to continually mount tapes trying to find one that MVS didn't reject because of the date. With scratch mounts typically accounting for as many as 50% or more of all tape mounts, these kinds of problems cry out for an automated solution.

Here's where a tape volume management system comes in, using the following types of techniques. Information about the installation's tape volumes is maintained in an inventory data set owned by the management system. All permanent tape data sets are assigned expiration dates when they are created; if a date isn't assigned by the job, the management system will assign one by default. When a volume is mounted, but before a job is allowed to write on it, the management

---

[10]Technically, a private tape is used to hold permanent files, and a scratch tape to hold temporary files, but in practice the terms are often used interchangeably.

system verifies the volume's eligibility for scratch use by referring to its inventory. Eligibility for scratch use is based on criteria such as the number of days since the existing data set was written on the tape, or the number of days since the data set was last accessed, or the fact that the installation ran a job to uncatalog the data set. If the volume is ineligible for scratch use, a message is issued asking the operator to mount another volume.

On command the volume management system can produce a "scratch list": a report of tape volumes eligible to satisfy future scratch requests. This allows operators to know which tape volumes can be mounted to satisfy those requests, and to periodically gather such tapes into one easily accessed location.

Tape volume management systems generally provide additional functions beyond those described above. For example, ancillary information about a data center's tape volumes is usually maintained in the inventory. Useful information includes the name of the job that created the data set currently on a tape volume, the time and date the data set was created, whether the tape should be sent off-site and where, and more.

(Reference: none.)

QUESTION 10—OPERATIONS IN A SYSPLEX

A single MVS image (a single copy of MVS) can be controlled at one or more operator consoles. For capacity reasons, management reasons, and availability reasons, many installations support multiple images of MVS, whether on a single processor (perhaps through PR/SM logical partitioning), or on multiple processors, or a combination of both. While multiple MVS images can share resources such as tape and DASD devices, historically each image required dedicated operator consoles. Describe how console operations can be enhanced by an installation through implementing an MVS sysplex.

Note: The following description applies mainly to JES2 environments. JES3 has always supported a single operational image for console operators. However, JES3 can take advantage of other sysplex facilities.

The operations of multiple MVS images can be enhanced through connecting these images together into a "system complex," or sysplex. The physical connections are channel-to-channel communications (provided, for example, by ESCON channels). Management of the sysplex is provided by the *cross-system coupling facility (XCF)* component within MVS.

An immediate operational benefit is that an operator console attached to any processor in the sysplex can direct messages to and receive responses from any MVS image. In this way, an installation can support a single operational image and consoles can be shared by all systems.

Consider an example. Without a sysplex, operators supporting tape activity from multiple MVS images would normally have to monitor a separate console for each system for tape-related messages. In a sysplex, on the other hand, all tape-related messages from all systems could be routed to a single console, saving space and increasing operator efficiency.

Examples of other benefits of a sysplex (not restricted to JES2 environments) include the following:

A shared external clock called a sysplex timer provides consistent timing across all images.[11] The sysplex timer eliminates the need for an operator to set the time of day manually during the IPL process, speeding IPL and eliminating a source of operational error.

The MVS Global Resource Serialization (GRS) component manages shared data sets. The GRS Resource Name List contains the names of data sets to be protected across shared systems. In a sysplex environment only, this list can be changed dynamically by an operator command, allowing for improved system availability.

XCF allows the installation to specify a policy for managing an XRF (Extended Recovery Facility) takeover; XRF is a facility that, for example, allows a standby CICS subsystem to take over the processing of a failed CICS subsystem.[12] The policy can allow a standby CICS in one PR/SM logical partition to dynamically acquire processor storage from another PR/SM logical partition at the time of the takeover. Having a predefined policy minimizes operator activities required when a takeover occurs, improving availability.

---

[11]The sysplex timer is normally required in a sysplex. However, the sysplex timer is optional in the special cases of a sysplex consisting only of a single MVS image or consisting only of MVS images all executing within one processor. In these cases, if the sysplex timer is not installed, then the internal time-of-day clock provides synchronization.

[12]See "Question 103—Extended Recovery Facility (XRF)" for a discussion of XRF.

PDS library members such as program load modules and TSO CLISTs can be maintained in processor storage for enhanced performance. This capability is provided by the MVS Virtual Lookaside Facility (VLF). If the PDS is shared by multiple MVS images, then when the PDS is changed by one system, the other sharing systems must be notified so they can keep their memory-resident members current. This notification is provided by the TSO/E VLFNOTE command. In a sysplex, this command is automatically sent to all systems; in a nonsysplex environment, the command must be entered manually on each system.

(References: 92, 95.)

QUESTION 11—MANAGING CONSOLE MESSAGE TRAFFIC

One day you find yourself in a computer room. Looking over the console operator's shoulder you notice the rapid flow of message traffic, clearly more than the operator could be reading. In talking to the operator you learn that she ignores most of the messages anyway, and that the number of unimportant messages often makes it difficult to notice the important messages. Further, you learn that many of the replies to messages are standardized. What can you suggest to the installation as ways of better managing this message traffic?

Improved management of console message traffic is part of a strategy toward achieving automated systems operations.

An easy technique to reduce message traffic is to refrain from issuing unneeded messages in the first place, when that option is available. An example is avoiding the *MVS MONITOR JOBNAMES* command, since this causes messages to be issued that are essentially redundant with messages issued by JES.

Another technique useful in reducing message traffic is dispersing messages to different consoles according to function—for example, tape mount and disposition messages could be routed only to a console residing in the tape drive area, reducing traffic to the master console. This dispersion is implemented by assigning only certain route codes to each console, so that only associated messages are displayed (MVS components assign route codes to messages they issue).

The above techniques have been around for a long time. But, as systems have grown in capacity, message traffic has increased to the point where more sophisticated techniques are required. These are being provided in several ways.

The ability to reduce message traffic is assisted by the Message Processing Facility (MPF) that is part of MVS. One function of MPF is to suppress messages as specified by a SYS1.PARMLIB member defined by the installation. Reference 84 contains lists of messages to consider for suppression. Note that messages suppressed by MPF are still written to the hard-copy log and so are available for future reference. In addition to message suppression, MPF allows the installation to highlight key messages (such as by blinking) to make them more noticeable to an operator.

Console operations can be further enhanced by automating replies to messages. For example, system programmers can write MPF exit routines to provide programmed replies, relieving the operator of that burden.

In addition, the NetView product supports CLIST (Command List) and REXX (a System Application Architecture language) procedural languages to help an installation automate routine replies to messages.[13] NetView also supports message handling through routines written in high-level languages, which can provide better performance than the interpretive CLIST and REXX languages. In particular, NetView contains special support for KnowledgeTool, an expert system offering.

The AOC/MVS (Automated Operations Control/MVS) program product is a NetView application that builds on NetView's generalized automation facilities by offering capabilities tailored to the MVS environment. For example, AOC/MVS can automate the startup, restart, and shutdown of MVS subsystems. As another example, AOC/MVS can detect MVS messages that indicate that a system data set, such as an SMF data set, is full, and submit a job to offload the data set to tape.

MPF, NetView, and AOC/MVS can be used in combination to provide comprehensive automated console operations. MPF, by virtue of receiving control relatively early in the life of a message, can reduce system overhead through early suppression or early automated response. When needed, MPF exits have the advantage of being able to gather data from MVS internal structures to assist in decision making. NetView offers the advantages of high-level language support, which includes ease of writing and maintenance. AOC/MVS builds on NetView's facilities to offer automation tailored to the MVS environment.

---

[13]The older MVS/OCCF product also supports CLISTs, but NetView is more functional and should be considered more strategic.

We'll complete this discussion by mentioning that the CICS Automation Option/MVS and IMS Automation Option/MVS program offerings build on NetView and AOC/MVS facilities to help automate operation of the CICS and IMS transaction processing environments.

(References: 4, 5, 6, 84, 90, 125.)

QUESTION 12—REMOTE SYSTEMS OPERATION

To reduce costs, I / S management would like local console operators to also support a new departmental processor to be located at a remote site. The current local system and the planned remote system both run MVS. The existing data center has traditionally only implemented channel-attached consoles. What alternatives are available to allow local operators to operate the remote system?

This discussion will look at remote operations solutions that allow a local operator to control a remote system in the same basic way the operator would control a local system. That is, these solutions can be viewed as allowing consoles to be located at a greater distance from the computer than allowed for channel-attached devices.

Initializing and Monitoring Remote Data Center Hardware

The first aspect of remote operations to be addressed is turning the hardware power on and off at the remote site, and monitoring the remote site for unusual changes in the environment that could affect hardware function.

These functions can be handled by IBM SystemView SiteManager Services. SiteManager Services consist of various selectable modules; the overall service works like this. A hardware unit at the remote site can switch power on and off to data processing equipment such as processors and control units. Sensors can detect unusual conditions such as high temperature, smoke, or water. If an unusual condition is detected, a message is sent to an attached PS/2, and can then be sent via a modem to a remote location such as a message pager or a NetView focal point. Optionally, an alert can be sent to an IBM Monitoring Center, which will take customer-approved actions.

Initializing a Remote MVS

Once a processor and its associated equipment are powered on, the next step is to get the operating system going. This normally requires someone manually to "push some buttons" on the processor, such as by typing information into a hardware system console. But there are solutions that allow this to be done remotely.

1. The Target System Control Facility (TSCF) program product is designed to allow a local site, called the focal point, to initiate power-on-reset (POR) and initial program load (IPL) functions at one or more remote sites, called target sites.[14] TSCF runs partly as a NetView application on the local, focal[15] point system, and partly as a program in a PS/2 computer at the remote, target site. The TSCF programs in the host and in the PS/2 communicate with each other, allowing a NetView operator to control and monitor initialization and shutdown, as well as normal system function, of target systems.

   Here is the intended scenario of remote operations using TSCF. TSCF under NetView at the focal point, in communication with the PS/2 at the target site, first displays screens from the target's hardware system console to the focal point operator. This allows the operator to initiate functions such as power-on-reset and IPL. Next, TSCF displays screens from the target's operator console to the focal point operator, allowing the operator to respond to prompts from MVS during the IPL process. TSCF provides the ability for the installation to automate much of this process; for example, tasks needed to activate a target processor, from power-on-reset through responding to IPL messages, can be performed by TSCF in response to a single ACTIVATE command.

   The PS/2 program is packaged with TSCF and is downloaded from the host system to the PS/2. The TSCF program in the PS/2 attached to the target system emulates the hardware system console or operating system console or, more likely, both. For hardware system console emulation, attachment is directly to a port in the target system (e.g., a port in the 3092 processor controller in the case of a 3090 processor complex). For MVS operator console emula-

---

[14]The single TSCF product supersedes an earlier set of products: Inter-System Control Facility (ISCF), ISCF/PC, and 3090 Automated Console Application for ISCF.

[15]Please excuse the alliteration.

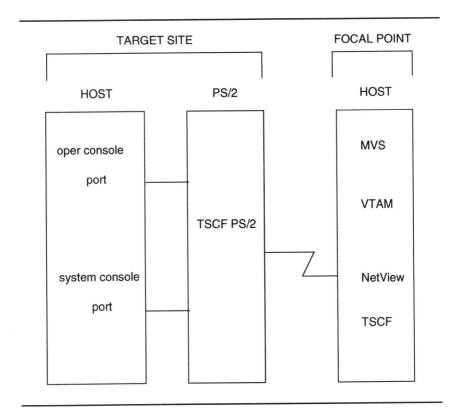

Figure 2.1.   Target System Control Facility configuration.

tion, attachment is via a channel-attached non-SNA 3X74. The PS/2 communicates with the focal point system using an SNA LU6.2 (program-to-program) protocol. See Figure 2.1.

Target processors supported by TSCF include selected models of the ES/9000, 3090, 4381, and 308X processor families.

2. Some processor models offer unique remote operations facilities. The 4381 provides a Remote Operator Console Facility (ROCF); the 9370 and ES/9000-9221 provide a Remote Operator Facility (ROF). While TSCF should be considered the strategic remote operations product of choice to control system initialization, specialized processor facilities such as these may be useful for processor models not supported by TSCF.

Operating a Remote MVS after Initialization

Now that MVS is initialized at the remote site, what are the alternatives for console operations?

1. A 7171 ASCII Device Attachment Unit can be attached to a channel on the remote system and connected over a teleprocessing link to an ASCII display terminal at the local site. The 7171 emulates ASCII terminals as 3278s attached through a 3274-41D, which is supported by native MVS console support.

   In this approach, there is no communication between the two systems; the local site is just taking advantage of the 7171's ability to make a remote terminal appear to be a locally attached 3278.

2. A TSO/E terminal connected remotely to the target system may be used to provide (somewhat primitive) operator console capabilities. Keep in mind that since TSO/E depends on a telecommunications subsystem, it is not available during system initialization or shutdown, meaning TSO/E cannot support all aspects of remote console operations.

   Let's contrast various TSO/E facilities for operator functions.

   The basic TSO/E OPERATOR command supports only a small subset of MVS operator commands and so is not practical for supporting remote systems.

   For JES2 installations, the System Display and Search Facility (SDSF) program product that runs under TSO/E allows operator commands to be submitted to the system. However, this capability within SDSF is only intended for occasional use and does not support usability features associated with standard operator consoles. For example, under SDSF, messages from the system, including responses to entered commands, can only be viewed by using SDSF to scroll through the system log that is maintained in the JES2 spool data set. Because of such characteristics, SDSF is really not practical for use as a full-fledged console.

   As of MVS/ESA SP Version 4, authorized TSO/E users have access to nearly all MVS operator commands. This is accomplished through TSO/E's use of an MVS facility called "extended MCS consoles." MCS, which stands for Multiple Console Support, is the facility within MVS that provides basic operator console management. Standard MCS support is limited to non-SNA channel-attached consoles; extended MCS consoles expand that support by allowing more consoles than the basic MCS limit of 99 and by providing a set of services that any authorized program can use to interact with the system to send operator commands and receive messages. The TSO/E

CONSOLE command supports these services, allowing authorized TSO/E users to enter MVS operator commands and display associated responses.

However, TSO/E terminals used in this way lack some of the usability characteristics normally associated with MCS consoles, and so may not be practical for full operator support of remote (or local) systems. For example, while MCS will display a message on an MCS console as soon as the message is sent, TSO/E will not display a message on a TSO/E terminal if the terminal is in a "waiting for input" state.

3. The following solution is the most powerful as it provides the platform for automated operations.

The NetView program product can provide centralized monitoring and control of remote data processing sites (the targets) from a single focal point site. An operator at the focal point site can issue commands to target systems and view the responses, and also respond to messages generated by target systems.

After TSCF has finished system initialization as described earlier, NetView would be started on the target system. From then on, a focal point operator would control the remote system through NetView-to-NetView communications, rather than through TSCF, to take advantage of NetView's extensive automated operations capabilities.

The Automated Operations Control/MVS (AOC/MVS) program product is a NetView application that builds on NetView facilities to enhance automated operations of local or remote systems. For example, AOC/MVS can display a screen that names all remote locations, each in a color that identifies the location's status. Green might indicate no problem, while red alerts the operator that the site is experiencing some kind of problem; the operator can "tab" to the name in red and press a PF key to display additional details.

Additional products are available that build on NetView and AOC/MVS to provide an even more comprehensive automated operations solution.

The CICS Automation Option/MVS and IMS Automation Option/MVS licensed programs build on NetView and AOC/MVS facilities to help automate operation of, and provide a single point of control for, CICS and IMS transaction processing environments.

(References: 1, 5, 12, 56, 125, 127, 128, 135.)

3

Data Management

The data management function provides the means to organize, store, catalog, and retrieve all the information, including programs, processed by MVS. Information is organized as data sets, which are collections of logically related data records.

A data management facility is basic to any operating system. Even the relatively unsophisticated operating systems available for the first personal computers provided, at a minimum, a basic filing system.

QUESTION 13—VSAM DATA SET ORGANIZATIONS

Briefly describe the four types of VSAM (Virtual Storage Access Method) data set organizations. Where applicable, name a non-VSAM access method that has a similar function.

There are four VSAM data set organizations.

1. *ESDS.* A VSAM Entry Sequenced Data Set is a sequential data set. New records are added only to the end of the data set. Records can be accessed sequentially, or randomly by specifying a record's relative byte address (RBA), which is an offset into the data set. Deletion of records is not supported directly, but applications could

implement a special flag (e.g., a bit) to indicate that a record is logically deleted.

The ESDS organization is similar to the MVS physical sequential data set organization, which can be accessed by access methods such as QSAM (queued sequential access method) or BSAM (basic sequential access method).[16]

2. *RRDS*. A VSAM Relative Record Data Set consists of a number of fixed-length "slots," each of which has a unique relative record number (1 to N) and contains one logical record. Records are added and retrieved by specifying the appropriate relative record number. VSAM maintains information that indicates whether slots contain data or are empty (never filled, or deleted).

The RRDS organization is similar to the (now rarely used) MVS direct data set organization, which can be accessed through the Basic Direct Access Method (BDAM).

3. *KSDS*. A VSAM Key-Sequenced Data Set consists of an index component and a data component. The records in the data component must have unique keys, that is, a field in each record that uniquely identifies the record. The index component contains key values and pointers to the associated records. Through the index, records can be accessed either randomly or sequentially.

The KSDS organization is similar to the MVS indexed sequential data set organization, which can be accessed through Indexed Sequential Access Methods, such as QISAM (queued ISAM).

4. *LDS*. A linear data set is a VSAM data set with a fixed control interval size and block size of 4096 bytes. One use of an LDS is for the MVS Data in Virtual (DIV) function. Linear data sets are used by DIV to contain data such as tables and arrays that are processed by being mapped directly into virtual storage (note that the control interval size and block size are both equal to the MVS page size).

The function provided by DIV and linear data sets is rather unique, and no other data set organization really provides a similar type of capability.

(References: 3, 72.)

---

[16]When an application opens a data set, it selects an *access method*: the technique the application wants to use to read and write to the data set. For example, QSAM provides a record level interface, while BSAM provides a block level interface. That MVS offers a choice of access methods for some data set organizations helps demonstrate the distinction between how a file is physically organized and the techniques used to access that file.

QUESTION 14—REORGANIZING A VSAM KSDS

Installations sometimes run special utilities to "reorganize" certain types of data sets, such as VSAM key-sequenced data sets. Can you explain what is accomplished by reorganizing a VSAM KSDS?

VSAM KSDS data sets use an index structure that allows records to be found randomly or sequentially. VSAM also attempts to keep records physically in ascending order (based on each record's key) by attempting to insert new records between existing records if there is sufficient free space to move existing records around easily. When that free space is exhausted, additional free space is dynamically formatted within the data set in a process called a control interval (CI) split or control area (CA) split. This dynamic reorganization allows the insert to succeed, but with the consequence that some records with consecutive keys won't be physically adjacent to each other (indexes are adjusted to maintain the correct logical order). This has little effect on performance when accessing records randomly, but can add additional seeks to sequential processing that can degrade performance. Further, the CI and CA split processes take a relatively long time, which also can negatively impact performance.

Also, as a data set grows, new DASD extents may be added. Since these new extents are generally not adjacent to the original extent, more seeks or longer seeks for both direct and sequential processing would occur than if the data set resided in one continuous extent.

The IDCAMS utility REPRO or EXPORT/IMPORT commands will reorganize a KSDS data set as follows:

- Reload data so that it is physically in sequential order.
- Allow for consolidation of extents.
- Reestablish the CI/CA free space specifications to allow future inserts to proceed with reduced need for CI/CA splits.

(Reference: 72.)

QUESTION 15—ISAM AND BDAM DATA SETS

MVS supports many data management access methods, including ISAM and BDAM, which have been available since the earliest releases of the operating system. What reasons can you give to motivate MVS installations to work toward eliminating ISAM and BDAM type data sets?

Installations should work toward eliminating ISAM and BDAM data sets for reasons such as the following:

ISAM:

- Has been "functionally stabilized" for a number of years.
- Is not supported by DFSMShsm.
- Is not supported in programs compiled by VS COBOL II.
- Is not supported by CICS 1.7 and later releases.
- Is not supported by IMS after IMS Version 2, Release 2.
- Generally does not perform as well as VSAM.
- Is not supported on system-managed storage volumes.

BDAM:

- Is not supported in programs compiled by VS COBOL II.
- Generally does not perform as well as VSAM.
- Has only an unblocked format. This either uses DASD space inefficiently, or forces the application to manage blocking and unblocking of records.
- Can have device dependencies that may make data set movement and device conversion difficult (BDAM records may contain absolute cylinder-track-record addresses). On the other hand, VSAM data organizations use a relative byte address (RBA) technique to address locations within a data set. The device independence of the VSAM RBA technique makes it easier to move VSAM data sets to a different location on a DASD volume or to a new device type.
- Is not supported on system-managed storage volumes when the BDAM data set is marked unmovable (DSORG=DAU).

(References: 19, 102.)

QUESTION 16—CROSS-SYSTEM DATA SET SHARING

An operations manager reports that while data sets were in use by one system, these same data sets were deleted by a second, sharing system, causing all sorts of havoc. How could this have been prevented?

Before we discuss solutions to the data set sharing problem, we need to review how MVS serializes access to data sets. We'll look at data set serialization from the point of view of a job and its JCL, but note that programs that allocate data sets dynamically without JCL are handled in a similar fashion.

MVS device allocation processing uses the MVS ENQ mechanism to control access to data sets. Basically, MVS issues an ENQ request (via the ENQ macro instruction) for each data set specified in JCL at the time a job is initiated. The request is for either shared or exclusive control of a data set, depending on JCL parameters. Corresponding DEQ requests are not issued until the last job step that references a given data set is completed. So a job's data sets are allocated to that job for a period of time that starts before the data set is open and ends sometime after it is closed.

Assume MVS has allocated a data set to a given job with either shared or exclusive control. If a second job on the same MVS system tries to allocate that same data set with exclusive control (in order to change or delete it), when MVS issues the ENQ macro the ENQ service denies the request. Thus the second job is not allowed access to the data set, and integrity is preserved.

That's easy within a single system since MVS is using a set of control blocks in virtual storage to track and enforce all ENQ requests. However, because the ENQ request is unknown to other sharing systems, those systems would allow a delete request to proceed. The formerly allocated DASD space could then immediately be used for a new, different data set. Unfortunately, the original job still accessing the original data set wouldn't know that, which could lead to all sorts of surprises. The problem is wider in scope than just unexpected deletions—two systems could be updating the same data set at the same time, causing integrity problems unless special care is taken.

The situation in the question could be prevented in at least four ways.

1. Applications could issue RESERVE requests to protect data sets. However, the RESERVEs would have to remain in effect from

OPEN until CLOSE time. This could be a rather long duration in many cases, with disastrous consequences for performance considering that RESERVE is a lock on the entire volume on which the reserved data set resides. Thus this solution is not very practical. Note that MVS itself issues RESERVEs of *short* duration to protect critical data sets such as VTOCs.

2. Another way to manage the problem is by scheduling all requests against a given data set from one system only, thus ensuring ENQ protection. This requires cooperation among users or system exit routines for enforcement.

3. JES3 can be used to manage a complex of systems that share the same DASD. In this case, JES3 can optionally control data set allocation and provide the data set integrity we need.

4. The MVS Global Resource Serialization (GRS) function handles the problem by propagating ENQ and RESERVE requests across sharing systems that are connected by channel-to-channel communications. Some installations have implemented non-IBM products that perform functions similar to GRS but use a shared disk as the vehicle to communicate between systems.

Note that sometimes it *is* desirable to have programs on the same or different systems concurrently updating the same data set. Shared catalogs are an example where this is true for system data sets; data bases are another case where concurrent sharing is desirable. Programming conventions are then needed, possibly relying on serialization facilities such as GRS or RESERVE/RELEASE, to coordinate processing so that data set integrity is maintained.

(References: 36, 72, 80, 89, 98, 110.)

QUESTION 17—SENDING DATA SETS TO REMOTE SITES

An MVS data center is being split into two separate data centers in different locations. Management anticipates the need to send data sets back and forth between the two sites. What alternative methods are available to accomplish this?

Methods to transmit data sets between two remote MVS systems vary from manual methods to using JES Network Job Entry to using programs designed to support transmission of data sets over a teleprocessing link.

1. *Manual delivery methods*. Files can be copied to tape, and the tapes transported between sites. This method may be practical if the amount of data to be transported is small and timeliness is not critical. If the data centers are close enough, company personnel might be able to deliver the tapes. Otherwise an outside delivery service could be used.

2. *JES2 or JES3 Network Job Entry (NJE) facilities*. These facilities are native to JES2 and JES3. NJE is normally used to transfer jobs and SYSOUT from one MVS system to another but can be used to transmit sequential data sets as in-stream data within a job. Unfortunately, this limits the data sets to a sequential format with records of 80 bytes each. Tools are described later that use NJE for transmission but which use their own formatting techniques to work within the normal JCL record length restrictions.

   Here's an example of how NJE could be used directly to transfer a data set between two systems. A user or program at a source node could create an IEBGENER utility job, placing the data set to be transmitted as //SYSUT1 DD * in-stream data. The //SYSUT2 DD statement would name a data set at the target node to receive the data. Transfer of the data set is thus completed when the job is executed on the target node.

   NJE uses JES spool to hold the job, including in-stream data, at both the source and target nodes, so data set size is limited by spool capacity. Spools at any intermediate nodes are also used (store-and-forward), unless VTAM (SNA) is being used to support data transmission (in a JES3 network, this requires the MVS/Bulk Data Transfer program).

3. *TSO/E Transmit and Receive*. TSO/E users can use the TRANS-MIT and RECEIVE commands to transfer data sets and messages between users on different nodes. The JES NJE network is used for communications. A single sequential data set, partitioned data set, or partitioned data set member can be transmitted via one TRANS-MIT command.

4. *Data Extract (DXT)*. This program product also supports file transfer via NJE. DXT supports VSAM KSDS and ESDS organizations, physical sequential files, and DL/I and DB2 data bases. Support for file transfer is provided by an option that extracts desired data and formats it within JCL's 80-byte constraint. The user can place this data in a job and transfer it to another node via standard JES JCL parameters. A DXT utility can be run on the target node to reformat the data into a sequential data set. Other utilities can then be used to reload the sequential data into desired data structures.

5. *MVS/Bulk Data Transfer (BDT), File Transfer Program (FTP), and NetView FTP MVS.*

These programs

- Require a VTAM/SNA link between sending and receiving nodes. These two nodes must have compatible programs installed (e.g., compatible levels of BDT). Copies of these programs are not required at any intermediate nodes.
- Do not use an intermediate spooling device; this can be an advantage over NJE since the size or number of data sets in an NJE network is limited by JES spool capacity.
- Provide data compression during transmission.
- Provide a checkpoint facility so that interrupted transmissions can be restarted; checkpointing is not supported by NJE but can be an important time saver during transmission of very large files.

The MVS/Bulk Data Transfer program runs only in MVS systems. Supported data set types are sequential, partitioned, and selected members of a partitioned data set. BDT can be invoked from batch jobs, operator consoles, or TSO/E terminals (an ISPF panel is provided).

The File Transfer Program sends VSAM KSDS and ESDS files and physical sequential files between systems, which may be MVS, VSE, or VM systems—the sending and receiving node need not be the same operating system.

NetView FTP is the successor to FTP and adds additional function such as an interactive ISPF interface, the ability to transfer entire partitioned data sets as well as individual members, and improved performance.

NetView FTP should be considered the product of choice, unless a function unique to BDT, such as JES3 SNA NJE support, is required.

(References: 16, 35, 68, 86, 87, 104, 107, 130.)

4

Storage Management

Most MVS installations devote a large portion of their data processing budget to storage hardware, storage management software, and storage management personnel. The demand for storage has been increasing every year as new applications begin production and additional users become active. It takes time and effort to install and effectively use storage. Automated storage management techniques and products can help more efficiently manage this resource by improving performance, availability, space utilization, device installation, and user productivity.

QUESTION 18—SYSTEM-MANAGED STORAGE

Installations are facing the problem of managing an ever-increasing amount of auxiliary storage. IBM has taken major steps to assist in the management process by supporting a system-managed storage environment. What does "system-managed" mean? What products are involved in IBM's implementation?

Definition

System-managed storage means that the system determines data placement and automatically manages data availability, performance, space reclamation, and security. Based on user-defined requirements, the system matches the logical needs of the data to the physical characteristics of the storage devices and ensures that each device is used effectively. In other words, the system takes over many of the storage management tasks previously done by users.

Implementation in DFSMS/MVS

The name of the collection of IBM software products that work together to support system-managed storage is DFSMS/MVS: Data Facility Storage Management Subsystem/MVS. DFSMS/MVS is a single product that includes the following components available as a single package or in selected subsets called offerings.[17]

DFSMSdfp   DFSMS/MVS Data Facility Product. Manages active data (access methods; utilities). The Interactive Storage Management Facility (ISMF) within DFSMSdfp provides an interactive interface to storage management facilities for use by storage administrators and other end users.

DFSMSdss   DFSMS/MVS Data Set Services. Manages data movement (copy; dump/restore; convert a volume to system-managed storage format).

DFSMShsm   DFSMS/MVS Hierarchical Storage Management. Manages low activity and inactive data (migration/recall; backup/recovery).

DFSMSrmm   DFSMS/MVS Removable Media Management. Provides inventory management and protection of assets for removable media (e.g., tape volumes).

---

[17]Prior to the availability of DFSMS/MVS, "DFSMS" was the name used for a collection of products including MVS/DFP, DFHSM, DFDSS, DFSORT, and RACF. The packaging of components into a single, enhanced DFSMS/MVS product facilitates installation and maintenance and is more representative of the functional integration among the DFSMS/MVS components. While DFSORT (sort/merge) and RACF (resource authorization) are not DFSMS / MVS components, these products continue to provide functions that are key to any data processing installation. Note that because DFSMS/MVS was just beginning to be shipped at the time of writing, references at the end of various topics still cite the DFSMS level of publications.

While installations can use selected subsets of the DFSMS/MVS components, the total DFSMS/MVS package provides the most complete implementation of system-managed storage.

DFSMS/MVS components are designed to support a set of *constructs* managed by DFSMSdfp; these constructs are named objects created by an installation to define policies used to manage its data sets. Constructs are assigned to a data set when it is first created, on DASD or tape, and may be maintained or changed if the data set moves.

It must be emphasized that constructs are assigned on a *data set* basis. This is one of DFSMS/MVS's strongest features. Prior to DFSMS/MVS (and for volumes not yet converted to DFSMS/MVS format), most storage management tools generally manage data sets on a volume basis. For example, at one time, the policy of having DFSMShsm automatically delete all data sets that have gone unreferenced for 365 days would have applied to all data sets on a given volume (exceptions would have to be handled through installation-written exits). In contrast, DFSMS/MVS allows each data set to be assigned a unique expiration policy. There is no need to worry about placing data sets on specific volumes just for policy considerations.

People, Products, and Practices

As powerful as these software-provided techniques are, system-managed storage, in IBM's view, consists of more than just software. It is the interaction of people (e.g., storage administrators), hardware storage devices, systems software, and installation policies and practices. Let's consider an example of how all these factors come into play.

An installation has implemented a data set that supports a large number of interactive end users—having the data set constantly accessible is extremely important. Normally the DASD volume containing the data set would be a single point of failure: a hardware failure of the media would require restoration of a backup copy on a spare volume, a rather time-consuming procedure. In a DFSMS/MVS environment, however, this exposure can be eliminated. When the data set is allocated, the installation can assign a "storage class" construct to it that specifies AVAILABILITY=CONTINUOUS. The system will then place the data set on a dual copy (duplexed) volume behind a 3990 cache subsystem, eliminating the volume as a single point of failure. Note the interaction of the hardware supporting the function, the software that allowed easy use of the function, and the people who agreed on and implemented the policy of having the important data set make use of the function.

Separating Logical and Physical Considerations

DFSMS/MVS separates the logical requirements of data (e.g., its format as it appears to a program, or the policy for managing the data) from the physical characteristics of devices on which the data is stored. This is an extremely important facet of DFSMS/MVS, with the benefit of simplifying the process of converting from one device type to another. Consider what many installations had to go through when converting from 3350 DASD to 3380 DASD in the early 1980s. At that time, most installations were faced with a lot of existing JCL, TSO/E CLISTS, and even programs that were sensitive to hardware characteristics of the 3350. For example, JCL statements such as the following were common:

```
//DISK DD DSN=A.B.C,UNIT=3350,VOL=SER=TSO123,SPACE=(TRK,(2))
```

This statement depends on there being a 3350 volume available with the indicated volume serial number. Two tracks are requested because the user estimated that the data set was 24K bytes in size, and remembered that a 3350 track holds only about 19K bytes.

When the data sets on one or more 3350 volumes were moved to a 3380 volume, which had a track size of about 47K bytes and often a different volume serial number, such JCL statements either used space inefficiently or didn't work at all. Thus the data center had to work with users to ensure such JCL was changed before the data on the 3350 volume could be moved to a 3380 volume. This elongated the time it took to install new DASD.

In a DFSMS/MVS environment, the UNIT and VOL parameters can be omitted by the user, or if present in "old" JCL, then they can be ignored by the system. SPACE for a data set can be requested as a number of records of a specified average size or even omitted by the user and assigned by the system in many cases. These kinds of capabilities remove device dependencies from JCL and programs, meaning conversion to new device types can be accomplished without involving users.

(References: 23, 28, 29, 102, 111, 124.)

QUESTION 19—CENTRALIZING STORAGE MANAGEMENT

Question 18—System-Managed Storage discussed the meaning and value of system-managed storage. The technical support group at an installation is convinced of the value of this approach and wants to move toward implementation. One concept that is new to them is the IBM recommendation that storage management be centralized under a single "storage administrator." Explain what this means and why centralized storage management is important in a system-managed storage environment.

One of the most important actions an installation can take to prepare for system-managed storage is to centralize control of its physical storage resources.

In many installations today, storage management is not centralized but is dispersed among various users (or departments) who may be responsible for such tasks as backup/recovery, cleanup of old data, compression of partitioned data sets, and so on in addition to their normal jobs. Further, users are often tied to the physical device characteristics of "their" volumes—for example, their JCL may specify UNIT=3390 or VOL=SER=MYVOL1. Such dependencies make conversion to new disk devices difficult to manage.

DFSMS/MVS is designed so that a centralized storage administrator, which may be one person or a group of people, is responsible for translating data set service level requirements into the DFSMS/MVS constructs that tell the system how to manage the data sets (meaning how often to back up data sets, when they can be migrated, what performance they require, etc.). The service level requirements for any particular data set or group of related data sets are determined by negotiations between the storage administrator and the users. The storage administrator specifies the management policies to the system, which then implements them. So we say that DFSMS/MVS is system managed but administrator controlled.

Centralization of storage management also places control of the physical storage media under the storage administrator. Users still own the data but have no dependencies on the underlying media—for example, JCL is interpreted by the system in a device-independent fashion. The process of converting to a new device type is then very simple and can be done by the storage administrator (the owner of the devices) without the need to involve users (the owners of the data).

There are at least two ways in which centralized control of storage management can reduce costs.

First, the number of people needed to administrate storage is likely less than in a decentralized approach (though it may not be easy to prove since that might mean accounting for all the time individuals otherwise do their own manual storage management tasks such as deleting old data sets). At a minimum, it is certainly easier to maintain a high level of skill among a consolidated group of storage administrators.

Second, centralized resources can be shared among users, minimizing waste. For example, in a decentralized organization volumes are owned by individual users or groups. It is usually (politically) difficult if not impossible for a group that has run out of space to use the free space on volumes belonging to another group. So the group generally has to acquire another entire volume, which might be much more space than is needed, while other available space in the organization continues to go unused.

All of this isn't to say that centralization is without drawbacks. From the point of view of an individual who "owned" several DASD volumes, for example, there may be some additional risk that needed space isn't available on demand, or there may be a requirement for additional interaction with the storage administrator from time to time. However, from the point of view of the business as a whole, the benefits should be clear.

Centralized control of system resources is really nothing new. As an example, consider the processor resource. The processor is "owned" by the data center, yet provides a capacity that is shared by many users. One way that systems programmers administer this capacity is by defining MVS performance groups with differing performance characteristics. Important jobs are assigned performance groups that give them better use of processor capacity than less important jobs. Users have to negotiate with the system programmers which jobs are considered important and which are not.

Centralization can be largely accomplished prior to migrating to a DFSMS/MVS environment, or it can be implemented as part of that migration.

(References: 29, 102, 111, 124.)

QUESTION 20—STORAGE POOLING

Many installations manage their DASD volumes in a decentralized manner. The data center / technical support group owns the "system" volumes (SYSRES, paging, spool, etc.), but each user department owns the volumes on which its data resides. IBM, however, recommends that all volumes be centrally managed using a "pooling" concept. Describe what storage pooling is all about and what the benefits are compared to private volume ownership.

The idea of *pooling* is not unique to DASD, but refers to any set of shared resources that are managed in a centralized way. For example, JES2 and JES3 manage pools of local printers and assign them to SYSOUT data sets; the jobs that create SYSOUT do not themselves select the printers, but merely specify the attributes (forms, number of copies, and so on) that they need and let JES handle it. JES then has information about all printing requests, allowing it to control printers efficiently.

Storage pooling (sometimes called volume pooling) brings the pooling concept into the DASD arena.

From reference 102:

A *storage pool* is a predefined set of DASD volumes, or DASD and optical volumes, belonging to an object storage hierarchy, used to store groups of related data. Pooling allows you to match the logical needs of your data to the physical characteristics of storage devices without requiring users to know or understand your installation's hardware configuration. With storage pooling, users can efficiently store and retrieve data without being aware of space limitations, device characteristics, or volume serial numbers. Thus, pooling is one of the first steps in implementing system-managed storage. By designing and implementing storage pools for your installation, you can prepare for the future as well as solve current storage management problems.

And,

Ideally, you should be able to let DFSMS/MVS manage all of your data in one large pool. With one pool the system can automatically balance performance and space utilization without a lot of manual intervention. Because there is a larger pool of free space for new data set allocations, you have fewer out-of-space ABENDs. Data sets can be allocated on any volume in the installation without requiring users to know specific volume or device characteristics. Finally, with only one pool of volumes, device installation is simplified.

However, in reality, having only one pool is not viable. Most installations must cope with the needs of many different users using many different data types. One solution is to set up multiple storage pools with management criteria tailored to the type of data in the pool. With this type of pooling you can implement a common management policy for all of the data in each pool.

See reference 102 for recommendations about establishing a pooling structure.

Prior to DFSMS/MVS, storage pooling could be implemented through the use of "esoteric" unit names in JCL. For example, to put a new data set in the primary pool managed by DFSMShsm, a user might specify UNIT=SYSDA in JCL, omitting a volume serial number. Systems programmers would have previously specified to MVS which volumes are in the SYSDA pool, and MVS assigns one of those volumes to the new data set.

In a DFSMS/MVS environment, every new data set is assigned a DFSMS/MVS construct called a "storage group." A storage group contains a list of volumes eligible to hold the data set (plus other parameters beyond the scope of this discussion). As an example, all data base data sets might be assigned to a "data base" storage group. In contrast to the pre-DFSMS/MVS implementation of storage pooling, the assignment of a data set to a storage group eliminates the need for users to specify an esoteric unit name in JCL—the assignment of the storage group is instead made by an installation-coded procedure that receives control during the allocation of new data sets.

These are some of the major benefits of implementing storage pooling:

- *More efficient space usage.* If volumes are privately owned, when one user (which may be a group or department) runs out of space, he will probably not be allowed to use the space on a volume belonging to another user, but might instead have to acquire a new volume somehow. Pooling, on the other hand, would allow free space to be shared among users, eliminating this inefficiency and possibly reducing storage subsystem costs.
- *Device independence.* The DFSMS/MVS storage group construct and the older UNIT=esoteric-name allocation parameter both allow

data sets to be created without having to specify a volume serial number or device type. This allows volume serial numbers to be easily changed without having to coordinate changes to JCL. Combining two or three small DASD volumes onto one large capacity volume is a typical case that requires changes to any JCL statements that are sensitive to the affected volume serial numbers.

- *Improved performance.* If users allocate data sets to pools rather than to specific volumes, then there is more flexibility to move data sets around in order to meet performance goals.
- *Easier volume management.* Pooling keeps data sets that can be managed in similar ways on the same volumes. DFSMShsm, for example, manages data sets that are on specified volumes, that is, an installation assigns certain volumes to be managed by DFSMShsm. With pooling, then, it is easy to assign to DFSMShsm those volumes that it can manage, minimizing concern about exceptions. As another example, data bases are often best maintained in their own pool, since they often have strict performance requirements and may require carefully managed placement on selected volumes; further, DFSMS/MVS helps ensure that unauthorized data sets can't be placed in the data base pool.

Should an installation that does not pool storage today implement a pooling scheme prior to conversion to DFSMS/MVS? Implementing a pooling structure at any time generally involves moving existing data sets around to volumes assigned to the appropriate pool. But pooling prior to DFSMS/MVS generally also requires JCL changes (e.g., to specify UNIT=poolname). Therefore, installations planning near-term conversions to DFSMS/MVS may find it easier to convert to a pooling structure as they convert to DFSMS/MVS.

(Reference: 102.)

QUESTION 21—STORAGE MANAGEMENT OF ENTERPRISE-WIDE DATA

The dramatic decrease in the cost of computing power and storage over the last few years has meant that information processing, historically performed under control of a centralized data center, is increasingly being performed by individual users at workstations. In particular, numerous files containing key business information now reside only on small, distributed computer systems. Users are busy creating and using these files but may not have the time, the discipline, or the tools to manage these files the way host-based data is managed. Yet organizations are more and more aware that this enterprise-wide computerized data is a business asset. The cost to an organization if such files are lost could be very high. How can a centralized MVS/ESA system help manage the files distributed on workstations throughout an enterprise?

The IBM ADSM (Adstar Distributed Storage Manager) program product is designed to manage files stored at workstations or other distributed processing environments. ADSM makes available to workstations policy-based storage management facilities similar to those available to data sets in a DFSMS/MVS environment.

ADSM allows an MVS/ESA system to act as a file backup and archive server for client workstations from many manufacturers running varied operating systems.

Here's a scenario of how a user at a workstation would use the services of ADSM.

The user invokes a workstation program to select an ADSM service, such as file backup (the workstation program is part of the ADSM product and was installed earlier by a storage administrator).

The user then selects a *management class* policy from a list of such policies created by the ADSM storage administrator and authorized to that user. A management class might specify, among other things, how many backups can be maintained and under what conditions they can be deleted by the system.

The user can request backup of a single file, a group of files, a directory of files, or an entire disk. The backup can be limited to files that are new or changed since they were previously backed up. The backup can occur immediately, or it can be scheduled to occur at a later time if the workstation supports a scheduling capability. ADSM manages the backed up files in a hierarchy of DASD and tape devices attached to the MVS host. Data is compressed to reduce costs.[18]

---

[18]This storage hierarchy is similar to that supported by DFSMShsm but is actually an independent implementation. This independence allows the ADSM product to be implemented in a similar way in heterogeneous operating system environments.

If the user needs to restore a backed up copy of a file for any reason (perhaps the user accidentally deleted the original copy), then the user simply invokes the workstation program and requests the restore. The request is forwarded to ADSM at the host, and the backup copy is returned to the workstation.

In addition to backup/restore, ADSM also supports an archive/retrieve facility (analogous to DFSMShsm migrate/recall). Users can archive files that they anticipate will not be needed for some relatively long period of time. The files are moved to the host, and the workstation copies are deleted. The user can retrieve the files by command at any time. Archiving files in this way not only frees client disk space for other uses, but can lower storage costs by placing the data on relatively inexpensive tape storage at the host.

It is interesting to note that users can retrieve files backed up or archived by other users, if authorized to do so, so that ADSM can provide a method of file transfer between workstations not normally connected by a communication link.

In summary, ADSM can help bring the data management disciplines of backup and archiving, historically only available to mainframe based files, to files distributed on computing platforms throughout an organization.

(Reference: 26.)

QUESTION 22—DFSMSDSS LOGICAL AND PHYSICAL PROCESSING

DFSMSdss supports both "logical" and "physical" processing. Describe the difference between these two types of processing. When should installations use one type or the other?

"Physical" processing is sensitive to device geometry (track size, tracks per cylinder) and so moves data only between devices of like-geometry (e.g., different 3390 models). "Logical" processing, on the other hand, is not sensitive to device geometry and can move data between devices of different geometries (e.g., 3380 and 3390).

DFSMSdss physical dump processing requires that the user specify the serial numbers of the volumes to be dumped. A physical dump contains images of each source volume's tracks and so depends on device geometry, meaning that the dump can be restored only to a like-device type. Physical processing is very fast (compared to logical processing) because physical processing minimizes seeking and can read large amounts of data—up to one cylinder—at a time. Further, physical processing does not require catalog references.

On the other hand, DFSMSdss logical dump processing treats data sets as complete entities and formats the dump data set to be independent of device geometry. For example, a 3380 volume could be dumped via DFSMSdss logical dump processing and restored to a 3390 volume, or vice versa. Data sets can be selected by either volume serial number or by a data set name filter, e.g., all data sets beginning APPL2 regardless of the volumes on which they reside. Treating data sets as entities may require catalog references to find the data sets and DASD seeking to gather noncontiguous extents, making this processing slower than physical processing.

Why are there two kinds of processing, and when is each appropriate?

Physical dumping is most appropriate for full-volume backup and recovery, for example, onsite backup of DASD volumes in case of an HDA (head disk assembly) failure. This is because full-volume backups are a time-consuming activity at most installations, making speed important (however, IBM's Concurrent Copy function allows dumping to occur asynchronously to other processing, making this less of an issue).

On the other hand, logical dumping can support preparation for disaster recovery—the device independence of logical dumps means there is no dependency on the device types at the disaster recovery site. Because dumps for disaster recovery may be taken less often than (physical) dumps for volume recovery, performance is less critical.

The following cases exploit the ability of logical processing to collect data sets via the catalog according to a data set name filter, regardless of the volumes on which they reside. Logical dumps can be used to create a single dump copy of a data set that spans volumes, such as a sequential striped data set or a traditional multivolume data set. Logical dumping can also be used to gather in one dump data set (on a tape) related data sets that are to be moved to another location.

(References: 17, 102.)

QUESTION 23—DFSMSHSM SPACE MANAGEMENT

A systems programmer is frequently getting calls from users who are experiencing out-of-space ABENDs on DASD volumes. The programmer usually solves the problem by deleting old data sets (or trying to get users to do so), running a utility to compress partitioned data sets, and using other manual techniques. How could DFSMShsm help manage space more efficiently?

Out-of-space conditions can happen when space on volumes is nearly completely allocated, or partitioned data sets are full, or for other reasons. DFSMShsm has several techniques to help automate space management and prevent out-of-space conditions from occurring. Some of the more significant techniques are listed below.

Migration and Volume Threshold Management

Data set migration[19] is a very powerful function in DFSMShsm. Migration manages data set placement based on long-term patterns of reference (i.e., days or weeks). DFSMShsm can detect data sets that have gone unreferenced for an installation-specified number of days and move those data sets, in a compacted format, to designated DASD or tape volumes called "migration" volumes. When a user (or job) attempts to access a data set that has been migrated, DFSMShsm will "recall" the data set to its original form, without requiring the user to take any explicit actions. Managing data sets in this way provides additional free space for new and growing data sets.

DFSMShsm migration can just be "let loose," but additional efficiencies are possible through controlling migration according to an installation's objectives for providing free space. This is called *volume threshold management*. For example, assume that an installation has determined that out-of-space conditions are avoided if at least 25 percent of the space in a storage pool is available first thing in the morning. DFSMShsm can be told to review DASD volumes once every night and migrate unreferenced data sets only until at least 25 percent of the space on each volume in the pool is available.

In this way, DFSMShsm only migrates unreferenced data sets until

---

[19]The process is sometimes called "archiving."

the threshold is met. This avoids using processor and I/O resources to migrate (and later recall) data when there is little to be gained by doing so. After all, if there is enough free space already, there is no value in moving data sets around to provide more.

With that introduction, let's look at the philosophy of migration and threshold management in a little more detail.

Nonvolatile storage devices (e.g., magnetic media) can be viewed as forming a hierarchy ranging from relatively fast, expensive cached DASD to uncached DASD to relatively slower, less expensive tape. Migration is a technique that moves data sets efficiently within the device hierarchy, based on how often the data is used. Except for a possible delay during recall, this process should have no other impact on applications or users.

A typical scenario for migration goes something like this. When a data set goes unreferenced for some time (two weeks, for example), DFSMShsm moves the used space in a compacted form to a designated DASD migration volume. A good candidate volume is a high-capacity, uncached DASD volume with relatively low-performance characteristics; since it will be used to contain unreferenced data, optimal performance is not so important. In any case, if the user later references the data set, recall is a fast DASD-to-DASD copy. If the data set remains unreferenced (perhaps for several months), DFSMShsm migrates it to tape, a much less expensive medium than DASD. Since the data set has gone unreferenced for so long, it is unlikely that the tape will have to be mounted in order to recall the data set, but DFSMShsm will request that the tape be mounted if necessary. This whole process is automatic—users and applications need not take any actions to migrate or recall their data.

The scenario uses a three-level hierarchy: the primary DASD volumes containing the active data sets, the DASD migration volumes, and finally the tape migration volumes. This three-level hierarchy has significant advantages over a two-level hierarchy of only primary DASD volumes and tape migration volumes. In practice, such a two level hierarchy can force an installation to migrate data only after a long period, perhaps several months, in order to reduce the work and delays caused by tape mounting. Since DFSMShsm supports DASD as an intermediate level in the hierarchy, migration to DASD can occur after much less time, perhaps after just a few days, because tape mounts aren't needed for migration to or recalls from DASD. And DASD-to-DASD movement is fast by its very nature. Thus, a three-level hierarchy—in practice—generally frees up DASD space earlier than a tape-only migration scheme, which, after all, is the whole point of migration in the first place.[20]

DFSMShsm manages space very efficiently on migration volumes:

> Only used space is maintained (i.e., space containing data, as opposed to allocated but unused space).

> Used space itself can be compacted using the Huffman Frequency Encoding compaction algorithm.

> On DASD migration volumes, multiple small data sets can be "packed" onto a minimal number of tracks, even onto a single track. This contrasts to the standard MVS scheme of always allocating space for a data set in whole numbers of tracks, regardless of data set size. The small data sets are managed as records within a DFSMShsm data set called a Small Data set Packing (SDSP) data set.

Through these techniques, migrated data sets generally only require 50 percent or less of the space they originally occupied. So efficient space management can reduce a data center's overall DASD space requirement.

As mentioned above, the process of migration can be controlled by using volume space thresholds. There are two thresholds that can be assigned to DASD volumes, a high and a low threshold. In DFSMS/MVS, thresholds are specified in the storage group construct and apply to each volume in the storage group. In nonmanaged environments, these parameters are specified as DFSMShsm parameters.

The low threshold value is used to indicate when to initiate daily volume migration and when to stop it, avoiding work when there is already plenty of free space on the volume. For example, migration might be initiated once every night for a set of volumes when it is more than 80 percent full; migration will continue until that low threshold value is reached.

The high threshold value has two uses. First, it is used by an optional DFSMShsm facility called *interval migration.* In interval migration, DFSMShsm checks allocated volume space against the high

---

[20]It should be mentioned that DFSMShsm does allow an installation to migrate selected data sets directly to tape. This might be appropriate for data sets that are known not to be needed again for a long time. But, in practice, the three-level hierarchy should provide the greatest efficiencies for the bulk of the data set population.

threshold every hour. If allocated space is above the high threshold, DFSMShsm will migrate eligible data sets until allocated space is below the low threshold; this avoids repeatedly thrashing around a single threshold value. Interval migration is intended as a "safety valve" for unanticipated or very infrequent short-term peak space requirements. The second use of the high threshold is by MVS data set allocation which attempts to honor the high threshold when selecting volumes for new data sets. This helps to balance free space somewhat evenly across volumes, providing for the growth of existing data sets.

Expiration (Deletion)

DFSMShsm can expire (that is, delete) data sets that have gone unreferenced for an installation-specified number of days. In addition, DFSMShsm can automatically delete data sets that have been assigned expiration dates that have passed. Deleting data sets that are not needed makes the space they occupy available to other data sets.

On DFSMS/MVS-managed volumes, each data set can be assigned a management class indicating that the data set can be deleted by DFSMShsm based on criteria such as on a specified date, or after a specified number of days since it was created, or after a specified number of days since it was last referenced, or never.

MAXEXTENT Processing

DFSMShsm can detect that partitioned or sequential data sets have expanded beyond a specified number of extents and automatically reformat each such data set into a single large extent. Any unused space is automatically released, and partitioned data sets are automatically compressed. The secondary allocation quantity is preserved, meaning that MAXEXTENT processing allows data sets to continue to grow indefinitely into new extents. Further, reformatting a data set as a single extent can reduce seek processing, which can improve performance.

A Note on Volume vs. Data Set Management

In a DFSMS/MVS environment, most space management techniques can be applied at the data set level: different data sets on the same DFSMS/MVS-managed volume can be assigned unique space management policies. This is in contrast to non-DFSMS/MVS volumes where DFSMShsm generally manages all data sets on a given volume in the same way.

For example, in a non-DFSMS/MVS-managed environment, DFSMShsm deletes data sets on a given volume based on criteria associated with the volume as a whole, and fewer techniques are available than in a DFSMS/MVS environment. Installations that continue to manage data sets on a volume basis sometimes set aside some DASD volumes just to contain data sets that have a relatively short maximum life span; a utility is run periodically against each volume to delete all data sets created over "n" days ago.

(References: 18, 20, 102, 120, 124.)

QUESTION 24—DFSMSHSM AVAILABILITY MANAGEMENT

DFSMShsm automates the management of data set backup and recovery processing. Compare the way backup/recovery processing is traditionally handled in the absence of automation to the benefits DFSMShsm offers.

DASD data set and volume backup and recovery processing is traditionally handled in the following way. Data center personnel manually submit jobs that invoke a program such as DFSMSdss to back up entire volumes onto tapes. The backup cycle may be every night or every few days, possibly differing for each volume. The data center tracks which volumes are on which tapes in some form of a manual log and/or saves the SYSOUT listings from the backup jobs for use as a log.

Assume that a DASD volume is damaged and that the backup version of the volume needs to be restored. Someone in the data center searches the log for the volume serial numbers of the tapes that contain the most recent backup version. DFSMSdss is then run to restore the volume.

Sometimes, a user just needs a single data set restored—for example, a TSO user may have accidentally deleted a data set. When this happens, the user calls someone in the data center who can restore the data set. This is done either by restoring the entire volume to an empty device, then copying the desired data set to the target volume, or, if the dump/restore program supports it (as DFSMSdss does), by restoring just the desired data set directly from the full-volume dump. Note that this process involves personnel other than the affected user and may take some time to coordinate.

Let's contrast this to automated availability facilities in DFSMShsm.

The installation can have DFSMShsm automatically perform backup processing on command or at a given time on selected nights. DFSMShsm supports the backup of entire disk volumes as well as the backup of individual data sets. Let's discuss these capabilities in a bit more detail.

Full-Volume Backups

DFSMShsm can invoke DFSMSdss to perform full volume-backup functions according to installation specifications (e.g., each Sunday for volume A and every night for volume B). DFSMShsm interacts with DFSMSdss in such a way that DFSMShsm is informed of all data sets being dumped, and tracks them and the associated tape volume serial numbers in a special data set. The volume can be recovered by a command to DFSMShsm.

Incremental Backups

Incremental backup means DFSMShsm only backs up data sets that have changed (as indicated in the VTOC) since the last time they were backed up. Further, DFSMShsm can compact backup data sets to minimize the number of tape volumes required. And, DFSMShsm can manage data sets from multiple DASD volumes on a single tape.

DFSMShsm tracks the location of all backup versions of data sets. When a user needs to restore a data set, she can issue the DFSMShsm HRECOVER command under TSO, specifying the data set by name and a desired version or date. DFSMShsm will automatically perform the restore. Except for the possibility of an operator mounting a tape, no other personnel are involved.

What are the advantages of incremental dumps compared to full-volume dumps? Since the number of data sets that have changed is usually only a subset of all data sets, it usually takes less time and less tape volumes to save only those data sets. This is especially important in installations with many DASD volumes or with minimal time available in which to perform the backup process. So it might seem that everyone should use incremental dumps rather than full-volume dumps. However, there is a problem: What if an entire volume becomes unavailable due to an HDA (Head Disk Assembly) failure and must be recovered?

It is fairly easy to restore a disk volume from a full-volume dump. However, if only incremental data set backups are available for recovery, an indefinite number of tapes would need to be accessed to restore all data sets; some data sets may have been changed yesterday, but others not for weeks or months. The recovery process would not be easy to manage. Fortunately, DFSMShsm offers two good solutions to this problem.

1. Incremental backups and full-volume dumps together:

    One way the problem can be solved is by using the techniques of full-volume dump and incremental backup together. DFSMShsm manages the operation, invoking DFSMSdss for the actual physical movement. This takes advantage of the automation capabilities of DFSMShsm and the speed of DFSMSdss.[21]

    According to installation parameters, full-volume dumps are taken perhaps once a week and changed data sets are backed up daily. Via a single command, the installation can request DFSMShsm to recover a volume. DFSMShsm does this by restoring the most recent full-volume dump (actually, DFSMShsm invokes DFSMSdss to do this) and recovering all data sets changed since the date of the full-volume backup.

2. Guaranteed backup frequency:

    Another solution uses the *guaranteed backup frequency* parameter in the DFSMS/MVS storage group construct. For volumes in a storage group with the guaranteed backup frequency option specified, DFSMShsm will ensure that every data set is backed up at least once every n days even if it hasn't changed since the last backup; n is set by the installation. Guaranteed backup processing requires that DFSMSdss be used as the data mover for DFSMShsm backup processing. For ease of retrieval, all backups of data sets within the storage group are kept on a minimal number of tape volumes. This technique ensures that a volume can be recovered from incremental backups and that only a manageable number of tape volumes need be mounted. With this scheme, a full-volume dump would not be necessary.

On command, DFSMShsm can recover an individual data set regardless of whether the most recent copy is in a DFSMSdss full-volume dump created under DFSMShsm control, or is on a DFSMShsm-controlled (incremental or guaranteed) data set backup volume. Note that the ability to recover a data set from a full-volume dump is subject to some constraints that do not apply to recovery from a DFSMShsm backup volume; see reference 20. For example, the volume to which the data set is restored must be the same device type as the volume that was dumped.

---

[21]DFSMShsm must invoke DFSMSdss for full-volume dumps. DFSMShsm can optionally invoke DFSMSdss for incremental backups or can make the backup copy itself.

Point-in-Time Backups

To ensure that backup copies of data sets are very current, users often create their own ad hoc schemes. For example, assume that a batch job makes a major change to a data set. The job may make a backup copy of the data set immediately so that if the data set is lost before the usual installation backup cycle comes around (which may be hours or days later), the data set can be restored from the backup copy—often a faster process than rerunning the job. This kind of "point-in-time" backup is usually made onto a tape, often using a naming convention such as BKUP.mydata set. Many jobs doing this same thing means there are numerous tape mounts for this ad hoc backup processing.

A better alternative (except, perhaps, for very large data sets) is for the job to include a simple step that invokes DFSMShsm. DFSMShsm would immediately place a backup copy of the data set on a DFSMShsm-managed DASD volume. Periodically, DFSMShsm would move all such backups (perhaps from dozens or hundreds of jobs) onto a minimal number of tape volumes. DFSMShsm will manage the backup copies and any future recovery, just as described above. The advantages DFSMShsm offers include the managed tracking of the backups and the elimination of a separate tape mount for each backup request, which means reduced job delays, reduced need for tape volumes, and reduced operator intervention.

Similarly, TSO users can issue the DFSMShsm HBACKDS command to backup their data sets at any time, rather than create their own ad hoc copies (which are usually on DASD and not always on different volumes than the originals).

A Note on Currency

Keep in mind that using DFSMShsm and DFSMSdss, or other products, to provide full-volume and incremental backup capabilities does not necessarily make recovered data sets current—updates may have been made since the time of the last backup. Generally, only data base management systems and other specialized functions offer the ability to automatically track and restore changes to records as soon as they are made.

(References: 18, 20, 21, 102.)

QUESTION 25—REDUCING BACKUP PROCESSING TIME

Installations generally run jobs to create backup copies of their DASD volumes during off-shift hours. With the increasing use of online systems that have high availability and performance requirements, the so-called "window" of time during which these systems can be quiesced and backup jobs run has been shrinking. What actions can installations take to help reduce the amount of time required for backup processing?

There are several actions that can help reduce the length of time required for backup processing. Some are hardware solutions, some are software, and some are procedural.

- Use concurrent copy. Concurrent copy is the most powerful solution to the backup problem. With Concurrent Copy, DFSMS/MVS and the IBM 3990 Storage Control work together to take a point-in-time dump of one or more data sets, or even an entire volume. Conceptually, the dump is completed almost instantaneously. This means that jobs that modify the data sets being dumped can proceed without waiting for the physical dump process to complete.
- Ensure that backups are not made for disk volumes that do not require constant backup. For example, system data sets on the SYSRES (i.e., IPL) volume generally don't change. Some system data sets such as SYS1.LOGREC and page data sets do not require backup processing.
- Eliminate any redundant backup processing. For example, it may be the case that a volume containing only data bases is backed up by specialized data base utilities as well as by a full-volume backup process; since the specialized utilities are probably needed for data base recovery, the full-volume dump may be unnecessary.
- Review the frequency of backup for volumes that do require backup. Some volumes may only need to be backed up weekly, rather than every night.
- Review the number of volumes being backed up concurrently to see if the number can be increased.
- Install faster DASD. Data can be dumped from a volume only as fast as it can be read. 3390 DASD, for example, with a data transfer rate of 4.2MB/second, can dump data 40 percent faster than 3380 DASD, with a 3.0MB/second data transfer rate.

- Consider 3480 or 3490 tape cartridge subsystems.

  The speed of these tape subsystems better matches the speed of DASD. Tape subsystems with slower data transfer rates than the DASD being dumped could degrade dump performance. In particular, selected models of 3490 subsystems support the high transfer rates available when attached to ESCON channels.

  Cartridge loaders can be used to pre-load scratch tapes for dumps, reducing operator time.

  The effective capacity of a cartridge can be significantly increased through three capabilities. This is important because it reduces the number of cartridges required to be mounted to hold large data sets such as full-volume dumps. A standard tape cartridge might only hold about 200 megabytes of data while the capacity of a DASD volume is measured in gigabytes.

  1. The Improved Data Recording Capability (IDRC) can increase cartridge capacity by up to three to five times or more.
  2. 3490 Enhanced Capability models (3490E) use high-density recording techniques that double the capacity of a cartridge. And by writing data bi-directionally (front-to-back, then continuing back-to-front), rewind time for full cartridges is virtually eliminated.
  3. The 3490E models support an Enhanced Capacity Cartridge System Tape that further doubles the capacity of a cartridge through use of a longer tape.

  Together, these techniques can increase the effective capacity of a cartridge by up to 12 times or more! And these capabilities also improve throughput as well.

- Optimize use of DFSMSdss. The DFSMSdss DUMP command can retrieve data from DASD in various size increments, from one track to one cylinder at a time. Setting the OPTIMIZE keyword on the DUMP command to read an entire cylinder of data at a time can reduce dump time.

  Further, using the DFSMSdss COMPRESS parameter will encode the dumped data, reducing the number of tape volumes needed to hold the dump, which can also improve performance by reducing the number of tape mounts needed.

- Reduce the amount of dumping done for disaster recovery purposes. This can be done using DFSMSdss logical dumping or DFSMShsm Automatic Backup and Recovery (ABARS) processing. See "Question 27—Disaster Recovery Considerations."

- Use DFSMShsm to replace full-volume dumps by a backup process that only backs up changed data sets rather than entire DASD volumes. See "Question 24—DFSMShsm Availability Management."

(References: 17, 18, 51, 102.)

QUESTION 26—RECOVERING WASTED DASD SPACE

One of the tasks of storage administrators is to see that DASD space is used efficiently. Inefficient use of space could make it appear that space capacity is exhausted when in fact additional free space could be made accessible with a little effort. Create a list of ways space can be wasted, and in each case identify tools or procedures to help use space more efficiently.

The list below identifies some of the major ways in which DASD space can be used *in*efficiently. In each case, practices or products are identified that can help in recovering wasted space.

• *Allocated but unused space.* This can result when a data set's records do not completely fill the extents allocated to the data set. This usually occurs when a user is not sure how much space is needed for a new data set and so requests some large amount that "feels" like more than enough for current needs and future growth. If the unused space could be released, then it would be available to other data sets to use. As long as the data set was allocated with a secondary space quantity, then it will still be able to grow in the future.

   Here are some ways to release allocated but unused space for sequential and partitioned data sets.

When a data set is created in a DFSMS/MVS environment, it can be assigned a management class that specifies the installation policy for releasing allocated but unused space. For example, the policy might indicate that unused space should be freed as soon as the data set is closed, or that it should be freed during DFSMShsm's primary space management processing. Further, the policy can specify that space should only be released if the data set was created with a secondary space quantity so it is able to grow to additional extents if need be in the future. Because this management class support is integrated into the system and enforcement is automatic, it may be the best technique to implement.

The release attribute can be specified when allocating data sets via various system interfaces, including JCL DD statements, the TSO/E ALLOCATE command, and the dynamic allocation SVC. Unfortunately, this tends to require more discipline from users than is realistic to expect.

Installations can write MVS exits to request release of unused space. This probably requires the most work to implement. DFSMSdss supports a RELEASE command that can release allocated but unused space for selected data sets or all data sets on a volume.

When DFSMShsm migrates a data set, it frees the allocated space on the primary volume at that time and only places used space on the migration volume. When the data set is recalled, only used space is allocated if a secondary allocation quantity was originally assigned (DFSMShsm does not want to inhibit possible future growth).

DFSMShsm MAXEXTENT processing releases unused space through migrating and immediately recalling data sets that have grown beyond an installation-specified number of extents.

The ISMF (Interactive Storage Management Facility) CONDENSE and RELEASE commands will release unused space for data sets that are assigned secondary space quantities. CONDENSE invokes DFSMShsm to perform the release by migrating and immediately recalling the data set. RELEASE invokes DFSMSdss to release unused space in place.

- *Partitioned data set "gas."* New members in a PDS are always placed physically after the current last member. Over time, deletions and replacements of existing members will cause fragmentation ("gas"). In order to be able to reuse this space, the PDS must be reorganized in a process called *compression*.

  PDS gas is an old problem for which many solutions have been developed.

  The best solution is to eliminate the need for compression in the first place. That can be done by replacing PDS data sets with the newer PDSE (partitioned data set extended) data set format. PDSE data sets are functionally compatible with PDSs but are designed to reuse imbedded free space so that periodic compressions are not required; PDSEs offer other advantages over PDSs as well.

Historically, the IEBCOPY utility has been used to perform PDS compression. Data sets must be individually specified by name.

The DFSMSdss COMPRESS command will eliminate PDS fragmentation; it can process all or selected PDSs on a given volume.

DFSMShsm will automatically compress a migrated PDS when it is recalled.

DFSMShsm MAXEXTENT processing will automatically compress PDSs that have grown beyond an installation-specified number of extents; such data sets are automatically detected during automatic volume space management.

The ISMF CONDENSE and COMPRESS commands will perform the compress function against selected data sets. CONDENSE invokes DFSMShsm to perform the compression, and COMPRESS invokes DFSMSdss to perform the compression.

- *Uncataloged data sets.* On DFSMS/MVS-managed volumes all data sets are cataloged—this is enforced by the system. Many installations have a policy that all data sets on non-DFSMS/MVS-managed volumes must also be cataloged. This policy can be enforced by using DFSMSdss periodically to delete any uncataloged data sets. This is done by issuing the DFSMSdss DUMP command with the DELETE keyword and a filter that selects only uncataloged data sets. The dump can be targeted to a DD DUMMY data set; DFSMSdss detects this and will not actually waste any time doing I/O to read selected data sets before deleting them.
- *Old, unreferenced data sets.* DFSMSdss can be used to delete data sets that have gone unreferenced for some number of days, via the DUMP command with the DELETE keyword.

DFSMShsm offers sophisticated techniques to do this automatically.

DFSMShsm can delete data sets based on how many days they have gone unreferenced. It will search for such data sets once a day, without the need for anyone to enter a command or schedule a batch utility.

Alternatively, DFSMShsm migration support can detect data sets that have gone unreferenced for some number of days (not so many days that the data set should be arbitrarily deleted) and move them to a special migration volume (disk or tape) in a compacted form. Migrated data sets that continue to go unreferenced can be deleted automatically. See "Question 23—DFSMShsm Space Management" for a discussion of DFSMShsm migration.

- *Expired data sets.* MVS supports the assignment of an expiration date to a data set. However, this just prevents accidental change or deletion of the data set before that date—there is no mechanism native to MVS that automatically deletes a data set when its expiration date is past.

  DFSMSdss can select expired data sets through its filtering capability and delete them on command. DFSMShsm can do this automatically every night. In particular, DFSMShsm can migrate data sets after they remain unreferenced for some time (but have not yet expired), and automatically delete such migrated data sets when they finally do expire.

- *Fragmented DASD space.* Over time, as data sets are allocated, as they grow into new extents, and as they are deleted, space on DASD volumes becomes fragmented. This may make it hard to find contiguous space for new data sets, especially if they are relatively large.

  DFSMSdss supports a DEFRAG command that can reduce volume fragmentation through repositioning extents on a volume. This repositioning is done directly on the volume in question, without the need for an intermediate storage medium. Invocation of DEFRAG can be automated as follows. DFSMShsm calls a user exit routine for each volume processed by the DFSMShsm space management function. One parameter passed to the exit is a "fragmentation index" that indicates the extent to which the volume is fragmented. Installations can supply an exit routine that submits a job to invoke DFSMSdss DEFRAG when the index indicates that the volume is severely fragmented.

- *Cylinder allocation.* Users often specify cylinders as their unit of space when creating new data sets, partly because "everyone has known for years" that this improves performance for large sequential data sets (better techniques are discussed below). While release processing, discussed above, could eliminate unused cylinders, it cannot recover the unused tracks in the last or only cylinder of data sets allocated in cylinder units.

  The potential performance benefit of cylinder allocation applies mainly to processing large sequential data sets. When allocation is in units of tracks, the system traditionally constructed channel programs that caused MVS to get control via a hardware interrupt before the channel program proceeded from one track to the next in order to check if that next track was part of the data set. Allocation in units of cylinders allowed the channel program to be constructed so that an interrupt was only required after accessing all records in the same cylinder.

However, advances in storage management techniques and in DASD control units make the practice of cylinder allocation for performance generally unnecessary.

1. MVS allocates space for DASD data sets in units of cylinders, tracks, average block length, or average record length. The DFSMS/MVS data class construct only supports the average record length option; whether space is specified in a data class or directly in JCL, average record length should be considered the strategic technique. Certainly, specifying average record length (and number of records) seems the most natural way to request space. After all, how big is a track or a cylinder? Most users probably don't know, and, anyway, it depends on the device. Using average record length rather than cylinders provides a device-independent space request.

2. 3990 Storage Control units and 3880 DASD cache controllers support the Define Extent channel command that eliminates end-of-track and end-of-cylinder interrupts altogether, regardless of the original unit of allocation. This is accomplished by including a range of valid extents with the channel program, so that the control unit itself can check for valid access without having to ask MVS to do so.

-   *Block sizes*. Current DASD technology requires gaps of space between adjacent records on the same track, primarily for timing purposes. Since gaps occupy space that could be occupied by data, most access methods, such as VSAM and QSAM, support the ability to organize adjacent records into contiguous *blocks* on the disk. Applications are generally unaware of this blocking when using a record level interface provided by the access method. However, in practice, the block size, or blocking factor, is often determined by values specified in JCL or hardcoded in programs.

    Small block sizes use DASD space inefficiently, causing a data set to occupy more space than would be required for large block sizes. Reference 131 contains tables that indicate the efficiency of various block sizes for 3390 devices. For example, a small block size of 80 bytes would use only about 12 percent of a track, while a block size of 8000 bytes would use about 94 percent of a track! And fewer blocks means less physical I/Os to read and write records sequentially, improving performance as well as optimizing the use of space.

Reblocking of existing data sets can be performed by DFSMShsm and DFSMSdss. Installation exits can be used to set the block size of new data sets. The best way to set the block size of a new data set, however, is to omit it altogether or set it to zero for selected data set types, which will cause the system to determine an efficient block size automatically—for example, half track block sizes for sequential data sets—which is really the best way to handle things. This is particularly true since what is an efficient block size on one device may not be efficient on another. Let the system handle it.

- *Uncompressed data.* MVS/ESA Version 4, Release 3 introduced data compression services integrated into the operating system. Selected data types can be compressed through an algorithm implemented in software; on some ES/9000 processors the algorithm is implemented in hardware that can significantly reduce the processor utilization required for compression/decompression logic.[22]

While the amount of compression will vary depending on data patterns, typically a 50 percent or greater reduction in data can be achieved for supported data types. Data types that support MVS-based compression include DB2, IMS/DB, and DFSMS-managed VSAM, QSAM, and BSAM data sets. Some independent software vendors have announced products that use the MVS or hardware services to provide data compression for these and other data types as well.

While there is some administrative work needed to implement compression, and the impact on processor utilization should be evaluated, compression/decompression is normally transparent to application programs. There are also secondary benefits to data compression such as reduced channel and control unit utilization.

(References: 17, 70, 73, 80, 102, 131.)

---

[22]The data compression algorithm implemented in MVS is based on the ZivLempel technique, which replaces redundant character strings by short bit strings. For example, each occurrence of "Chicago, Illinois" in a database could be replaced by a 12-bit code.

QUESTION 27—DISASTER RECOVERY CONSIDERATIONS

A growing corporation recognizes the importance of data processing to the daily running of the business. In reviewing the ability of the business to continue running, were a physical disaster to occur at the data center site, the corporation decides to ensure that data processing can be resumed at a remote site. One part of the overall disaster recovery plan specifies that the corporate data center must periodically prepare copies of key data sets to be sent to the remote site. What basic techniques are available to make copies of DASD data sets in preparation for disaster recovery?

The following is a basic overview of techniques that can be used to prepare copies of DASD data sets for shipment to a remote site.

Note that this discussion focuses only on one piece of a comprehensive disaster recovery plan.

- *Full volume physical dumps*
  One scheme is simply periodically to take full volume dumps onto tapes of all DASD volumes in the data center. This can be done using DFSMSdss physical dump processing, perhaps under control of DFSMShsm. The tapes would then be stored at the remote site. This may be practical for small data centers with few volumes. Large data centers may find that the time to take the dumps is prohibitive, or that the recovery site is not large enough to support restoring copies of all volumes. Further, physical dumps require that source and target DASD volumes have the same device geometry (e.g., both are 3390s).
- *Logical dumps of applications*
  The data center may decide to reduce the amount of data to be collected for disaster recovery and only send copies of the most critical applications to the recovery site. Further, it may be decided to allow for restoration of the data sets onto device types different from those installed at the corporate data center. DFSMSdss logical processing can be selected to do this. DFSMSdss logical processing allows data sets to be selected via a filtering criteria (e.g., all data sets beginning with PAYROLL.). DFSMSdss locates data sets through a catalog search and so can gather them without the user having to specify the volumes on which they reside; multivolume data sets are handled automatically. The data sets can be restored

by DFSMSdss onto DASD device types that may be different from the source device types.

- *DFSMShsm Aggregate Backup and Recovery Support (ABARS)*
  ABARS can back up user-defined groups of data sets, where a group usually represents one application, and assist in recovery at a remote site. ABARS is more sophisticated than DFSMSdss logical processing.

  An "aggregate group" is defined by a storage administrator interactively through ISMF (Interactive Storage Management Facility). The aggregate group specifies a description of the aggregate (e.g., "payroll application"), data set names or filters, identification of any tape data sets that should accompany the aggregate, instructions to guide the recovery process, and the destination of the group. The DFSMShsm ABACKUP command is issued to create the aggregate; the command uses DFSMSdss to create the data set copies, and DFSMShsm itself to make copies of data sets that happened to be migrated (DFSMSdss logical processing by itself cannot handle migrated data sets). The DFSMShsm ARECOVER command is issued to recover the aggregate at the remote site.

(References: 17, 20, 102.)

QUESTION 28—REDUCING TAPE PROCESSING

An operations supervisor expresses concern about the size of the data center's tape library and the number of operators needed to handle tape mounts. What recommendations can you make to address this concern?

There are several steps that can be taken to help minimize tape processing. Some or all can be implemented as needed.

1. Use 3490/3480 tape cartridge subsystem technology to replace older "reel" technology.[23] Compared to older technology, 3490 and 3480 subsystems can save floor space for tape drives as well as for tape libraries, provide increased capacity on tape volumes, improve

---

[23]Given the widespread acceptance of cartridge technology, Hollywood won't be able to rely much longer on filming spinning reels of tape to show that "the computer" is doing something important.

reliability that can reduce job reruns due to tape-related errors, improve performance, and reduce power/cooling requirements.

2. Use cartridge loaders.[24] Cartridge loaders reduce manual mounting by supporting premounting of up to six cartridges per drive for new data sets. New data sets require mounting empty tapes referred to as "scratch" tapes. In practice, as many as 50 percent or more of all mounts call for scratch tapes, so speeding the mounting of just those tapes can have a significant impact on reducing average mount times. Since each 3490/3480 drive can have its own cartridge loader, multiple drives can be automatically loading cartridges at the same time, reducing delays.

3. Use high-capacity tape volumes. Increased tape volume capacity can reduce the number of volumes required to hold large data sets such as DASD volume dumps, reduce the overall number of tape mounts required, and reduce library space. There are three advances in IBM tape cartridge subsystems that independently increase cartridge capacity beyond that advance initially delivered in the mid-1980s— and these advances can be combined for maximum benefit.

The Improved Data Recording Capability (IDRC) is a data compression technique implemented within tape subsystem hardware. IDRC can significantly increase the amount of data that can be placed on a single cartridge, typically by a factor of 3 to 5.

The 3490 Enhanced Capability models (3490E) double the capacity of tape cartridges compared to previous models through the use of high-density recording techniques (36 tracks consisting of 4 bytes plus parity bits versus 18 tracks on base 3490 and all 3480 models). And by writing data bidirectionally (18 tracks front-to-back, then continuing on 18 different tracks back-to-front), rewind time for full cartridges is virtually eliminated.

Finally, the 3490E models support an Enhanced Capacity Cartridge System Tape that further doubles the capacity of a cartridge through use of a longer tape.

4. Move small data sets to DASD. Implementing this item can often significantly reduce tape processing.

Typically, most tape volumes contain only one file. It is often the case that the file may be fairly small compared to the capacity of a tape volume. For our purposes here, let's call data sets under 10

---

[24]Cartridge loaders were originally called automated cartridge loaders (ACLs). On 3490 subsystems, they are also referred to as integrated cartridge loaders since they are designed as integral parts of the drive frames.

megabytes in size "small." A single 3390-2 volume (1.9 gigabytes capacity) could hold hundreds of such data sets.

The following are some benefits of moving small data sets from tape to DASD:

Reduced requirement for library space.

Reduced tape mounts and thus decreased wait time by applications.

Reduced requirement for tape operators, or at least reduced time spent by operators mounting tapes, allowing them to spend their time doing more productive tasks.

Reduced need for tape drives.

Reduced need for additional tape volumes for growth.

Increased availability, in that an installation may choose to back up disk volumes and thus the data sets on them, something that is rarely done for tape data sets.

A JCL change would be sufficient to cause future creation of appropriate data sets to be on disk rather than tape. JCL referencing existing tape data sets should not have to be modified if the data sets are cataloged. A better solution exists in a system-managed storage environment under DFSMS/MVS, where automatic class selection routines coded by the installation can redirect small data sets from tape to DASD, without necessarily requiring JCL changes at all.

This scheme could be enhanced through the use of DFSMShsm. DFSMShsm would allow the oldest, unreferenced data sets now on DASD to be migrated to tape. But wait a minute, didn't we just move these data sets off tape? Yes, but in this case DFSMShsm can place multiple data sets on one tape in compacted format, so the number of volumes is still greatly reduced, and the space freed by migration could be used to contain still more small tape data sets. Further, under control of the installation, DFSMShsm only migrates data sets that have gone unreferenced for so long that they will likely not be accessed again in the future, minimizing tape mounts.

DFSMS/MVS includes a Volume Mount Analyzer program that helps identify the best data sets to move from tape to DASD.

5. Use DFSMShsm to manage the point-in-time backups that are often created by batch jobs.

Assume that a batch job makes a major change to a data set. The job may make a backup copy of the data set immediately so that if the data set is lost before the usual installation backup cycle comes around (which may be hours or days later), the data set can be restored from the backup copy—often a faster process than re-running the job.

This kind of "point-in-time" backup is usually made onto a tape, sometimes using a naming convention such as BKUP.mydata set. Many jobs doing this same thing means there are numerous tape mounts for this ad hoc backup processing.

With DFSMShsm, however, a special job step can be used that requests DFSMShsm to make a backup of the data set on DASD rather than tape. Once a day, DFSMShsm will batch together all such backup copies and write them, optionally in compacted format, to a minimal number of tapes, thus reducing mount activity and tape requirements.

(References: 18, 37, 49, 51, 102.)

QUESTION 29—DFSORT PERFORMANCE

Sorting has been an important application since the early days of data processing. Sorting may account for as much as 25 percent of processor resources plus significant I/O subsystem resources in many installations. So the performance of a sort program can be very important. Can you identify features of DFSORT that help you improve performance of sort jobs?

The following discussion reviews some of the more significant DFSORT performance features.

370-Extended Architecture introduced instructions specifically designed for use by DFSORT. DFSORT uses these instructions to improve the performance of its fixed-length record sorting algorithm.

DFSORT is designed to optimize the use of processor high-speed buffer storage.

DFSORT offers Hipersorting and dataspace sorting, techniques that sort data using processor storage as much as possible, reducing physical I/O activity and elapsed time.

DFSORT can use DASD for temporary work files. DFSORT optimizes its performance on DASD devices through awareness of DASD geometry (bytes per track, tracks per cylinder).

DFSORT uses the Read Track channel command on the 3990 Storage Control to reduce processor time.

DFSORT uses cached control units efficiently. DFSORT can provide enhanced performance through its use of the Cache Fast Write mode of the 3990-3 Storage Control. In this mode, DFSORT writes its work files to cache at cache speeds without waiting for or requiring writes to the backing DASD.

DFSORT uses the EXCPVR SVC for I/O to reduce processor time. When using EXCPVR, DFSORT will perform a single page-fix operation at initialization time, and a single page-free at termination time, rather than a fix/free operation for each I/O. It is practical to exploit storage in this way given the current availability of large processor storage sizes.

DFSORT includes a replacement for the standard IBM IEBGENER utility for copying data sets. The DFSORT version of this program offers significantly improved performance.

Demonstrating DFSORT Capabilities

The market for sort programs is very competitive. The ultimate proof of performance is how well a given package performs in a real production environment. Reference 30 will help you design a fair, effective sorting benchmark.

(References: 22, 30, 38, 54.)

QUESTION 30—STORAGE MANAGEMENT—SYSTEM SOLUTIONS

A unique value of IBM is its ability to provide integrated "system solutions." IBM's hardware and software development organizations work together to provide a set of integrated products that deliver comprehensive solutions to customer problems. Give as many examples as you can to illustrate how IBM integrates the hardware and software storage products supported by MVS.

The following list identifies ways in which IBM hardware and software storage products interact with each other. This list is not complete, and you may identify additional items not cited here.

- DFSMS/MVS supports the concurrent copy function in the 3990 Storage Control. Concurrent copy allows point-in-time dumps of data sets and volumes to be taken quickly so that other work can proceed with integrity (that is, changes can be made to the data without affecting the point-in-time contents of the dumped copy). The DFSMSdfp storage class and management class constructs allow a storage administrator to specify that a new data set is eligible for concurrent copy. DFSMSdss provides the external interface to invoke concurrent copy processing.

- DFSMShsm supports the DFSMSdfp management class construct that can be assigned to new data sets in a DFSMS/MVS-managed storage environment. This interaction allows DFSMShsm management techniques to be tailored to the data set level, as opposed to the volume level.

- DFSMShsm makes a backup copy of the associated RACF discrete profile (if one exists) when it backs up a data set.

- DFSMShsm can optionally invoke DFSMSdss as a high-speed data mover for functions such as migration and recall in place of DFSMShsm's native facilities. Using DFSMSdss in this way also adds support for more data set types than DFSMShsm supports natively, such as PDSE. DFSMShsm can also invoke DFSMSdss for full volume dump/restore processing. DFSMShsm will recover an individual data set on command from its own backup volumes or from a DFSMSdss volume, whichever contains the latest copy, transparent to the requestor.

- DFSMShsm uses the high-speed search capability of the IBM 3480/3490 cartridge tape subsystems. DFSMShsm can create on a cartridge one physical file that in fact includes many data sets; this is called *singlefile format* in DFSMShsm. In this format, DFSMShsm uses high-speed search to locate any particular data set (for recall or recover) without tying up channel and control unit resources. Not only does this improve performance, but it also uses the space on cartridges more efficiently by reducing the number of data set labels.

- DFSMShsm helps improve operator productivity by supporting use of IBM 3480/3490 tape subsystem cartridge loaders. Typically, when DFSMShsm's migration or backup processing to tape has ended, tapes mounted for these functions will not yet be full and will be the first tapes to be selected when processing resumes the next day. DFSMShsm can optionally mark such partially full tapes as full anyway, so that all subsequent mounts for migration or backup processing call for empty tapes that can be satisfied from primed cartridge loaders.

- The DCOLLECT command in the IDCAMS utility in DFSMSdfp extracts information about volumes and data sets into a single file for reporting. DCOLLECT interacts with DFSMShsm to extract information about migrated and backed up data sets. The Service Level Reporter (SLR) product has a built-in capability to produce reports from DCOLLECT output.
- The ISMF application runs under ISPF in TSO/E. It is part of the MVS/DFP product. ISMF can invoke DFSMShsm, DFSMSdss, ICKDSF, DFSORT, DCOLLECT, and DASD cache management functions through full-screen menus, eliminating the need for users to create JCL in many cases.
- DFSMShsm and DFSMSdss support the RACF erase-on-scratch option for data sets protected with that attribute.
- DFSMS/MVS supports the performance and availability features of IBM DASD subsystems. When a new data set is allocated, MVS will determine where the data set should be placed based on installation-specified service requirements. For example, if an installation assigns a storage class that specifies AVAILABILITY=CONTINUOUS to a new data set, DFSMS/MVS will place the data set on a dual copy (duplexed) volume under a 3990 Storage Control. In a separate process called *dynamic cache management*, DFSMS/MVS communicates with 3990 cache controllers dynamically to turn caching on or off for data sets the installation has indicated should only be cached when it would not degrade the performance of more important data sets.
- RACF provides authorization control over the use of DFSMS/MVS class constructs and storage administrator functions.
- MVS device allocation can detect the presence of cartridge loaders on IBM cartridge tape subsystems and will always prefer satisfying requests for scratch tapes from such drives.
- DFSORT exploits special capabilities in XA and ESA-mode IBM processors. In these modes, the processors support instructions designed for use by DFSORT to improve the performance of its fixed-length record sorting algorithm.
- DFSORT can provide enhanced performance through its use of the Cache Fast Write mode of the 3990 Storage Control. In this mode, DFSORT writes its temporary files to cache at cache speeds without waiting for or requiring writes to the backing DASD.
- DFSMSdss and DFSORT use the Read Track channel command in the 3990 Storage Control to improve performance by reducing processor time.

(References: 17, 18, 20, 22, 37, 70, 73.)

QUESTION 31—BENEFITS OF STORING IMAGES ON OPTICAL MEDIA

Historically, digital computers have generally been limited to storing and processing coded data such as alphanumeric text. Permanent storage media has predominantly been magnetic disk and tape. Some estimates indicate, however, that as much as 95 percent of the information used in an enterprise is in fact noncoded data such as microfiche or paper. High-density optical storage media is increasingly being employed to store noncoded visual data such as pictures and documents. What are the benefits to an organization of storing and managing images in this way?

Image processing solutions such as IBM's ImagePlus product family, which manages digitized images of scanned documents, can offer the following general benefits to an organization.

- *Cost savings*
  The total cost of managing paper documents, including storage space, storage equipment (file cabinets, folders, perhaps movable racks), and personnel, may be greater than the costs of an automated image-processing solution. Storage space for paper documents can become quite large, especially if old documents must be retained for legal reasons.

  Increased productivity is another cost savings. Documents stored in a computer system can be retrieved at electronic speeds. There is no need for a person to walk to a file cabinet to retrieve, and later to return, a document, or to write an order for a clerk to do that work.
- *Improved customer service*
  The time to search for a document is reduced. Customers who phone a business with a query don't have to wait for a manual search for a paper document to be performed and a phone call returned.
- *Availability/access to information*
  Paper documents can become lost. When one person is using a paper document, it is usually unavailable to other persons. Images managed by a computer system can't become lost in this way, and backup copies could be made. Image processing also makes it possible for multiple users to access the same document at the same time.

(Reference: 44.)

5

Catalogs

Catalogs have always been an integral part of MVS. They provide an inventory of permanent data sets and the volumes on which they reside, eliminating the need for users to track this information themselves. This allows users to access data sets by name only, providing device independence and ease of use. New catalog types have been introduced over the years. While ICF catalogs are the most strategic and provide the best function and performance, older catalog types remain supported for compatibility.

QUESTION 32—TYPES OF CATALOGS

Name the three types of catalogs supported by MVS and briefly describe each type.

MVS supports three types of catalogs:

* Integrated Catalog Facility (ICF) Catalog
* VSAM Catalog
* Control Volume (CVOL) Catalog

CVOL catalogs are the oldest type of catalog and originated in the MVT (Multiple Variable Tasks) operating system from which MVS evolved.

CVOLs support all MVS data set types except for VSAM, which was not introduced until MVS.

VSAM catalogs (comprised of VSAM master and VSAM user catalogs) were introduced with MVS as a single catalog type to support both VSAM and non-VSAM data sets. CVOLs continued to be supported for compatibility. In practice, because CVOLs performed better than VSAM catalogs, VSAM catalogs were mainly used for VSAM data sets only, while CVOLs continued to be used for all other data set types. Thus prior to ICF catalogs, most installations supported both CVOL and VSAM catalogs.

ICF catalogs were introduced in the early 1980s as a single, efficient replacement for both CVOL and VSAM catalogs. VSAM and CVOL catalogs continue to be supported for compatibility.

IBM made the following statement in 1983 in announcement letter 283-141.

> CVOL and VSAM catalog stabilization: The integrated catalog facility catalog...is a functional replacement for VSAM master catalogs, VSAM user catalogs, and OS control volume (CVOL) catalogs, with improvements in reliability, recovery, performance, and usability.
>
> The integrated catalog facility may be used to replace all catalog functions and facilities. OS control volume catalogs and VSAM master and user catalogs are functionally stabilized. Catalog functional enhancements, if any, will be provided by the integrated catalog facility.

(Reference: 71.)

QUESTION 33—BENEFITS OF ICF CATALOGS

An installation expresses concern about the amount of time required to convert existing catalogs to ICF catalogs. What are some major benefits of ICF catalogs that motivate conversion from other catalog types?

Some major advantages of ICF catalogs:

- *Enhanced function/ease of management.* Newer functions in MVS and associated products requiring catalog support are only being implemented for ICF catalogs. Here is a partial list of such functions.

VSAM catalogs have the restriction that only one VSAM catalog can control the VSAM data sets on a given volume. For example, if a system uses a VSAM master catalog, various system VSAM data sets such as the SMF data sets are cataloged in that master catalog. This ownership restriction means that any other VSAM data sets on the same volumes as the SMF data sets must be cataloged in the VSAM master catalog only. This restriction is removed for ICF catalogs.

ICF catalogs can easily be split apart and merged together.

ICF supports more control interval sizes for VSAM objects than the older VSAM catalogs. This can improve the utilization of space on DASD volumes.

DFSMSdss and DFSMShsm support VSAM data sets more completely if they are cataloged in an ICF catalog. For example, DFSMShsm supports data set migration and recall of VSAM data sets only if they are cataloged in an ICF catalog.

Certain data set organizations must be cataloged in ICF catalogs. DB2 tables, VSAM linear data sets, and PDSE data sets are examples.

As of MVS/DFP Version 3, ICF catalogs support alias names of up to four levels—for example, data sets beginning A.B.C can be cataloged in one ICF user catalog, while those beginning A.B.D can be cataloged in another.

- *System-managed storage.* Data sets that are brought under the control of DFSMS/MVS must be cataloged in ICF catalogs. Because of the significant benefits of the DFSMS/MVS environment, this may be the single strongest reason for converting to ICF catalogs. See Question 18—System-Managed Storage—for more information on DFSMS/MVS.
- *Performance.* Generally, ICF catalogs perform catalog requests (e.g., LOCATE, DEFINE, DELETE) faster than VSAM or CVOL catalogs.
- *Recovery.* Since catalogs are resources shared by many applications, catalog outages can have a significant impact on system availability. ICF catalogs provide many benefits with respect to recovery.

VSAM catalogs contain logical information about VSAM data sets such as owner and retention period, and physical information such as extent information and pointers to areas within a data set.

The process of recovering a damaged VSAM data set or catalog may cause the data set and the information about it in the catalog to become out of sync; for example, the extent information in a restored copy of a catalog may not match the actual extents now occupied by referenced data sets. VSAM detects this condition through its maintenance of time-stamps in VSAM catalog entries and the VTOCs of owned volumes; if the time-stamps don't match, VSAM denies OPEN requests. When this happens, a systems programmer must take actions to correct the problem.

On the other hand, the ICF structure stores physical information about a VSAM data set on the same volume as that data set in a file called the VSAM Volume Data Set (VVDS). The VVDS can be thought of as an extension to the VTOC. Full volume backup/restore and data set EXPORT/IMPORT functions will keep the VVDS and its data sets in synchronization automatically. Similarly, restoring an ICF catalog does not alter the currency of the physical information in the VVDS. All of this eliminates the need to maintain the time-stamps. Consequently, the process of VSAM data set and catalog recovery is easier to manage in an ICF environment.

In addition to this ease of recovery, the ICF Recovery Utility (ICFRU) can be used to bring the restored copy of a catalog up to date; no comparable facility exists for VSAM catalogs or CVOLs. See Question 36—Integrated Catalog Forward Recovery Utility—for more information.

Another advantage of ICF catalog recovery involves processing of *aliases*. Basically, the master catalog contains alias names for each user catalog or CVOL (the names are defined by the systems programmer). The aliases are the high-level qualifiers of the data set names in the user catalog; for example, if a user catalog has an alias of "APPL3.", then all data sets beginning "APPL3." are cataloged in that user catalog. If IMPORT is used to bring an older VSAM catalog into a system for recovery purposes, then any aliases associated with that catalog must be manually redefined by the systems programmer. However, for ICF-catalogs only, EXPORT maintains associated aliases and IMPORT redefines them automatically.

Finally, DFSMSdfp supports the ability to temporarily "lock" ICF catalogs so that they can be recovered without first shutting down any subsystems that have OPENed them. DFSMSdss uses this facility when copying and restoring ICF catalogs.

(References: 17, 21, 71, 112.)

QUESTION 34—ICF CATALOG STRUCTURE

Briefly describe the major components of an ICF catalog structure, both within a given ICF catalog and between catalogs.

The major components of an ICF catalog structure are the Basic Catalog Structure (BCS) and the VSAM Volume Data set (VVDS).

The BCS is a VSAM key-sequenced data set (KSDS), which contains information about data sets including volume, device-type, DFSMS/MVS class names, and other information. The BCS does not contain details about physical data set organization such as extent location, but rather high-level information that tends to change infrequently, at most, during the life of a data set; this simplifies the recovery of volumes and catalogs.

More detailed data set information is maintained on the same volumes as the data sets in structures called the VVDS and VTOC.

VTOC stands for Volume Table of Contents. Every volume has a VTOC that is created when the volume is formatted for use by the operating system. The VTOC contains extent information and data set organization information for all data sets on its volume and thus serves as a directory to those data sets.

VVDS stands for VSAM Volume Data set. The VVDS is a VSAM entry-sequenced data set (ESDS) that can be thought of as an extension to the VTOC. The VVDS was originally created as a place to maintain additional information about the organization of VSAM data sets, and, as such, there is a VVDS on every volume containing VSAM data sets, including the volumes containing a BCS. Moreover, *every* DFSMS/MVS-managed volume has a VVDS that is used also to contain the names of the DFSMS/MVS classes assigned to each of the data sets on the volume.

ICF catalogs relate to each other in the following way. In a single MVS system there is always one *master* catalog. The master catalog typically points to one or more *user* catalogs. The hierarchy is limited to these two levels. When MVS needs catalog information (such as the volume that data set APPL1.LIBRARY resides on), it begins its search in the master catalog. The information is either in the master catalog or in a user catalog the master catalog points to. For example, an installation can choose to have all data sets that begin "APPL1." be cataloged in a single user catalog; the master catalog will then have an entry called an *alias* for APPL1 that points to that user catalog. One possible catalog structure is illustrated in Figure 5.1.

(References: 71, 124.)

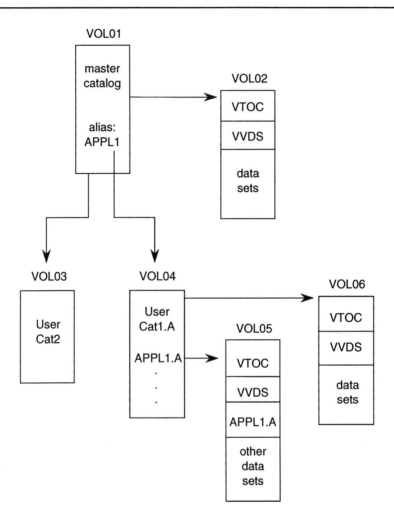

Though not shown, even catalog volumes contain VTOCs and VVDSs. Also,
volumes containing catalogs can contain other data sets as well; such

Figure 5.1. A possible ICF catalog structure.

QUESTION 35—MANAGING ICF CATALOGS

Describe basic considerations for managing an ICF catalog structure in terms of security, size (number of entries), number of catalogs, recovery, sharing, and performance.

- *Security.* The master catalog should only contain pointers to system (e.g., SYS1.) data sets and connections to the user catalogs that will contain application data set information. This makes the master catalog fairly stable so it can be easily recovered and secured against update. Restricting updates ensures that users cannot arbitrarily create new high-level data set name qualifiers, helping to control naming conventions.
- *Size.* The space required for a BCS can be estimated based on the size and number of different entry types. There is no "best" catalog size, at least not in terms of numbers of entries. Because if a catalog is unusable, applications dependent on the catalog can't run, it makes sense to limit the number of entries or to limit the scope of entries to a small number of applications. Also, from a performance point of view, the more entries in a catalog, the busier it might be. Finally, too large a catalog can increase the number of index levels, which can also degrade performance.
- *Number.* There is no straightforward answer as to the number of catalogs an installation should have. A guideline to consider: from control, performance, backup, and recovery points of view, it is desirable for each major application or each individual department to have its own catalog.
- *Sharing.* Catalogs can be shared by multiple systems. Note, however, that a master catalog cannot be shared by multiple systems, at least not in its role as a master catalog, because there are unshareable data sets such as SYS1.LOGREC cataloged in the master catalog.
- *Performance.* There are many considerations here, including the following.

    Catalogs, particularly catalogs used by TSO users, can be highly active data sets. Thus, for best performance, they should be kept on volumes separate from other highly active data sets. Also, catalogs are generally excellent candidates for caching, especially given their relatively small size.

    Place the catalog, VTOC, and VVDS close together on a volume, to reduce seek time.

A catalog may expand into multiple noncontiguous extents over time, which can cause additional or longer seeking. If this occurs, EXPORT/IMPORT should be used to reorganize the catalog by consolidating extents.

MVS/ESA can reduce catalog I/Os by keeping frequently referenced catalog entries in a data space and by improved algorithms for managing shared catalogs. Even so, sharing of catalogs by multiple systems may impact system performance. To serialize access to shared catalogs, MVS uses the RESERVE/RELEASE mechanism. Because a physical RESERVE is a lock on an entire volume, for best performance actual sharing should be minimized. Global Resource Serialization (GRS) should be considered in order to convert physical RESERVEs to a more granular serialization mechanism.

(References: 71, 89, 102.)

QUESTION 36—INTEGRATED CATALOG FORWARD RECOVERY UTILITY

An installation just went through the very difficult process of manually recovering a catalog. They realize that catalog recovery may again be needed in the future, but they would prefer to never have to go through manual catalog recovery again. Describe how the Integrated Catalog Forward Recovery Utility (ICFRU) can assist in automating the recovery of an ICF catalog.

ICFRU assists MVS users in recovering a damaged BCS (Basic Catalog Structure) within an ICF catalog environment to a correct and current status. When a damaged BCS is recovered by restoring a backup copy, the newly restored catalog does not reflect any changes to the original catalog since the time that the backup was made. The systems programmer must take manual actions to recatalog data sets created after the backup was made, delete catalog entries for data sets deleted after the backup was made, and reissue any ALTER commands (via the IDCAMS utility) that changed catalog contents. This process is called forward recovery. Reference 65 bluntly states

Depending on the tools at hand, this part of the procedure may well be the most difficult and time-consuming part of the catalog recovery. Without user program support this phase may consist of many steps, most of which are manual.

When an important resource such as a catalog is unavailable, probably the last thing an installation wants is to have to perform difficult, time-consuming, manual recovery procedures. Since catalog failures are rare, there will likely not be a lot of expertise around to speedily return things to normal. Fortunately, the forward recovery process can be largely automated by using the Integrated Catalog Forward Recovery Utility program.

An error-free backup of an undamaged basic catalog structure is used as the base for recovery. Catalog changes logged as SMF (System Management Facilities) records are selected and applied to this backup to create a new image of the catalog as it should now exist. This image of the catalog can then be reloaded to produce a current basic catalog structure.

You can view ICFRU as an insurance policy. You hope you never need it, but you're sure glad you have it if you do. Once this program is installed, it can be used to rehearse recovery procedures so that an actual recovery situation, difficult enough on its own, does not also require additional time for education.

(References: 65, 112.)

QUESTION 37—MASTER CATALOG AVAILABILITY

An installation is conducting a study in order to help them increase their system availability. The master catalog is identified as a single point of failure. What actions would you recommend to ensure that MVS can continue to run even if the master catalog is unusable?

There are two major techniques to address master catalog availability.

MVS allows an alternate master catalog to be specified by the operator at IPL time. It is the installation's responsibility to create and maintain a copy of the master catalog in case the original master is not available (because, say, the disk volume on which it resides could not be accessed).

Another technique is to use the dual copy facility of the 3990 Storage Control. This technique would automatically maintain a duplicate copy of the entire volume on which the master catalog resides, eliminating the need to keep the two catalogs synchronized manually. If data cannot be accessed from the primary volume, the 3990 automatically accesses that data from the secondary volume. This technique is more general than just providing an alternate master catalog since it protects the entire volume, and many data sets deemed critical to system availability could also be placed on that volume.

(References: 54, 71.)

6

Time Sharing Option/ Extended

There are many online, interactive subsystems that run on large systems. The Time Sharing Option/Extended, TSO/E, provides users a personal view of a shared MVS system.

For systems programmers and system administrators, there are tools for system maintenance and systems management. For application developers, there are tools for program development and testing. For end users, there is access to decision support and other productivity tools.

QUESTION 38—COMPARING TSO/E AND OTHER TRANSACTION ENVIRONMENTS

An application development organization is planning to rewrite major transaction-based applications that drive the business. The new applications are expected to be in place for years, just as the ones they are replacing have been, so even the most basic design decisions are being carefully reviewed. One of the earliest topics under discussion is the transaction environment in which the applications should run. Candidate environments include TSO/E, VM/CMS, CICS, IMS/TM, and APPC/MVS. Describe the major highlevel differences between these subsystems and describe the types of applications for which each is designed.

Let's start with the basics. Nonbatch transactions can be conceptually viewed as follows:

1. A person at a terminal enters some information, perhaps a command or an entry on a full-screen menu or a click of a mouse to select an icon.
2. The information is sent to a controlling subsystem (TSO/E, et al.) on a host system.
3. The controlling subsystem passes the information to an application program for processing.
4. The application program processes the information, perhaps accessing data on auxiliary storage, then sends back a response to the user at the terminal.
5. The cycle repeats.

This scenario is generally called *transaction processing*. This scenario is also referred to as *online* transaction processing, especially for short, repetitive transactions such as order entry, or as *interactive* processing, especially for more complex, less repetitive processing, such as ad hoc database queries or computer-based modeling applications.[25]

Historically, in transaction environments the user is at a non-programmable terminal in direct communication with a large mainframe. Increasingly, the user may be at a programmable workstation, running programs within the workstation and submitting transactions to be run remotely at the mainframe. Programming in the workstation may simply make the workstation appear as a nonprogrammable terminal to the mainframe. Or, programming in the workstation and host may be designed to work together to implement what appears to be a single application from the user's point of view, in which case the above scenario is increasingly being called *cooperative processing*.

In trying to get our hands around the differences between the various application environments, it will help to group together the environments according to the above terminology. TSO/E and CMS are generally considered interactive environments, CICS and IMS/TM online environments, and APPC/MVS a cooperative processing environment.

---

[25]These terms are not used consistently in the industry and are often used interchangeably.

MVS TSO/E and VM/CMS

TSO/E runs under the MVS operating system. The Conversational Monitor System (CMS) runs as a guest machine under the VM operating system. The general strategy of TSO/E and CMS is to provide an environment that can be used for

- Application development and testing.
- Information Center and decision support applications for end users.
- Maintenance of the system by systems programmers.

The TSO/E and CMS environments include many commands provided by IBM; installations can also add their own commands. Both TSO/E and CMS have been available for many years and are used extensively by many installations around the world.

There are many similarities between TSO/E and CMS. From the point of view of many users, there may seem to be few significant differences between these subsystems. Many products run in both environments, including ISPF, ISPF/PDF, GDDM, DCF, and compilers. Many non-IBM products also run in both environments. A major advantage of TSO/E is the ability to access the extensive function of the underlying MVS system. A major advantage of CMS is its ability generally to support more concurrent transactions on a given machine than is possible in a TSO/E environment.

CICS and IMS/Transaction Manager

CICS and IMS/TM are sometimes called DC (Data Communications) or TP (Teleprocessing) monitors.[26]

In contrast to TSO/E and CMS, CICS and IMS/TM provide environments in which primarily user-written applications (perhaps developed under TSO/E or CMS) can run and access data bases. These environments provide access to a subset of MVS function—for example, not all MVS data set types are supported as data bases.

Unlike TSO/E and CMS, CICS and IMS/TM provide extensive fa-

---

[26]Note that this high-level discussion applies to the current CICS/ESA and IMS/ESA products, as well as to their predecessor products. The current IMS/ESA product consists of two components: IMS/Transaction Manager (IMS/TM), and IMS/Database Manager (IMS/DM), which supports a hierarchical data base organization. Earlier versions of IMS used the terms IMS/DC and IMS/DB.

cilities for data base integrity, such as automatic backout of changes in case a transaction does not terminate normally. Subsystem availability is enhanced through support for the MVS Extended Recovery Facility (XRF). A very significant point is that CICS and IMS/TM provide for concurrent access to data bases by multiple users who are reading and updating the data; in contrast, while multiple TSO/E (or CMS) users can read a single data set at the same time, a single TSO/E user must have exclusive control of a data set in order to update it.

Major differences between CICS and IMS/TM include the following:

- IMS/TM supports IMS/DM (DL/1) and DB2 data bases. CICS supports these as well as VSAM files.
- IMS/TM supports a "fast path" function that offers very high system throughput rates.
- CICS provides portability through following System Application Architecture (SAA) standards. CICS products currently run in the MVS, VM, VSE, and OS/2, and other environments, providing a common application programming interface.

APPC/MVS

APPC/MVS is the newest transaction environment, available beginning in 1991.

APPC stands for Advanced Program-to-Program Communication, referring to the SNA LU6.2 protocol that underlies the communications supported between APPC/MVS and programs outside of APPC/MVS.

APPC/MVS can play a significant role as MVS increasingly supports large-scale services in client/server environments. In particular, APPC/MVS provides an environment for what is called *cooperative processing*. In cooperative processing, an application's logic is split between two or more computing systems. A common example of cooperative processing is a user running application programs in a programmable workstation. These programs do some local processing such as managing an interactive graphical interface providing high-usability characteristics, and also invoke programs on remote processors, perhaps in an APPC/MVS environment, to access data from large shared data bases as well as to use other facilities. Alternatively, a program in an MVS system could run under APPC/MVS in order to initiate communications with programs in remote programmable workstations, to collect statistics on workstation activity, or to distribute useful information. Programs in each computer cooperate to provide a single application solution.

APPC/MVS provides a rich platform for cooperative processing applications. Programs that run under APPC/MVS have access to all MVS facilities, including standard MVS data sets. Further, APPC/MVS programs can invoke TSO/E commands and can communicate with subsystems such as IMS, CICS, and DB2.

Programs that run within APPC/MVS are expected to be written by users and/or software vendors. These programs can use Systems Application Architecture (SAA) programming interfaces[27] so that they are portable to other SAA platforms; of the other environments, only CICS offers portability. Optional programming interfaces that take advantage of unique capabilities within MVS, such as data spaces, are also provided.

An example of a system facility that uses APPC/MVS is the Distributed FileManager facility that, as of this writing, IBM has stated it intends to deliver in a future release of DFSMS/MVS. Distributed FileManager supports the SAA Distributed Data Management (DDM) architecture that provides record-level access to files on distributed systems.

APPC/MVS provides an extremely powerful environment whose importance should grow significantly over time.

(References: 95, 126.)

QUESTION 39—MANAGING TSO/E STEPLIBS

Programmers frequently test new versions of programs under TSO/E by placing these programs in special libraries that are accessed by a STEPLIB DD statement in the logon procedure. Describe the reasons for this technique, what its limitations are, and identify an IBM program that enhances STEPLIB management for TSO/E users.

Let's begin by reviewing the function of the STEPLIB facility.

When requested to access a program, MVS normally searches for that program in a list of libraries specified in the LNKLSTnn member of SYS1.PARMLIB. Through JOBLIB and STEPLIB statements, jobs can specify the names of one or more libraries that MVS will search before searching the LNKLST libraries.

A TSO/E user is viewed by MVS as a job step and can have a STEPLIB DD statement in his or her logon procedure. A common rea-

---

[27]The SAA interface in APPC/MVS is the Common Programming Interface—Communications (CPI-C).

son to do this is so that the user can test programs with the same names as production programs without affecting users of the production programs. A secondary reason is that having a STEPLIB can improve performance when the user is frequently accessing the programs in the STEPLIB library, since that library is searched first.

Unfortunately, standard system facilities for managing STEPLIBs are not very flexible. Once a TSO/E session is active, there is no way to change the libraries named on the STEPLIB DD statement, or to terminate STEPLIB processing for the session, short of logging off and then logging on with a new logon procedure. If a STEPLIB is allocated but no longer needed during a session, performance may suffer because MVS will continue first to search STEPLIB libraries for programs and commands before searching the normal LNKLST libraries.

The MVS/TSO Dynamic STEPLIB Facility Program Offering can solve this problem. This product provides an ISPF interface that allows TSO/E users to allocate dynamically, change, or unallocate the STEPLIB assigned to their sessions. This eliminates the need for installations to create and maintain special LOGON procedures containing the STEPLIB DD statements.

(Reference: 103.)

QUESTION 40—DIALOG MANAGEMENT

An installation is planning to write an in-house interactive application under TSO/E to provide various services to their data processing professional staff. What product would you recommend the installation use to provide basic dialog management for this application?

The application should be designed to use the Interactive System Productivity Facility (ISPF). ISPF is a dialog manager.

A dialog is a "conversation" between a person who is using a full-screen terminal and a computer that is executing a program. The user communicates with the program by entering information in response to inquiries (prompts) that the program presents on the screen. Responding to the user's input, the program can invoke a routine, file the user's input in a data base, display information from a data base, or take some other action. After each interaction, the program prompts the user to enter additional information. The process is repeated until the user ends the dialog.

The user sees the dialog as a series of panels or menus. ISPF provides facilities to invoke functions selected on panels and to pass control from panel to panel. Selected functions can be implemented by an installation through programs written in languages such as COBOL, C, or assembler, and/or through REXX or CLIST procedural languages.

Most TSO/E installations are already somewhat familiar with dialogs through their use of the ISPF/PDF (Program Development Facility) product that provides editing and other environmental services useful to data processing professionals. PDF is itself a dialog that is implemented using the ISPF dialog manager. PDF, among other functions, provides facilities to assist installations in creating and testing their own dialogs to run under ISPF.

IBM generally designs new interactive applications for the TSO/E environment to run under ISPF. Examples include RACF, SMP/E, and the ISMF storage management facility in DFSMS/MVS. Installations generally add these applications to the standard list of options available on the ISPF/PDF main menu. It would be natural for an installation's home-grown application to become another option for users to select from this menu.

(Reference: 58.)

QUESTION 41—MANAGEMENT OF APPLICATION DEVELOPMENT LIBRARIES

A particular installation has for years had a relatively lax process of application development. However, they recently had some major problems in their production runs. After some research and a lot of aggravation, the cause was identified as multiple developers unknowingly changing the same programs at the same time, and placing the programs into production libraries before testing had been completed. To avoid this happening again, the installation wants to incorporate change management disciplines into their application development process. Identify facilities within the ISPF/PDF product for TSO/E that can help the installation better manage its application development efforts.

There are two facilities within ISPF/PDF to assist installations with management of their application development projects.

1. *Software Configuration and Library Manager (SCLM)*
   SCLM can assist in managing an application development environment. The main idea is to support a hierarchical structure of program libraries that are part of the same application. A library's position in the hierarchy corresponds to a stage in the development cycle such as modification, test, or production. Programs move up through the hierarchy as their status advances during the development process.

   SCLM serves as the basis for IBM's Application Development/ Cycle (AD/Cycle) library functions. While the sophistication and discipline imposed by tools such as SCLM might not be needed by, say, a single systems programmer writing a small system exit, SCLM can provide the structure and control necessary for complex software projects with many application developers.

   Some of the facilities within SCLM include the following:

   Organizing application software components into a *project database* consisting of a set of hierarchically ordered *groups*. A group is made of one or more related libraries (partitioned data sets). For example, at the bottom of the hierarchy can be a group for each application developer. There are separate libraries in each group for source modules, object modules, and program listings. Higher-level groups would combine object modules from these groups into load modules.

   Editing and browsing library members using an enhanced version of the standard ISPF/PDF editor.

   Ensuring that only one user at a time can change a software component.

   Compiling and linking programs according to a defined structure of software components (the structure is called an *architecture*).

   Promoting members through the group hierarchy. For example, once a program in a development group is compiled without errors, it could then be promoted to a test group.

   Reporting on the project data base. For example, reports on software components can provide statistics on the number of lines of code in program source modules. Reports on data base activity can provide information on promotions.

2. *The Library Management Facility (LMF)*
   LMF was the only library management facility within ISPF/PDF before SCLM was introduced. LMF provides many though not all of

the functions of the newer SCLM. SCLM should be considered the facility of choice.

(Reference: 60.)

QUESTION 42—INTERACTIVE DEBUG TOOLS

Traditional compilers translate a program written in a high-level language into machine language—it is the machine language program that is actually executed. In order to assist with testing programs written in high-level languages, interactive debugging tools have been developed. These tools allow a user at a terminal to monitor execution of a program, temporarily alter the logic flow of the program, and examine and alter intermediate results, using symbols and terminology meaningful to the source language programmer.

What interactive debugging tools does IBM provide that run under TSO?

The following interactive debugging tools are available under TSO/E.

1. *COBOL Interactive Debug.* This program product provides interactive debug capabilities for programs written in OS/VS COBOL.
2. *Cross System Product.* CSP, which consists of two programs, CSP/AD for application development and CSP/AE for application execution, is IBM's fourth-generation language for data processing professionals. CSP/AD includes an interactive test facility.
3. *INSPECT for C/370 and PL/I.* INSPECT provides interactive debugging facilities for C/370 and mixed PL/I-C/370 environments.
4. *OS PL/I Version 2.* The Interactive Test Facility allows interactive testing and debugging of PL/I application programs.
5. *TSO/E TEST command.* This command is part of TSO/E and supports interactive testing of programs written in assembler language.
6. *VS COBOL II.* This COBOL compiler exploits 31-bit addressing, and includes an integrated interactive debug capability.
7. *VS FORTRAN Version 2.* Like VS COBOL II and PL/I, this program includes both the compiler and an integrated interactive debug facility.

(References: 126, 130.)

7

Security

Data in computer systems is increasingly being recognized as an important business asset. At the same time, computer systems are being accessed by a growing number of people; people from different departments within a company or even from different companies may be able to access the same system. Much publicity has been given to issues ranging from concern over privacy to the threats to computer systems that go by such exotic names as viruses, worms, and Trojan horses. Because of all these factors, organizations are becoming increasingly interested in implementing security practices to prevent accidental or intentional destruction, modification, or disclosure of critical information.

QUESTION 43—STATEMENT OF MVS SYSTEM INTEGRITY

IBM Programming Announcement letters for new releases of MVS or products that run within an MVS environment often contain a statement about "MVS System Integrity." What is the definition of System Integrity for MVS?

The following discussion is extracted from IBM announcement letter P81-174, Statement of MVS System Integrity, dated October 21, 1981. Reference 91 has a discussion of MVS system integrity and how it relates to system security.

At the time the MVS system control programming became available, it was stated that all known System Integrity exposures had been removed from MVS. This statement was based on IBM's knowledge of System Integrity at that time. Because it is not possible to certify that any system has total integrity, it was expected that additional exposures would come to light. Therefore, it was also stated that APARs describing additional exposures would be accepted. Since the release of MVS, a number of APARs on MVS System Integrity problems have been accepted as valid.

Since development of MVS began, a System Integrity Programming Standard has been in place within IBM and specific design and coding guidelines for System Integrity have been in use. As APARed integrity problems have been investigated and corrected, understanding of System Integrity has increased, more effective use has been made of the design and coding guidelines, and procedures have been established to make application of these guidelines a formal part of the design/development process.

System Integrity is an important characteristic of MVS. IBM continues in its efforts to verify and enhance the integrity of MVS and to respond promptly when exposures are identified. IBM will accept all APARs that describe exposures to the System Integrity of MVS or that describe problems where the installation of the indicated release of any of the programs listed below introduces an exposure to MVS System Integrity, as defined below.

[The list is omitted in this extract.]

System Integrity is defined for MVS as the inability of any program not authorized by a mechanism under the customer's control to:

1. circumvent or disable store or fetch protection,
2. access an OS password-protected or a RACF-protected resource (RACF is the Resource Access Control Facility), or
3. obtain control in an authorized state; that is, in supervisor state, with a protection key less than eight (8), or Authorized Program Facility (APF) authorized.

MVS System Integrity does not specifically include data protection between concurrently executing applications within a single address space (e.g., one CICS/OS/VS application's instorage data from another CICS/OS/VS application). The level of protection in such situations will be addressed in product documentation.

Program documentation, subject to change as IBM deems appropriate, informs the customer of what action must be taken and which facilities must be restricted to complement the System Integrity support provided by MVS. Such actions and restrictions may vary, depending on system, configuration, or environment. The customer is responsible for the selection, application, adequacy, and implementation of these actions and restrictions, and for appropriate controls.

MVS integrity is concerned simply with preventing an unauthorized program from bypassing certain basic system mechanisms. It is not concerned with such items as

Data integrity—accidental damage as a result of a hardware, programming, or user error.

Lack of security function—RACF or equivalent product is required to verify user identify and authorization to access resources.

Performance or availability—MVS integrity is not concerned with an unauthorized user's capability to affect system performance and availability through excessive use of system resources such as processor time or DASD space.

(Reference: 91.)

QUESTION 44—CONTROLLING SYSTEM ACCESS

Online transaction systems such as TSO/E, CICS, and IMS/TM are active in nearly all MVS installations. Users from different departments within a company, or even from different companies, may be able to access the same system. For security, a user's identity can be verified before access to the system can be permitted. Describe the basic facilities provided by RACF (the Resource Access Control Facility licensed product) to verify a user's identity at logon/sign-on time.

Most online systems have historically supported the ability to require users to enter a password to log on to the system successfully. RACF augments this function in several ways, some of which are described below.

RACF can require the user to change his or her password after a certain number of days have elapsed to better ensure password secrecy. Password syntax can be limited by installation-specified rules, for example, minimum password length. In addition, when access is allowed, RACF will display the previous time and date that access was granted so that the user can determine if security was compromised.

RACF can also limit logon and terminal access to certain hours within each day and to certain days of each week.

RACF optionally supports an Operator Identification Card as further proof of a user's identify. This is a badge-like card with magnetically encoded data. During logon, RACF prompts the user to place the card in a reader, which is a small device that transmits the data on the card to the system. RACF can then read the data and verify it as if it were a form of password.

(Reference: 114.)

QUESTION 45—CONTROLLING DATA SET ACCESS

In MVS, data sets are the facility for permanent data retention. Data sets are the basic structure used to implement program libraries, catalogs, system files, and user files. Clearly, protecting data sets against unauthorized access and against accidental or intentional change or destruction is of vital importance to the successful functioning of any enterprise. Briefly describe the data set password protection feature that has been available in MVS since its earliest days, and contrast the limitations of that mechanism to the data set security functions provided by RACF.

In native MVS, a data set can be assigned a read and/or write password to control access. Password processing has been around since the earliest days of the operating system and has seen few if any enhancements.

When a job or TSO/E user tries to access a password-protected data set, the MVS operator, or the user in the case of TSO/E, is prompted for the corresponding password. This can result in delays to the user or job, requires tracking of passwords that may be known to many people, and depends on the operator to determine if the requesting program is really authorized or not. A further drawback is that MVS ignores passwords assigned to DFSMS/MVS-managed data sets.

Because of these and other issues, and the need for automated security mechanisms in today's data processing environments, password processing for data set protection is really no longer acceptable.

RACF is IBM's product to provide automated, comprehensive security throughout an MVS environment.

RACF offers a rich set of functions to control access to data sets (as well as to other resources). RACF associates resources with "profiles." In the case of data sets, a profile may refer to a single data set or generically to a group of data sets such as all data sets beginning with "SYS1." Each profile contains a list of users and the access each user has to the data set. In addition, a Universal Access Code (UACC) can be specified that defines the access authority of users not in the list. So, for example, a profile can specify a list of three users who have authority to update a data set and also indicate, via the UACC, that all other users may only read the data set.

In contrast to a prompting scheme, RACF's verification is automated; this can improve system performance. RACF offers other performance enhancements over MVS password protection. The MVS data set password protection mechanism requires I/O requests to a special data set to retrieve the password for comparison against the value the operator or TSO/E user specifies. While RACF access to a profile may require I/O, RACF can reduce or eliminate those I/Os in some cases. For example, copies of profiles may optionally be maintained in virtual storage and so will tend to stay resident in processor storage if frequently accessed.

(References: 80, 91, 114, 115.)

QUESTION 46—CONTROLLING PROGRAM ACCESS

An installation is concerned about preserving the integrity of its system against accidental or intentional damage. The concern in this case is not about keeping unauthorized users out of the system, but rather keeping users who are authorized to use the system from accessing all available functions. Specifically, they want to restrict the use of sensitive programs to only certain users. In addition, they want to restrict access to key data sets to specific programs. How would you recommend that they control program use to achieve these objectives?

In the past, the native password protection facility in MVS could be used to protect libraries of critical programs. The system operator or TSO/E user would be prompted for the password whenever a job tried to access these libraries.

This scheme has many drawbacks. Manual intervention is required to answer the prompts. Separate libraries would have to be managed for each set of programs requiring a unique level of authorization. And password protection is not enforced for DFSMS/MVS-managed data sets.

Some installations have tried to implement roll-your-own schemes to provide program authorization mechanisms. This often involves modifying the operating system and increasing the complexity of system maintenance.

Because of these and other drawbacks, and the need for automated security mechanisms in today's data processing environments, the above techniques are really no longer acceptable.

A better means to restrict access to programs to authorized users is to use the Resource Access Control Facility (RACF). The RACF program control function can be used to

- Prevent the copying of sensitive load modules (programs).
- Control the modification and maintenance of load modules (programs).
- Restrict the use of certain programs and commands to specific users.
- Allow access to data sets only through certain programs. For example, a user may only be allowed to modify a certain data set when executing one particular program.

For example, the RACF program control function can be used to restrict access of selected ISMF (Interactive Storage Management Facility) commands to storage administrators.

(References: 73, 80, 114, 115.)

QUESTION 47—PROTECTING ACCESS TO NONTRADITIONAL RESOURCES

Data sets were among the earliest system resources to be protected by security mechanisms. As systems have evolved, the number and types of resources have also evolved, and the number and variety of users accessing these resources has increased. System security and authorization facilities have been enhanced to define more precisely a user's authority to access only designated resources. RACF supports the ability to limit access to many types of resources to authorized users. How many such resources can you identify?

Below is a list of resources that an installation can protect by using the RACF licensed program. This list isn't intended to be complete, but rather to demonstrate the scope of what can be done.

Note that some program products include tailored security facilities, often predating those provided by RACF. The advantage of using RACF is in the consistency of the interface, in additional function such as auditing, and in providing a single point of control for security administration.

1. The RACF JESINPUT resource class controls which users can submit jobs to the system through various "ports of entry" such as internal readers and Remote Job Entry (RJE) stations.

2. The RACF JESJOBS resource class controls the job names that users can specify. For example, this can be used to enforce the policy that only a particular department is allowed to submit jobs with names beginning "PROJX," assisting operators in correctly identifying jobs.

3. The RACF OPERCMDS class provides control over the MVS commands that system operators can issue. For example, tape library and help desk operators do not need authority to all the powerful commands that a master console operator or systems programmer should be able to issue. For identification, operators can be required to log on to MVS, entering a userid and password similar to TSO users, if the installation so specifies in the CONSOLxx SYS1.PARMLIB member.

4. The RACF DLFCLASS resource class controls the use of hiperspaces by the MVS Hiperbatch facility. Hiperbatch can greatly improve job performance, but it also may require a large amount of expanded storage in the form of hiperspaces, with a potentially negative impact on the performance of other system activities.

    Similarly, the RACF FACILITY resource class can be used to control the use of hiperspace by the Batch LSR subsystem. Batch LSR allows users to improve VSAM performance by creating buffer pools in hiperspaces.

5. The RACF TEMPDSN resource class can be used to protect temporary data sets—that is, data sets that only exist for the life of a job. Normally, access to a temporary data set is automatically limited by MVS to the creating job; the data set is deleted when the job ends. However, if the system fails while a job using a temporary data set is executing, then, without RACF protection, it becomes possible for another job to access the temporary data set when the system again becomes active.

6. The RACF VTAMAPPL resource class can be used to protect access

to VTAM resources and facilities. SNA Logical Units (LUs) are represented by VTAM Access Control Blocks (ACBs). Without this RACF protection, any program could open an ACB and process communications directed to the associated LU.

7. The RACF APPCSERV resource class can be used to control which programs can declare themselves to be APPC/MVS servers.

8. The RACF FACILITY resource class can be used to protect many DFSMS/MVS facilities intended for use by a storage administrator. Examples are the DFSMSdss CONVERTV command that converts volumes to system-managed format, the IDCAMS (utility) DCOLLECT and SETCACHE commands, and the ability to activate a system-managed storage configuration.

9. The RACF STORCLAS and MGMTCLAS resource classes can be used to control access to DFSMS/MVS storage and management classes that specify data set management policies. This can also simplify the logic of the automatic class selection (ACS) routines that assign policies to data set allocation requests.

(References: 73, 74, 91.)

QUESTION 48—RACF AUTHORIZATION CHECKING

Once a user or job is allowed access to a system, that user will attempt to access various resources such as commands, transactions, data sets, or other programs in the process of doing his or her work. Many resources in the system may optionally be protected by RACF. When a user requests access to a potentially protected resource, the system will request that RACF determine if the user is authorized for that access or not. Describe the basic steps RACF goes through during authorization checking. Point out mechanisms RACF uses to improve the speed of this process.

RACF goes through the following basic series of checks to determine if a user is authorized to access a resource. Each check is executed in turn, until access is either definitely permitted at some point, or definitely denied.

Reference 115 identifies the numerous steps in the actual authorization algorithm; many details are omitted here for simplification. Examples will be used that refer to data set resources since these are the most commonly protected resources—but remember that RACF protects many other types of resources as well.

1. A RACF preprocessing exit (written by the installation) can grant or deny the request.
2. Global Access Checking (GAC) is invoked. In this process, RACF refers to an in-storage table of simple rules. GAC is intended to provide the ability for an installation rapidly to grant access to commonly referenced "global" resources. A rule in a GAC table can permit access, but not deny it. For example, a GAC rule might allow anyone to read the TSO/E SYS1.HELP data set. Another rule might be that a user can always access any data set that has a name beginning with that user's userid. Because GAC performs no I/O and does not keep statistics or perform logging, GAC tables permit a very fast verification of authorization.
3. The next check is based on the (optional) security labels assigned to the user and resource. Since the label for the resource is in something called the resource's profile, we need briefly to discuss profiles before proceeding.

Resources protected by RACF are described by profiles (users also have profiles). Two kinds of resource profiles exist. A "discrete" profile is one that protects a single resource such as a single data set. A "generic" profile can also specify the name of a single resource such as USER01.DATA.SET, or, more commonly, a filter such as USER01.** which in this case means all data sets that begin with the qualifier USER01. Generic profiles can reduce the need for a security administrator to create and maintain many profiles for resources with a similar name and identical security characteristics.

RACF can optionally maintain resource profiles in virtual storage which, if sufficient processor storage is available, will reduce the I/O processing that would otherwise be needed to access the profiles. This can improve system performance.

We can now continue with RACF's checking of security labels. The security label for the resource is contained in its profile and consists of a security level and one or more security categories.

Levels form an installation-defined hierarchy, such as PUBLIC, SECRET, and ULTRASECRET; each level is associated with a number. Access will be denied if the user's level is less than the level assigned to the resource; if a resource has a level of SECRET, for example, access would be denied to a user with a level of PUBLIC.

If access is not denied by checking security levels, then categories are checked. Categories are intended to be the names of one or more departments or areas in an organization that the resource belongs to and that the user is part of or is allowed to access, such as PROJECT101 or PERSONNEL. Access is denied if RACF finds any security category in the resource profile that is not in the user's profile.

4. If a user attempts to access a resource that RACF can easily determine belongs to the user, the request is granted. A data set is considered to belong to a user if the user's userid is the same as the high-level qualifier of the data set name.

5. Checking proceeds by examining the "access list" in the resource profile. The access list is a list of userids and the type of access each is allowed (e.g., userid USER01 can read the data set, while USER02 can alter the data set as well as read it). Access is granted if the user is specified in the access list with an access authority that supports the requested use of the resource; for example, a request to read a data set is granted if the access list specifies that the user has authority to read or to alter the data set.

6. A check is made to determine if the user is a member of a RACF "group" of users where the group is on the resource access list with sufficient access authority to grant the request.

   Groups allow users to acquire authority by virtue of belonging to the group. RACF groups can reduce the need to add or delete individual users to the access lists of resources shared by the group.

7. A "universal access authority" (UACC) in the access list is checked if it has been defined by the installation. The UACC applies to all users and groups not specifically named in the access list; for example, if the UACC authority is READ and the user (or the user's group) is not in the access list but only wants to read the data set, access is granted. It is important to check for a specific entry for the user or group first in case the specified authority to access the resource is NONE.

8. A check is made to see if the user has the "OPERATIONS" attribute. This attribute gives the user authorization to access a resource even if the user does not appear on the access list. However, if the user is on the list, the access list authority would override the fact that the user also had OPERATIONS authority.

9. If permission to access the resource has not yet been granted, RACF checks another access list in the profile called the conditional access list. The conditional access list contains users (and groups) and conditions under which those users (and groups) can access the resource. Examples of conditions are the user accessing the resource from a specific terminal or a specific JES2 RJE station. In the case of data sets only, a condition can limit access to a specific program. If the user is on the conditional access list, at least one

associated condition is met, and the requested access does not exceed the authority specified in the list entry, then access is granted.

10. A post-processing installation exit can grant or deny the request.

11. If access has not been explicitly granted or denied by this point, access is denied.

(References: 114, 115.)

8

Performance and Capacity Management: Concepts and Principles

While a computing system's functions are key to its success in the marketplace, it is the system's performance that can often mean the difference between ultimate acceptance or rejection of the system by users. Once familiar with how to use a system, it is the performance of that system that users confront on a daily basis. Although detailed performance and capacity analysis can sometimes be quite complex, there are many fundamental principles that are useful to keep in mind.

QUESTION 49—DEFINITIONS

Define the terms performance *and* capacity, *and describe the purpose of performance management and capacity management (also called capacity planning). How do these disciplines relate to the concept of "service level"?*

When most people in data processing talk about performance, they are usually referring to two measures of a computer system:

response time: *how fast* a unit of work completes, and

throughput: *how many* units of work complete in a given amount of time.

The term "response time" is generally only used when referring to interactive work (e.g., TSO or CICS transactions). It is the elapsed time from entry of a transaction at a terminal until a response is received.

"Turnaround time" is the term used to mean response time of batch jobs. It is the elapsed time from submission of a batch job until SYSOUT is available to the user.

"Throughput" applies to both batch and interactive work. It is the rate at which interactive transactions or batch jobs complete, e.g., transactions per second or jobs per hour.[28]

Performance management is the process of configuring the current system to provide satisfactory performance for current workloads. This includes reviewing measures of current performance (what the system is doing now), and changing (tuning) the way existing system resources are used in order to make performance more acceptable.

Capacity planning is the process of identifying a system configuration to provide satisfactory performance for projected future workloads. Capacity planning techniques vary from "whoops, the phone is ringing off the hook with complaints so I think we need more X," to projections based on historical trends, to projections based on estimated business volumes and application plans.

A key term in both these definitions is "satisfactory." Every business must determine for itself the rate at which work must flow through the system in order to meet business objectives. This can be expressed in terms of response time as well as throughput—e.g., the business may need to process 100,000 transactions a day, with an average response time of one second given the available personnel.

The actual work flow at any time is the *level of service* being delivered; service level objectives are the desired level of service. For example, you wouldn't buy a hand calculator that always took 20 seconds to give you a result; only a very rapid response time is a desired and acceptable level of service for that tool.

Service level objectives are often informal, as when the system is only considered not to be meeting objectives if users are loudly complaining. Better would be a quantified objective that is a standard to be met. In fact, a formal "service level agreement" can be developed between the data center and users, "guaranteeing" delivery of specific levels of service under various conditions (e.g., time of day or number of concurrent users).

In summary, performance management deals with monitoring and

---

[28]See Question 52—Throughput and Response Time—for a more detailed discussion of throughput and response time.

modifying the current system to meet the service level objectives for the current workload. Capacity management deals with planning future configurations that will enable the system to meet the service level objectives of future workloads.

(References: 9, 10, 11, 45, 101, 118, 119.)

QUESTION 50—MEANING OF "BOTTLENECK" AND "BOUND"

One characteristic of commercial data processing is that I/O is generally the major contributor to overall response time. What does it mean to have an "I/O bottleneck" or to be "I/O bound"?

Work on a computer requires time waiting for and using multiple resources including processor time, processor storage, data sets, and services performed by programs including the operating system. The most common meaning of "bottleneck" is the resource that contributes the largest portion of the total time it takes to complete a unit of work. The work is also said to be "bound" by that resource. Usually, that resource is only referred to as a bottleneck when the time to complete the work is longer than desired. The cause may be either that the resource is too slow by its nature or is too busy to service requests in a timely manner.

When analyzing causes of poor performance, it is important to identify the major bottleneck since reducing the time spent there offers the greatest potential improvement.

Let's look at an example. Assume that an online user experiences an average response time of five seconds. Analysis shows that the response time can be broken down into components:

```
1.5 seconds of communication/network time
 .5 seconds of processor time
3.0 seconds of I/O time
```

In this case, the I/O component of response time is the bottleneck since it is the single largest contributor to overall response time. It is also said that the work is "I/O bound." Reducing I/O time could have the most impact on improving response time in this case. Reducing processor time, even to zero, would have only a relatively minor impact on the user's response time.

(Reference: none.)

QUESTION 51—BALANCED SYSTEMS

The term "balanced system" appears in many IBM presentations and technical bulletins. What is a balanced system?

Work in a computer system (excluding the network) uses a combination of hardware resources: processor, processor storage, and I/O. The principle of balanced systems is concerned with how these resources should relate to each other for efficient performance.

Processor, processor storage, and I/O are not independent variables. For example, processor storage adequate for a given workload on a processor of a given speed may be inadequate for an increased workload on a faster processor.

Keep in mind that the term *balance* does not necessarily mean *equal*. After all, what size processor would be equal to a string of DASD? *Harmony* is closer to what we're after.

On a balanced system it is possible to use all resources efficiently at the same time. It is not the case that a very busy resource creates a bottleneck that constrains other resources from being used optimally.

One way to get our arms around the concept of balanced systems is to consider an example of an extremely *unbalanced* system. This example will be so extreme that no one could ever actually implement it, but it definitely makes the point.

Consider a machine running MVS with a large number of channels and devices but only enough central storage to hold the fixed-page requirement of MVS plus one more 4K page frame and no other processor storage. This means that all user programs and data, as well as some nonresident parts of MVS, all share this single frame.

How would such a system perform? Probably like swimming in tar. The system would constantly be handling page faults as the currently running (crawling?) program makes references to virtual storage areas not resident in central storage. This high page-fault rate would cause repeated execution of MVS storage management routines (processor busy overhead), plus a very high I/O rate to paging data sets.[29] In the situation we have created here, during the waits for page-ins MVS can't even dispatch the processor to run other work because there is no other

---

[29]When a system is spending a lot of time managing a high paging rate caused by insufficient processor storage to hold active pages, the system is often said to be "thrashing"—the system is very busy but is not accomplishing very much.

work in storage to run. System throughput is extremely constrained by the low amount of central storage available for pages.

The elapsed time to run even a single job would be greatly elongated compared to running the same job on the same machine with sufficient central storage to reduce or eliminate paging altogether. You could assume that this elongation would be unacceptable in practice, given any reasonable service level requirements.

Now, if central storage were gradually increased on our fictional machine, we would expect our job's elapsed time to improve gradually as paging decreased. Within some range of paging, performance would be considered acceptable by most people. Beyond a certain point, however, additional central storage will lead to only minimal improvements in performance. And at some point there will be sufficient storage to eliminate all paging whatsoever, so that any further additions to central storage would be of no value at all.

With this example in mind, we can draw some conclusions.

In an unbalanced system one or more resources are scarce relative to others, by definition. What alternatives are available to us within such an environment? We can decide to run enough work to use the capacity of the abundant resources, but then that work will experience poor performance due to long delays as it competes for the scarcer resources (bottlenecks). Or, we can decide to reduce the workload (through tuning or rescheduling) to the level that the scarcest resources can handle without causing long delays, but then the more abundant resources are left underutilized.

So, an unbalanced system tends to force us to choose between poor performance and inefficient use of resources, either of which can be very costly.[30]

From all that has been said, we can develop two principles for sizing resources for computer systems:

1. Provide sufficient resource to allow work to complete within required service objectives (e.g., response time).
2. Don't provide more resource than is required to meet service objectives if there is any cost in doing so.

---

[30]Note how the MVS System Resources Manager (SRM) determines whether to raise or lower the system multiprogramming level (MPL). The level is raised if the SRM determines that *all* resources it tracks are underutilized and is lowered if the SRM determines that *any* resource is overutilized, thus opting for better performance (for some work) at the expense of higher resource utilization.

A balanced system is one with resources configured within these constraints; Not too little storage, because that would impact our service; and not too much storage, since there is no payback for the additional resource, and storage is not free.

We need to add some "real life" qualifications to all this theory.

First, it is not reasonable to expect to be able to configure a system so that its resources will be in balance all of the time. As workloads vary through the day/week/year, what is a balanced configuration at one time won't necessarily be balanced at another time. It's natural that if enough resources are configured to handle the service level requirements of the heaviest workloads, there may be an overabundance of resources for other work. And even then, fluctuations in workloads may give rise to short-term bottlenecks.

Second, it's usually appropriate to configure more resource than is strictly needed today in order to support anticipated workload growth without having to constantly suffer the disruption of resource upgrades. Upgrading a processor every year or two may be acceptable, but doing so every month is probably not (even if such small incremental upgrades were available). In this case, we are still designing a balanced system, but for a future workload, while conceding that this may mean we are over-configured now.

Finally, jobs use a mix of resources (processor, channels, central storage, etc.); there could theoretically be more than one combination of resource sizes that would allow us to meet our service objectives. For example, a fast processor and slow devices, or vice versa, might each be balanced for a given workload. However, in practice, the possible mix is more limited. Performance of commercial workloads, for example, generally depends mainly on the speed and capacity of the I/O configuration and not so much on the speed of the processor.

In summary, a balanced system is one in which processor, storage, and I/O resources are sized so they can be used efficiently while supporting service level objectives.

(References: 7, 45.)

QUESTION 52—THROUGHPUT AND RESPONSE TIME

We often use throughput and response time as measures of overall system performance. Describe these measures and how they relate to each other.

Throughput and response time are high-level measures of system performance.

When we look at the system from a user's point of view, one thing we care about is *response time:* how much time it takes to complete a unit of work. For interactive work, this is usually the time from when the enter key is pressed after typing a transaction or command on the terminal until the first character of a response is displayed on the screen. For batch jobs, this is usually the time from job submission until output is available to the submitter—also called turnaround time. Common measures of response time are seconds per transaction and minutes or hours per job.

When we look at the system as a business asset (it IS a business machine, remember), we want to get the most value out of it that we can—in this case, the most work. This leads to a concern about *throughput:* the quantity of work we are able to complete on the system in some unit of time. Throughput can be measured on a system with only one user but is more commonly measured on systems shared by many users and jobs. Common measures of throughput are transactions per second and jobs per hour.

Note that the measures for response time and throughput are reciprocals of each other: time/work versus work/time.

We can gain more insight into the relationship between throughput and response time if we look at the effects on performance of *sharing* a computer system among many users. We will see why trying to improve both response time and throughput on a given system can often be antagonistic goals.

Now, sharing is a good thing. Few people can afford to buy their own large-capacity, high-speed processors and storage subsystems. But organizations, such as corporations and time-sharing services, can afford to do this by letting many people and departments share these machines, spreading the costs among a community of users.

However, sharing also raises all sorts of problems that must be handled (typically by the operating system) in some way. For example,

- Determining which program is to be given control at any time. After all, a single processor can execute only one program at a given moment; a single disk device can handle only one I/O request at a time.
- Preventing two users from trying to do the same thing at the same time, such as changing a file or using the same area of central storage.

Managing these issues affects response time. For example, when one program needs a data set that is in use by another program, it may have to wait. If the processor is busy with one job, others will have to wait their turn.

If there is only one user on a system, response time will be minimized. As we add more jobs and users to a system in an attempt to get more work out of our expensive resources, we increase sharing and contention, and thus increase response time for individual users. On the other hand, in order to improve response time it may be necessary to decrease throughput/sharing to reduce contention (although systems programmers are sometimes asked to "make things faster" without lowering sharing—often easier to ask than to do).

An analogy may help. Consider a long highway. Response time is the time to travel from the beginning to the end of the highway. As the number of cars traveling at the same time increases, throughput is going up. But as you probably know from experience, at some point the amount of traffic causes all cars to slow down. So increased throughput can cause a decrease in response time; and less traffic would improve response time.

An example of how IBM recognizes the tradeoff inherent in throughput and response time is the way that performance characteristics of different DASD devices are often compared. The comparison is in two parts. One part holds the response time constant and shows how throughput differs, while the other part holds the throughput constant and shows how response time differs. This approach acknowledges that complete performance descriptions must deal with both concepts.

In closing, let's consider a more subtle consequence of sharing systems. Sharing does not merely elongate response time but can make it less consistent. If there is only one user on a system, response time should be repeatable if the user does the same thing twice. If many users are sharing a system, however, demands on resources can vary considerably over time as users' requests contend (or interfere) with each other. For example, at one moment a job might find itself queued up behind ten other jobs trying to read data from the same disk drive, while just seconds later the same job may find its next request is serviced immediately. This random contention results in inconsistent response times. It is because of this lack of consistency that performance in practice is measured in averages and trends.

(Reference: 57.)

QUESTION 53—SUBSECOND RESPONSE TIME

An installation's users are unhappy due to long, erratic interactive response times. Installation management is aware of this but doesn't want to spend money to solve the problem "just to make the users happy." Can you identify benefits to a business, in addition to user satisfaction, that accrue by providing subsecond interactive response time?

The following quotation is from the beginning of reference 31, *The Economic Value of Rapid Response Time*.

When a computer and its users interact at a pace that ensures that neither has to wait on the other, productivity soars, the cost of the work done on the computer tumbles, employees get more satisfaction from their work, and its quality tends to improve. Few online computer systems are this well balanced; few executives are aware that such a balance is economically and technically feasible.

In fact, at one time it was thought that a relatively slow response time, up to two seconds, was acceptable because the person was thinking about the next task. Research on rapid response time now indicates that this earlier theory is not borne out by the facts: productivity increases in more than direct proportion to a decrease in response time.

The document goes on to describe, in words and graphs, the research that leads to these conclusions. As response time decreases below one second, the user and system interact most efficiently, users do not lose their trains of thought, and the rate of transactions per user-hour increases dramatically.

This means that, in addition to increased user satisfaction, there is a productivity benefit from subsecond response time: the same number of people can get more work out, or fewer people can get the same amount of work out.

(Reference: 31.)

QUESTION 54—MEASURING END USER RESPONSE TIME

Delivering satisfactory response time to interactive users is one of the most important tasks of a data center. Of course, response times must be monitored in some way in order to determine the service actually being delivered.

Unfortunately, the response times reported by subsystems such as RMF or CICS are not the same response times that terminal users see. Why is that true, and what tools are available to report the response times actually experienced by terminal users?

Not all measures of response time report the response time that is seen by the enduser. Consider RMF's reporting of TSO transaction response time. The time RMF reports is *not* the same response time the enduser sees. Instead, RMF is really reporting what is called "internal" or "system" response time, which includes the time that the transaction spends doing I/O and executing instructions (and waiting in queues to do those things), but does not include the time spent by a transaction in network transmission. Other subsystems, such as CICS, also report only the internal response time for transactions. The reason this is so is that these subsystems are simply reporting on the time that they are "aware" of the transaction; they do not control the network (VTAM does that) and have no information about the time spent using network resources.

Yet time spent in a communications network could be a major portion of the response time a user actually experiences. So it is clearly desirable to determine that time in order to know what service is actually being delivered.

The NetView product can help provide this information. NetView can interrogate the Response Time Monitor (RTM) that resides in an IBM 3x74 SNA control unit. The RTM measures the interval from the time the user strikes the enter key until the first character of output is returned from the system; the RTM can also measure other intervals. The RTM accumulates these measurements and, on request by a 3x74 operator, displays the average response times experienced by terminal users on the same control unit. These measurements can also be accessed by programs running in the host, including the Service Level Reporter (SLR) and NetView Performance Monitor (NPM) products, and displayed to network performance analysts.

NPM offers another technique for estimating enduser response time, useful for terminals without the RTM facility. This approach uses the SNA definite response facility (basically, an indicator in an SNA message header) in order to have the remote terminal (control unit) send an acknowledgment back when it receives a message from an application in the host. The measured transit time approximates the network transit time the user sees (it's an approximation because it can differ from the actual transit time of the original incoming message).

By comparing internal response times and enduser response times, the individual contributions of network time and internal time to overall response time can be identified. Both NPM and SLR can report this information, which is very useful when determining where the focus should be if response times are not meeting objectives.

(References: 105, 116, 117, 133.)

QUESTION 55—LOCALITY OF REFERENCE

Many performance efficiencies in information systems are based on the principle of "locality of reference." Describe this principle and cite examples of large system products that make use of locality of reference.

The principle of "locality of reference" refers to the observation that, after data is referenced, a high probability exists that it will soon be reused or that subsequent references will be in close proximity to it in space and time.

A good example of where this principle holds true is in the sequential access of data. After one record or table entry, say, is accessed, it is very likely that the following records or entries will soon be accessed. Interestingly, the principle holds true for other situations as well.

The management of data in a computer system can take advantage of this principle to improve performance. This is done by using a smaller amount of faster (and generally more expensive) storage media to contain data that is active or is anticipated to become active soon, and a greater amount of slower (and generally less expensive) storage media to contain less active data.

The following is a list of some of the functions and products that make use of locality of reference to provide increased performance.

- *MVS Paging.* A reason paging is an effective mechanism for managing processor storage is that generally only a portion of a program and the data it accesses are ever active within small intervals of time. Program loops and table searches are examples where this clearly holds true. Only these most active pages need to be kept in central storage, while the rest can be kept in less expensive expanded or auxiliary storage until they become more active.

- *DFSMShsm Migration.* From experience we know that data sets that have been referenced (opened) recently are likely to be referenced again soon, on the same day or within a few days. The corollary is that when data sets are not referenced for many days or weeks, they are likely to remain unreferenced for a long time. The process of migration compresses and compacts such unreferenced DASD data sets. This already uses any media more efficiently—in addition, the data set may be moved to less expensive media (e.g., tape). If the data set is referenced again, it is recalled to its original media in standard format. It may be highly active for many days, then become inactive again and remigrated.

  An example of this cycle is the editing of a document. Once an early draft is complete and printed copies are distributed, a document may be in review for a long time; DFSMShsm, after detecting the lack of activity against the data set, will migrate it. Some time later when the review is complete, the author will again reference the document in order to update it. DFSMShsm automatically recalls the document at that time. Eventually, the updated copy will also be migrated after DFSMShsm detects its nonuse after a period of time.

- *DASD Cache.* In the case of cache storage in DASD control units, a relatively small amount of electronic storage is used to improve DASD performance by storing the most recently referenced blocks and nearby blocks. A few megabytes of cache can often dramatically improve the performance of many gigabytes of data on a set of DASD devices. This is because only a small portion of the data sets on DASD are usually active at any time. Keeping the active portion in an electronic cache storage can improve response time by eliminating the relatively slow mechanical motion normally required to read or write data on a disk. In most installations most data sets can deliver improved performance when cached; an example of an exception is a very large data set that is accessed in an extremely random fashion, so that data read once is not read again soon enough to warrant maintaining it in the cache storage.

- *Processor High-Speed Buffer.* In the ES/9000 and other large processors, each central processor includes a cache (also called a high-speed buffer). The cache is a relatively small storage with a faster access time than central storage, used to hold portions of central storage that have been referenced most recently.

- *Expanded Storage.* Expanded storage is electronic storage in a processor that can be thought of as an adjunct to central storage. In MVS/ESA, expanded storage can be used to hold some types of frequently referenced data (through a facility called hiperspace), reducing the need to access that data on slower disk devices. Thus, expanded storage can act like a high-speed cache.

    VSAM supports expanded storage in this way, through allowing users to allocate large numbers of VSAM buffers in a hiperspace. Random processing of VSAM keyed data sets, in practice, often involves reading the same records more than once within reasonably short intervals of time. If a sufficiently large number of buffers are available, VSAM is able to save, in hiperspace, copies of many records recently read from DASD. This increases the probability of satisfying subsequent read requests from buffers in fast expanded storage rather than from slower disk drives.

Note that, in all the above examples, the way that the system manages active data in the faster storage media is by a least recently used (LRU) algorithm. To make room for the most active data, the LRU algorithm detects the least referenced data in the fast storage media and moves it to slower storage media (e.g., write of changed pages, DFSMShsm migration), or discards it altogether (e.g., unchanged pages, DFSMShsm expiration of old, unreferenced data sets, demotion of unchanged tracks from DASD cache).

(References: 18, 32, 38, 54, 72.)

QUESTION 56—MANAGING THE SHRINKING BATCH WINDOW

Businesses typically run online transaction processing during a period that includes, and likely exceeds, the standard "9 to 5" working day. Batch processing is usually scheduled within the "window" of time that remains, generally at night. One reason for this common practice is that some transaction processing systems and data base management systems do not support the concurrent sharing of data between batch and online processing; another reason is a concern about the negative impact on online response time if online transactions and batch jobs are concurrently accessing the same resources such as processor storage, channels, and even the same files.

Many businesses are attempting to increase the availability of

online access to data. For example, there is an increasing require-
ment to make centralized data bases accessible to online users in
different time zones. There is also an increased need to access data at
odd hours in order to provide improved customer service. These
business requirements result in pressures to decrease the amount of
time required for the batch window. What techniques can you sug-
gest to help reduce the time required for batch processing?

When approaching a batch window problem, it is helpful to stand back
a minute and try to understand the nature of the installation's batch
processing. What are the jobs doing? Are all jobs very similar or not?
Would improving the performance of just a few long-running jobs help,
or is the problem broader than that?

There are many techniques that can reduce the window of time
required for batch processing. The techniques identified below employ
technology that generally does not require changes to the batch programs themselves, meaning they can be implemented fairly quickly
and with minimum risk.

In practice, batch jobs in commercial environments are I/O bound,
and there is generally excess processing capacity during the batch window compared to other times. The techniques below focus on ways to
reduce the time batch jobs spend in I/O processing. Many of these techniques are discussed elsewhere in various parts of this book, so that you
might view this list as a summary of techniques that help address the
batch window problem.

1. *Using current program products*
   A lot of batch processing often relies on vendor program products.
   Sort processing and volume dump processing are two good examples. The performance of these programs is frequently being
   improved, so that just installing current releases can often help
   reduce batch processing time.
2. *Tuning*
   Tuning is frequently an inexpensive way to solve a performance
   problem. Tuning can be looked at as efficiently using the resources
   at hand rather than adding to them or replacing them with faster or
   larger resources.

   Let's look at some very simple and basic techniques that can
   have a huge payback. Clearly, however, this is not the entire tuning
   story.

   For sequential processing, using large block sizes can reduce the number of physical I/O requests and operating system overhead to process those requests. Clearly, it is faster to read one large block of 100 80-byte records than to read each record individually. On DASD, half-track blocking is a commonly used technique to provide good performance for sequential data sets while also using space efficiently. As an aside, in DFSMS/MVS the block size can be set automatically by the system, eliminating the need to change JCL whenever data sets are moved between devices of differing track sizes.

Another powerful tuning technique to improve the performance of jobs accessing sequential data sets, especially large data sets, uses a synergistic hardware/software capability called *sequential data striping*. In sequential data striping, successive tracks of a sequential data set accessed by BSAM or QSAM are spread ("striped") across from 1 to 16 DASD volumes attached to one or more 3990 control units. Successive tracks are read from or written to all volumes concurrently, providing a higher effective data transfer rate than would be possible if the data set resided on a single DASD volume. Sequential data striping is supported by DFSMS/MVS and by 3990s attached to the MVS image by ESCON channels.[31]

Here's a more traditional technique. When a single job, or multiple jobs running concurrently, access data sets on the same volume (or sometimes just on the same channel paths), performance may be improved by separating those data sets onto different volumes (or paths).

Sometimes there are sufficient resources already in place to allow an installation to increase the number of jobs running concurrently. This may be done by starting additional initiators or by changing SRM (System Resources Manager) multiprogramming level parameters.

3. *Reducing DASD processing time through DASD technology*
   For jobs that heavily access DASD, a simple time-honored approach to reducing the time of those jobs is simply to use faster DASD. Current technology such as 3390 DASD offers fast access speeds, high data-transfer rates (especially beneficial for the large chunks of data

---

[31]Sequential data striping is similar to, but different than, a RAID 3 (Redundant Array of Independent Disks) DASD subsystem design, often found in supercomputing environments. In RAID 3, the data is sent down a single channel, and striping occurs within the DASD subsystem. In DFSMS/MVS sequential data striping, the software manages the striping, and data is transferred across multiple channels to and from the target DASD volumes.

transferred during sequential processing), and four-path (DLSE) connectivity to reduce path delays. Four-path DASD may even make it practical to schedule some batch jobs concurrently with online processing in that the possible impact on online performance due to increased path usage by the batch work is reduced.

The greatest benefits are derived through using fast DASD with a cached DASD control unit front-end to mask delays inherent in DASD mechanical motion. The 3990 cache controller offers cache performance benefits for both read and write I/O operations. Through DFSMS/MVS, access to the cache can be controlled by the installation at a data set level. In particular, a facility called "dynamic cache management" helps ensure that designated data sets have priority use of the cache when cache demand is exceptionally high.

The 3990 cached control unit offers a high-performance function called *concurrent copy*. Concurrent copy makes it possible to take a point-in-time dump of a data set, a set of data sets, or an entire volume in just a few seconds (at least that's what happens from a job's point of view). This eliminates the long delays that otherwise occur to insure data being dumped isn't changed until the dump has been completed. Concurrent copy is supported by DFSMSdss.

4. *Reducing I/O processing through data in memory*
Processor storage can be used as a cache to hold the most frequently referenced data for many data types. Many techniques are available that can be used by batch jobs. Some of the techniques that are described in more detail in Question 88—Data in Memory—Exploiting Processor Storage—include the following:

Batch LSR, for random VSAM processing

Hiperbatch, for sequential VSAM and QSAM processing

Hipersorting, for sort processing

VIO in expanded storage, for temporary data sets

Virtual Lookaside Facility (VLF), for catalogs and programs

5. *Reducing tape processing time*
Batch is typically a heavy user of tape processing. Cartridge tape subsystems improve throughput significantly compared to the reel technology of the past and also provide dramatically increased availability, which reduces the time necessary for reruns due to tape media errors. In addition, the use of tape subsystem cartridge loaders can reduce mount delay times, even allowing multiple mounts to proceed quickly in parallel.

Multiple techniques can be used to increase cartridge capacity, reducing mounts and library space. The techniques can be combined to provide maximum cartridge capacity, thus reducing mounts and increasing job throughput.

The Improved Data Recording Capability (IDRC) on 3480 and 3490 cartridge subsystems can increase cartridge capacity typically by a factor of three to five times.

3490 Enhanced Capacity models (3490E) double cartridge capacity through the use of high-density recording techniques. In addition, 3490E models virtually eliminate rewind time for full cartridges (data is written front-to-back then continued back-to-front) and exploit the high data transfer speeds possible through ESCON channels.

3490E models can also double cartridge capacity through support for Enhanced Capacity Cartridge System tape volumes that use a thinner media to increase the amount of data a cartridge can hold.

A major portion of many batch windows consists of volume backup processing. Techniques to reduce this time are discussed in Question 25—Reducing Backup Processing Time.

Finally, in many installations a large portion of tape volumes contain only relatively small data sets. Placing these small data sets on DASD rather than tape may not require much DASD and can eliminate a lot of tape processing with its associated delays. No tape mounts are faster than fast tape mounts. See Question 28—Reducing Tape Processing for more information.

(References: 48, 51, 54.)

QUESTION 57—PENCIL AND PAPER ANALYSIS

A systems analyst is designing a new interactive transaction. Each invocation of this transaction is expected to use a negligible amount of processor time, issue ten I/Os to uncached 3390 DASD, and send approximately one full screen of information to a remote 3270-type terminal. A response time of under 3 seconds is mandatory. Could a 4800bps (bits per second) line speed be used? What about 9600bps? Making appropriate assumptions, could you do a relatively simple analysis to answer these questions?

The purpose of this question is to demonstrate that sometimes it takes only a few "pencil and paper" calculations to provide useful information about a performance question.

The response time for a single "typical" I/O request to any uncached, "reasonably performing" 3390 DASD volume could be estimated to be 25 milliseconds (.025 second) or less. (You might know this from experience, or you might use whatever DASD response time has been measured for the installation involved—such information is provided by RMF). So ten such requests would take about .25 seconds.

We are given the assumption that processor time is negligible. So we can very conservatively say that the total I/O time plus processor time is well under one second.

Let's turn to the time required to send the data to the display screen. The 3270 family of displays comes in several screen sizes, with 24 lines of 80 characters each being the most common, giving 1920 characters per screen. We can estimate the time it takes to transfer a full screen of data at different line speeds as follows:

For a 4800bps line:

```
(1sec/4800bits) × (8bits/1byte) × 1920bytes = 3.2 seconds
```

For a 9600bps line:

```
(1sec/9600bits) × (8bits/1byte) × 1920bytes = 1.6 seconds
```

A 4800bps line, taking over 3 seconds to send 1920 bytes of data, is unsatisfactory given our response time objective of 3 seconds, and our earlier estimate of processor and I/O time. A 9600bps line giving a transmission time of 1.6 seconds is probably sufficient, depending on the accuracy of this little exercise.

This is not a detailed analysis. It is not intended to be. It is easy to shoot holes all through this discussion: How accurate is our brief description of the transaction's use of system resources? Are the I/O requests really "typical" as we have assumed? Are there any implicit I/Os for index searches? What about additional line time for transmission protocols? What about delays waiting for the line and other network resources? And on and on.

Nevertheless, with a few simple assumptions you can often easily make significant conclusions about systems and avoid wasting time in a difficult, albeit more accurate and sophisticated, analysis.

(Reference: none.)

QUESTION 58—RESOURCE MEASUREMENT FACILITY (RMF)

The Resource Measurement Facility (RMF) product is a comprehensive tool for producing online and hardcopy reports about system performance. RMF contains three monitors: Monitor I, Monitor II, and Monitor III. Briefly describe the differences between Monitor I and II. Also describe how RMF Monitor III uses the "work flow" concept to identify performance bottlenecks in the system and how this contrasts to a traditional "rules-of-thumb" approach.

RMF Monitor I runs in the background, sampling system activity every second or so, and gathering information maintained by various system components. Data collected in this way includes processor utilization, DASD activity, internal response time for TSO transactions, and much more. The information is output in the form of hard-copy reports or SMF records at fixed intervals set by the installation (such as every 15 minutes). The hard-copy reports, or reports produced later from the SMF records, provide after-the-fact information about system performance. Monitor I output can be saved to provide a history of system performance for use in capacity planning.

RMF Monitor II collects snapshots of system activity for producing real-time reports on a display screen; hard-copy reports can also be requested. Much of the information is similar to what Monitor I provides, and information on individual address space activity is also available.

Let's move on to a discussion of the unique benefits that RMF Monitor III can bring to an MVS tuning effort.

A "traditional" approach to performance tuning relies on so-called rules of thumb (ROTs) to identify activities that are causing unpopular effects. For example, if users complain that response time is bad, analysts may later look at RMF Monitor I and Monitor II reports to identify any disk volumes that were busier (during the time reported on) than a 30 percent ROT. If any such disks are found, the analysts will take actions to lower device activity, hoping that will improve response time in the future.

This approach has some drawbacks. First, prior to Monitor III, RMF hard-copy reports have usually been available hours or days after a problem has occurred—the reports are more useful for trend analysis or after-the-fact analysis than for diagnosing problems as they occur. Second, ROTs are not very precise—the 30 percent rule mentioned is a generalization that may not apply to all situations. Finally, the cause of the problem may not have been the disk, but some other resource.

In contrast, RMF Monitor III identifies how resources are impacting performance in real-time, and makes this identification in a more precise manner than ROTs. Let's look at the philosophy behind RMF Monitor III.

The ultimate goal of the system is to get work out and to do so with satisfactory performance. Performance is determined by the speed at which resources can process requests and by the amount of contention for those resources due to other work in the system. So we can say that at any time a given job or user is either using some resource (e.g., executing instructions or doing I/O) or is being delayed due to other work using the resource.

If there is only a single job running in a system with sufficient resources, Monitor III says that its "workflow" is 100 percent—the job is progressing as fast as possible in the given environment. It is never waiting for access to a resource. At the other extreme, if a job is doing nothing because contention for a needed resource is infinite, its workflow is 0 percent. So workflow is a measure of job progress and of resource contention.

The workflow value indicates the percentage of time that a job is able to do work when it is trying to do work. If the performance of a job or TSO user is unsatisfactory, then the workflow can indicate why. If its workflow is high, then only faster hardware or a new application design can help. If, however, its workflow is low, you will want to know what resources the job is waiting for, how much time is spent waiting, and if the waiting is caused by a single job "hogging" the resource or is due to the number of concurrent requestors. Monitor III provides all this information.

Using a sampling technique, Monitor III looks at the state of jobs and resources in the system (i.e., it looks at various control blocks). It accumulates this data into reports. Some reports provide information on workflow, perhaps indicating that some job has a low workflow because it is always waiting in a long queue for an I/O device. Other reports provide information from the point of view of a resource, perhaps indicating that a processor is being "hogged" by a looping job.

Reports can be displayed on a terminal in real-time, or can be printed for later analysis. Armed with these reports, you know what to go after if you want to improve performance. If TSO response time is too high (for one user or for all users), Monitor III can be used to find out where the work is spending its time. You might see that waiting for page-ins is the major contributor to TSO response time. Other factors also contribute, but not as significantly. You may then decide to take action to reduce this delay. RMF does not tell you what action to take (so you still need to analyze alternatives), but at least you know what's going on, and finding out was not too difficult.

Let's walk through an example of Monitor III in action. A performance analyst is accessing Monitor III through TSO. Suddenly (the tension mounts) Monitor III displays a message indicating that job ABC's workflow is under 50 percent, meaning it is spending more than half of the time being delayed (the threshold is set by the installation). The analyst then enters a command requesting more information about the causes of ABC's delay. The resulting display shows that most of the delay is due to waiting for storage. Our analyst then enters a command to display a breakdown of how the storage resource is used by ABC. This next display shows that of all the ways ABC has been waiting for storage, most of its wait time is due to being "swapped out and ready." The analyst can then decide what to do about this; for example, the analyst might increase the multiprogramming level for TSO.

It is suggested that a Monitor III session be running in the operator control and help desk areas of a data center. The workflow of significant applications can be monitored continually. Performance problems may be identified and addressed *before* users are significantly affected.

(References: 94, 132.)

QUESTION 59—PRODUCING REPORTS FROM SYSTEM LOGS

In order to implement performance management and capacity planning, it's often necessary to be aware of current system activity and historical trends. MVS and major subsystems such as RMF and CICS write data about system activity in various logs, such as SMF.

Being machine-readable data, these logs are not directly readable by a human being. It is necessary for a program to process the data and produce reports. What IBM product would you recommend to aid in producing reports from system-generated logs?

The product is Service Level Reporter (SLR). You may want to think of SLR as a flexible tool for producing manageable reports from the large amount of information in system logs.

Reports can be used for performance monitoring, capacity planning (including future projections based on historical data), transaction billing, system and device availability tracking, service level monitoring, and other systems management reporting needs. SLR can report on system trends such as processor utilization over the last year or the number of CICS transactions per hour for every hour in a day.

SLR produces reports based on data in system or user logs. To SLR, a log is any sequential data set containing time-stamps, such as a sequential copy of an SMF data set. Reports can be created online under TSO or in batch; they may be in tabular or graphic form.

SLR collects records from existing logs and copies them into its own data base. This is done at a time specified by the installation. The SLR "starter set" includes definitions of the contents of logs for SMF, RMF, CICS, IMS, NetView, and other subsystems. This means that SLR understands the contents of the log records produced by these subsystems, so that users do not need to create definitions of the record formats. The format of logs not known to SLR can be defined to SLR by the installation.

Once records are in the SLR data base, reports can be created and tailored to specify the data to be included and how it should be displayed. It is even possible to combine data that originated in different logs into a single report; for example, processor utilization (from RMF) could be graphed against transaction rates from an IMS log.

(Reference: 117.)

QUESTION 60—BENCHMARK CONSIDERATIONS

An installation is deciding between one of two hardware products that provide similar function. In order to compare the performance of the two products, the installation has decided to run a benchmark. What general recommendations can you make to ensure that the benchmark provides useful information?

Remember that there are many factors other than relative performance that should be considered when evaluating products of "similar" function. Price, operating system support, environmental costs (power, cooling, floor space), maintenance costs, reliability, upgrade capability, vendor support, and so on, all come into play. Nevertheless, it is sometimes necessary to run a benchmark to provide comparative performance information. Below are some considerations that can help ensure fairness and comprehensiveness in designing and running a benchmark.

It should be agreed in advance what the criteria for the test are. For example, when comparing processors, MIPS (millions of instructions per second) is now commonly acknowledged to have little value as a measure of performance (see Question 63—Internal Throughput Rates (ITRs) vs. MIPs). It is better to measure the *work* (throughput) that the machine or system can accomplish.

When measuring the performance of a single machine, results should not depend on other attached devices. For example, in the case of a processor, the proper measure is *internal throughput rate* (ITR). ITR measures the ability of the processor to do work independent of the attached devices such as DASD. An example of ITR is transactions per processor-busy second.

When measuring the performance of an entire configuration, e.g., a processor and its I/O subsystem rather than just the processor alone—the proper measure is *external throughput rate* (ETR). ETR is a measure of the amount of work that can be processed by a complete data processing configuration. An example of ETR is transactions per second of elapsed time.

When possible, the machines being compared should be configured similarly, to approximate most closely an apples-to-apples comparison. For example, if two processors are being compared, then they should be configured with equal amounts of processor storage.

Similarly, the workload environments in which the tests are run should be as alike as possible. If there is other, unrelated work on the system at any time during the tests, results may easily be skewed. Relevant licensed program products should be at the same release levels, unless it is those products themselves that are being measured.

It is very important that the benchmark reflect the production environment in which the machine will actually run in the installation. Test data and programs should be as close to production status as possible. A synthetic test of any device may not reveal useful data if, intentionally or not, the test exploits some aspect of the machine that would rarely come into play given normal workloads. Let's look at some examples.

If the machines being compared are processors, the test should probably not consist of a small "kernel" of code, since that would not reflect production job streams or production use of the processor. Such a kernel would probably not be executing a representative set of instructions and would not use processor resources (e.g., high-speed buffer) the way such resources would normally be used.

If the processor contains multiple engines, the test should provide multiple streams of work (assuming that is true of the production workload) so all engines can be put to use.

If the machines being compared are disk devices with multiple paths, the workload should be designed to test the (potential) performance benefits of multipathing. A simple test that doesn't sufficiently utilize or stress the paths would not demonstrate the true performance capabilities of the machines.

In summary, performance benchmarks should be only one consideration in overall product evaluation. When a benchmark is required, care is needed to ensure the results are meaningful.

(References: 30, 57.)

9

Performance and Capacity Management: Processors

The processor continues to be thought of as "the computer"—the heart of a data center—and as such receives more attention than any other type of data processing hardware. Managing processor performance is an important task of performance analysts, and estimating processor capacity is a popular subject in the press as well as in data centers. Because the processor is usually the single most expensive piece of data processing equipment, processor capacity-planning often receives the most focus of all capacity planning efforts.

QUESTION 61—PROCESSOR PERFORMANCE CONCEPTS

A high-level customer executive who has limited technical knowledge has asked to see you. His staff has told him that a processor upgrade is needed in order to solve existing response-time problems. In their presentation, they said that the current processor was averaging 80 percent busy doing interactive work. The executive, being very budget conscious this year, wants to understand why the equipment must be replaced if it isn't 100 percent utilized yet. Assuming that you agree that the processor is the cause of response-time problems, how might you respond to this executive at an intuitive/conceptual level (i.e., using minimal arithmetic)?

Let's begin with a rather intuitive line of reasoning using a simple analogy, then discuss what is happening in data processing terms.

In this analogy, a computer's capacity is represented by a long highway, and a job or transaction is represented by a car. Traveling from the beginning to the end of the highway is equivalent to executing on a processor. If there is only a single car on the highway, it will be able to travel unimpeded at maximum speed (minimum response time). If a second car is added to the highway, it is unlikely that the two cars will interfere significantly with each other, and both should travel at or near maximum speed.

Now imagine adding cars to the highway one by one, so that traffic is constantly increasing. At some point, as you know from experience, the increased traffic will cause all cars to slow down as drivers become more cautious and aware of the traffic around them. Eventually, speed will be so reduced as to be unbearable to the drivers—and that will likely happen *before* the highway is filled 100 percent end to end with cars. To solve this performance problem, you could add lanes to the highway (add capacity), or convince some drivers to travel at different times (reschedule), or try to adjust everybody's expectations (raise response time service objectives).

This analogy can help you understand how multiple jobs running at the same time on a computer system lengthen the time it takes to run each job. The finite capacity of a computer can only support so many jobs and transactions before they begin to interfere significantly with each other, causing slowdowns that can become unacceptable *before* capacity is 100 percent saturated.

With this analogy in mind, let's discuss what is happening on the computer system in question.

The business has a certain amount of work to do on the computer system and has determined acceptable levels of response time to accomplish this.

The response time for a transaction is made up of time using and waiting to use the processor, as well as I/O and network resources. It is only necessary to consider increasing processing power when the response time objective cannot be met and the time spent using and waiting for the processor is a major cause. As we will see, this wait time can become very large for many transactions when processor utilization is high.

In general, any one transaction, if it is the only piece of work on the system, will complete in an acceptable amount of time. However, the number of transactions in the system at the same time has been increasing, as seen in the high level of processor busy time. Only one transaction can be executing instructions at any one time, so any other transactions in the system must wait (only strictly true for uniprocessors, but the point remains valid). The more work already running—the higher the utilization—the more likely that any new work will have to wait for other work to finish.

Let's look at specific examples of how utilization affects response time. Assume that the processor is busy 50 percent of the time, and that the next transaction to arrive goes to the end of the line (lowest priority).[32] From the point of view of that new transaction, the machine appears to be running at half speed. The new transaction will take about twice as long to run (just considering the processor) as if there were no line. Similarly, a low priority transaction running in a machine that is 99 percent busy runs as if the machine were reduced to 1 percent of its actual speed. Although 99 percent is barely double the 50 percent utilization, its effect on further reducing the apparent speed of the machine is much greater than a factor of two. So we can see that as processor utilization rises, response time also rises, but in a disproportionate nonlinear fashion.

The total time high-priority work spends using and waiting for the processor is essentially unaffected by work running at lower priority, no matter how much of the latter there is. (That's only true with respect to the central processor—the lower-priority work could cause delays in getting to other resources such as DASD.) On the other hand, the time low priority work spends waiting for the processor increases dramatically at high utilizations. Once the time spent waiting for the processor causes the response time objective to be exceeded, then a faster processor is needed. In this case, that point was reached at 80% utilization. If workloads or objectives had been different, that point may have been at a higher—or lower—utilization.

Besides the average response time issues, there are some additional subtleties you might want to consider.

> The current 80 percent busy is an average measure—some intervals of time would surely find the processor less than 80 percent busy, while, more importantly, others would find it at 100 percent

---

[32]The term "lowest priority" in this context does not necessarily mean less important. Processors can generally only execute one task at a time, and since there are many tasks in a system concurrently, they are tracked in an ordered list. When a new transaction is entered into the system, it generally goes at the end of the list and so can only execute instructions when the tasks ahead of it are finished or are waiting for something such as an I/O request to complete.

busy. While high utilizations elongate response time, frequent variations in utilization near the high end lead to erratic response times—unpredictable from transaction to transaction. This can cause user dissatisfaction.

When the processor is running near or at 100 percent for extended periods, you can expect there is work not getting done. Some work may be delayed, and some users may stop using the system rather than put up with the aggravation, all of which can build up what is called "latent demand." Again, this will lead to a very unhappy user community, to say nothing of stifled business productivity.

Data in Memory (DIM) techniques can help interactive work achieve acceptable response times at higher utilizations than might otherwise be possible. See Question 89—Data in Memory—Benefits of Exploiting Processor Storage.

It is generally good policy to not load a processor as heavily as possible, intentionally leaving some spare capacity. Such spare capacity could normally go unused or could be filled with less important work that is easily rescheduled; the spare capacity could be available on one shift or all shifts. The idea is to leave some room for unexpected peak loads as might occur if a subsystem was temporarily unavailable, then available, and users placed additional load on the system in order to "catch up."

Finally, in practice, it is possible—and, of course, desirable—to utilize the expensive processor resource efficiently. The trick to doing this is to manage to a predetermined maximum utilization for interactive work that will allow acceptable response times, then fill up the remaining processor capacity with batch work. Batch has the attribute that there isn't a person at the end of a terminal waiting for a quick response. Elongation of times for batch jobs may be very acceptable in many cases.

(Reference: 7.)

QUESTION 62—PROCESSOR CAPACITY PLANNING

Many installations with low data processing growth rates do not do much processor capacity planning to speak of, but just wait for processor utilization to approach 100 percent, and then look for any solution that adds capacity at low cost. Installations with service level objectives or less clearly predictable growth rates usually call for a somewhat more sophisticated planning procedure. Can you describe a few basic steps that apply to most any processor capacity-planning methodology?

Processor capacity-planning techniques vary from projections based on historical trends to modelling techniques such as queueing theory to benchmarking. The following steps are commonly applied in many processor capacity-planning efforts.

1. Break down the computer workload into "business elements," groups of jobs that support a particular portion of the business. A minimal set of business elements might be TSO/E, batch, and CICS or IMS. More meaningful might be the workloads generated by individual departments or major application areas (e.g., order entry). The idea is to be able to relate growth in data processing workload to growth in the business area generating that workload. The entire workload as a whole can be considered to be the only business element, which can be considered a special case.

2. Analyze the current workload to understand what the system is doing today. This is done by analyzing SMF data to learn how much processor resource is used by each business element. For example, the analysis might show that a processor has an average peak utilization of 80 percent, of which TSO/E contributes 30 percent, CICS 35 percent, and batch 15 percent.

3. Forecast future system usage. This would be based on estimates of how the business elements would grow (or shrink) over some period of time. It could be simply assumed that historical growth rates will continue into the future. Or, departments associated with business elements can be surveyed, hopefully providing more insight into the future than history alone. For example, department ABC, anticipating a major application development effort, might estimate that its TSO/E use will grow at a 50 percent compounded annual rate over the next two years. Or, the business as a whole might project a 20 percent increase in orders over the next year, which

could be translated into a growth projection for the CICS order entry application. These estimates would all be taken into consideration and translated by capacity planners into projected processor utilization. If the average TSO/E utilization during prime shift due to department ABC is 10 percent today, then that is projected to grow to 15 percent in one year's time.

4. Finally, project the future processor capacity requirement from the current use and projected growth. You would probably want to project that the current system will be adequate until a certain future date and that a processor of power x will then be required to support projected growth for some additional months or years.

You might picture the results in a graph something like Figure 9.1. This kind of organized view of the sources of processor growth can make it easier to justify the need for increased processor capacity. You can see where growth is coming from.

While the methodology is fairly straightforward, its implementation is not necessarily trivial. Each of the above steps could be expanded on in length, addressing issues such as defining the busi-

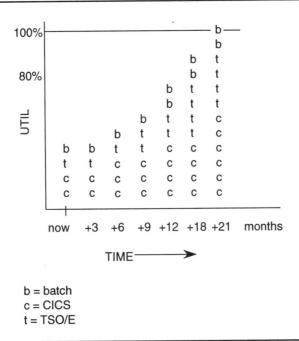

Figure 9.1.   Processor capacity projection based on business elements.

ness elements, determining the measurement period to represent current processor usage, computing the current processor usage of each business element, getting agreement on projected growth for each business element, evaluating latent demand, and so on.

Keep in mind that the above methodology does not specify at what utilization a processor should be considered out of capacity—this depends on service level objectives and on how delivered service is affected by processor utilization, all of which is fascinating but beyond the scope of this question.

(References: 9, 10, 11.)

QUESTION 63—INTERNAL THROUGHPUT RATES (ITRS) VS. MIPS

For a number of years, IBM has been reporting processor performance in terms of Internal Throughput Rates (ITRs). Explain why this is a more meaningful measure than MIPS.

Let's begin by examining MIPS, then move to a discussion of the benefit of using ITRs to measure processor power.

MIPS stands for Millions of Instructions Per Second. Or, for reasons about to be discussed, a Meaningless Indicator of Processor Speed. The idea behind MIPS is to provide a single number that indicates the power of a given processor. Very convenient, but, alas, the world isn't that simple. There are several drawbacks to MIPS as a means to compare performance of different machines, including the following.

- MIPS depends on machine architecture. For example, a personal computer and a 390-architected processor might both be rated as "50 MIPS" machines. Yet the personal computer will cost far less than the mainframe.[33] One reason is that not all machine instructions are created equal. It may take many instructions on a personal computer to accomplish what a single sophisticated instruction in a 390-architected machine can do. Also, it is important to realize that 390-architected machines often contain many "hidden" processors. For

---

[33]There are certainly other components of system price besides raw speed, such as elements that contribute to reliability, availability, and serviceability; device attachment capabilities; upgradability, and so forth.

example, each channel in high-end ES/9000 processors contains its own microprocessor; that offloads a lot of work that otherwise would be done by the central processors in the machine. Most public ratings of mainframe processor MIPS never take factors like this into account.

- MIPS can be misleading even for machines supporting the same architecture. Consider machines A and B of roughly equivalent speed, where A supports a certain function via a single microcoded instruction, and B supports the same function through invoking a machine language program that simulates the instruction. B's implementation will cause more machine instructions to be executed, leading to a higher MIPS rating, although A's implementation provides better performance.

    Here is an example that really happened. At one time, MVS handled the first page fault encountered in an address space by executing about 300 assembler language instructions. This sequence was replaced by a single microprogram. In a processor without the page fault assist microcode, each of the instructions executed to handle the page fault is counted in determining the MIPS value. In a processor with the new microcode, each time a qualifying page fault occurs, only one instruction is executed instead of 300. The one new instruction takes longer to execute than one of the original 300 instructions, but not as long as the entire set of 300 instructions. A hardware monitor would measure a lower MIPS rate on the processor with the new microcode, even though that processor is running more efficiently than before.

- Machine performance may vary with workload. For example, a numerically intensive application will execute a different set of instructions than a highly I/O bound application. A single MIPS number can't take this into account.

- Machine performance may vary with configuration. For example, the amount of processor storage can effect the paging rate and thus the mix of executed instructions. Similarly, Data in Memory (DIM) techniques use processor storage to reduce physical I/O requests with the frequent side effect of increasing a processor's capacity to do work. (DIM prompts the odd question: How many MIPS are bought by adding 64 megabytes of processor storage to a machine?)

Hopefully, you are now convinced that MIPS is of rather questionable value. Let's see if we can come up with something more useful.

The following statements are from reference 57.

There are a large number of attributes on which to base a comparison. To name of few of the features that assist a computer in running faster, consider:

- Processor cycle time
- Number of channels
- Implementation of channels
- Memory speed(s)
- Degree of parallelism
- Band width
- Size of the instruction set
- Internal buffering, etc.

These attributes and many other features of a processor contribute to its power and capacity. In the final analysis, however, it is how these features support the work that must be done that will determine the power of a specific processor for its users. The speed with which the processor performs its work determines its value. Given the intricacy of the processor complex and the range of work it is able to perform, the best way of determining its value is to measure the rate at which a representative workload can be processed . . .

The logical measure of a processor complex is the amount of useful work it can complete in a unit of time; in short, **throughput**. Throughput is a measure of performance expressed in units of work, which may be either jobs or transactions per second. Throughput is an expression of the purpose for which the machine was purchased in the first place—completed jobs. A simple count of the number of jobs completed divided by the time it took to complete them will yield a performance number expressed in jobs per second for a given workload executed on a specific processor. Measuring wall clock time results in a performance rating called "External Throughput"; measuring processor busy time results in a rating called "Internal Throughput" . . .

Internal throughput is defined as the number of completed jobs or transactions per processor busy second.

The idea behind Internal Throughput Rates is to provide a measure of processor speed for different workload types, *independent* of the remaining hardware system configuration (e.g., I/O subsystem). Only the processor busy time is considered. For comparison of TOTAL system configurations, the measure that should be used is External Throughput Rates: the number of jobs completed per *elapsed* second.

It must be noted that ITR values are dependent on the underlying operating system and subsystem. The ratings will vary across different operating systems (e.g., MVS or VM) and different subsystems (e.g., TSO/E or CICS or batch), and even different releases of these subsystems. This is because these programs incorporate different algorithms and vary in their use of processor facilities. Therefore, IBM's tables of ITR values always identify the software environment under which measurements were made.

As mentioned earlier, the instructions executed by a given job may vary depending on resource availability, e.g., the amount of available central storage. This could effect the ITR value. In order to prevent this from being a factor, IBM runs MVS and other benchmarks on configurations designed to remove these kinds of constraints. For example, time spent waiting for resources is avoided as much as possible. In this way, ITR is really an accurate measure of only processor power, independent of other resource considerations.

Remember that ITR is a rate. To compare the power of two processors, we look at the *ratio* of their ITRs (called an ITRR) for the same workload. Consider an example. Assume that for a CICS workload under MVS/ESA SP Version 4, the ITR of processor A is 100 and the ITR of processor B is 150. Then processor B has 50 percent more capacity in that environment than processor A. The ITRs of 100 and 150 have no absolute value in themselves. A different set of benchmarks in that same environment might have yielded values of 10 and 15, respectively. But, what is important is that the ratio of the ITR values stays the same.

In closing, let's return to MIPS for a moment. A more precise term for MIPS is "instruction execution rate," or IER. Processors are sometimes compared in terms of their IER *ratio*, or IERR; you see this in some IBM announcements, especially if the more precise ITR ratios have not yet been determined. As a single descriptor, IERR may not account for differences in performance under varying conditions. Yet, as a ratio it is certainly better than MIPS, and in practice is generally used only in fairly restricted contexts (e.g., when comparing two very similar machines for commercial processing, as opposed to, say, numerically intensive processing).

(Reference: 57.)

QUESTION 64—ITRS AND PROCESSOR UTILIZATION

Let's say that IBM has evaluated the performance of two uni-processors, A and B, when running a specific type of workload. The results show that the ITR (Internal Throughput Rate) of A is 1 and the ITR of B is 1.7 for this workload type. What reduction in processor time can be expected if a job of this workload type is moved from system A to system B?

The answer is the job should require about 41 percent less processor time on system B than on A. Let's see why.

Internal Throughput Rate measures the amount of work that can be run on a given machine in a unit of time. If the same workloads are run on both A and B, then their ITRs can be used to compare A's performance to B's performance in terms of throughput.

Let's assume the ITRs represent jobs per second (job/sec). Then when A runs 1job/sec, B runs 1.7job/sec. Simply consider the reciprocal (inverse) of these rates. This shows that when A runs 1sec/job, B runs 1sec/1.7job = .588sec/job. The time saved on system B is 1 - .588 = .412 sec. Now .412 seconds is 41.2 percent of 1 second, so a job could be expected to run in about 41 percent less processor time on system B than on system A.

Here's a way to help you see the "reasonableness" of this answer. Consider two machines, X and Y. Intuitively, if X's ITR is twice that of Y, then a given job should require half the processor time on X as on Y. That would be a 50 percent reduction in processor time. So an ITR ratio of less than 2, therefore, must give a less than 50 percent reduction in processor time, as in the calculation above.

Note that the logic used here depends on the fact that A and B are uniprocessors. If, say, A was a uniprocessor, but B gained its capacity over A through having multiple central processors (engines), there might not be any time reduction for the job when run on B if the job can only run on one engine at a time (i.e., if the job is what we call "single threaded"). B would get its power over A in this case by being able to run multiple jobs in parallel, compared to one at a time on A.

(Reference: 57.)

QUESTION 65—PROCESSOR TIME CAPTURE RATIOS

In calculating the processor time used by a given workload, a "capture ratio" is often applied to the processor (TCB and SRB) times reported by SMF. What is a capture ratio? Can you identify where a list of events that are not captured by SMF is documented?

SMF does not record (capture) all the processor time expended on behalf of each job. For example, time spent processing certain supervisory functions is not associated with any job. Functions for which time is not captured are identified in reference 96.

Because not all time is reported by SMF, if the processor times reported for all jobs run during some interval (e.g., one hour) were all added together, the sum would be less than the total processor time used over that interval (such total time is reported by RMF).

While reporting somewhat consistent times is useful for many applications such as billing systems, for other purposes, such as capacity planning, it is often desirable to apportion unaccounted processor time among jobs or workloads. To do this, the processor time reported by SMF must be adjusted by a so-called "capture ratio." For example, assume that a given job has a capture ratio of 80 percent. Then if SMF reports that the job used 60 minutes of processor time, the job more likely accounts for about 75 minutes of processor time expended by the system. In other words, 60 minutes only represents 80 percent of the actual processor time used by the job.

In practice, capture ratios are usually computed for broad workload categories such as TSO/E, batch, and CICS, rather than for individual jobs. These capture ratios can then be applied to each job in the workload category, if required.

Capture ratios vary by workload and even by release of MVS. The references for this question discuss techniques for estimating capture ratios for a given installation. Reference 57 gives sample MVS capture ratios that an installation can use as a starting point for estimating more precise values.

(References: 7, 9, 10, 57, 96.)

QUESTION 66—EXTENDING PROCESSOR CAPACITY

A currently installed processor is rapidly approaching maximum utilization. The system is fairly well tuned given existing resources and workload growth is expected to continue. What strategies can you identify to handle that growth?

Basic strategies to provide additional processor capacity include the following.

1. Investigate current releases of vendor software, especially operating systems and subsystems, since they often include performance and capacity improvements. This might add capacity at relatively low cost.
2. Move some of the workload from the out-of-capacity processor to other systems if any exist in the complex.
3. Reschedule current or future workloads. Typically, systems are busiest on first shift and less busy second and third shifts. There may be work that could be moved from first shift to the other shifts, thus increasing first-shift capacity. Batch jobs are often good candidates for such rescheduling.
4. Upgrade or replace the current processor with a more powerful model. More powerful doesn't always mean "faster" in the traditional sense. Adding processor storage and using Data in Memory techniques may add capacity for less cost than a model upgrade.[34] The ES/9000 Vector Facility could be considered for appropriate workloads.
5. Install a second, additional system, and break up the workload in some way to run on both systems.
6. If possible, modify the design of any particularly processor-intensive jobs that are significant contributors to overall utilization. This is usually not a practical solution to the capacity problem, especially if a near-term solution is required.

(Reference: none.)

---

[34]See Question 88—Data in Memory—Exploiting Processor Storage and Question 89—Data in Memory—Benefits of Exploiting Processor Storage.

QUESTION 67—UNEXPECTED PROCESSOR UTILIZATION

An I/S organization recently upgraded its processor since it was frequently running near or at 100 percent utilization during prime shift hours, and demand was expected to continue to grow. The new model was rated at twice the capacity of the previous model for the workload. Because of this, there were expectations that peak utilization would drop to about 50 percent when the new model was installed. However, utilization averaged 60 percent during prime shift beginning the first day. What could account for this?

The following are the most likely explanations of why a higher-capacity processor replacing a lower-capacity processor might be measured at a utilization higher than the ratio of capacities would predict.

1. *Change in the environment*
   A simple explanation might be that the workload changed. This could range from new applications, to more interactive users, to additional batch jobs. Perhaps system performance parameters such as the number of batch initiators were changed. In short, were the "before and after" measures comparing the same things?
2. *Latent demand*
   A typical reason that a new processor appears busier than expected after replacing a saturated system is *latent demand*. We can define latent demand for a processor as work that could run but is not being run for some reason.
   Latent demand may come from two sources. First, if the high processor utilization on the original system caused unsatisfactory response time, users may have simply stopped using the system as frequently as before. When the system is faster, those users are again submitting work.
   The second source of latent demand is a little more subtle. Assume that average processor utilization is measured hourly. Then an average for all of prime shift can be easily calculated. There will normally be a *peak hour* during prime shift where utilization is the highest of any hour and certainly higher than the average. That allows you to consider the peak-to-average ratio. For example, if prime shift average utilization is 70 percent, and the peak hour average utilization is 100 percent, then the peak-to-average ratio would be 100 percent:70 percent = 1.43:1.

History will show if the peak-to-average ratio stays fairly constant over time, and thus is representative of the way users submit work. If that is the case, then as workload growth raises the average utilization, the peak rises as well until it reaches 100 percent. The peak utilization will then stay near 100 percent even if the average continues to rise, because processors can't run higher than 100 percent busy. This means there is excess demand that isn't being met: work is being delayed within the system or is not being submitted by frustrated users. This unmet demand could be estimated as the calculated peak minus 100 percent. For example, given a 1.43:1 peak-to-average ratio, an 80 percent average implies a calculated peak of 114 percent; thus the latent demand can be estimated as 14 percent of the capacity of the current processor. This latent demand shows up as higher than anticipated utilization when a more powerful system is installed.

3. *PR / SM LPAR low utilization effect*

The use of a hardware logical partitioner can raise processor utilization due to the processor cycles used to manage multiple operating systems on one physical machine.

IBM's PR/SM LPAR (Processor Resource/Systems Manager Logical Partition) facility can raise processor utilization by a greater percentage at low utilizations than at higher utilizations. This is called a low-utilization effect. At low utilizations, a logical partition (operating system image) generally enters the wait state more often than at high utilizations, because there isn't enough work to keep the image constantly busy. Because PR/SM LPAR uses an efficient event-driven scheduler, when an image enters the wait state, control immediately passes to PR/SM microcode which looks for other partitions to dispatch. This avoids lost capacity due to unproductive idle time but is reflected as increased processor utilization.

The increase in utilization diminishes significantly at higher utilizations. Since the low utilization effect does not ultimately subtract from processor capacity, it should not be considered as a constant "overhead." Note that selected IBM processors support an LPAR Management Time Reporting facility that allows PR/SM's contribution to the utilization of each image, including increased low utilization, to be measured; RMF will report this measure, which can be useful for capacity planning.

(References: 7, 66.)

QUESTION 68—EFFECTIVELY USING AN N-WAY PROCESSOR SYSTEM

An installation is currently running on a uniprocessor. There is a clear need for additional processor capacity, and the next upgrade increment is to a two-way processor system. The installation is unfamiliar with n-way processing and questions whether their workload would run well on such a machine. What characteristics should workloads have to run effectively on n-way processors?

Before we answer this question, we need to clarify some terminology. The term CPC means central processor complex; you can think of this as a collection of one or more central processors (also called instruction engines), processor storage, and channels under centralized control. A CPC is also called a central electronic complex (CEC), or more simply, a processor or processor complex. A CPC with a single central processor is a uniprocessor, and a CPC with n central processors is called an n-way processor. If a CPC can be physically partitioned (through operator commands entered at the system console) into two processors, then the CPC is called a multiprocessor; each physical partition can run its own operating system.

Finally, some systems that cannot be physically partitioned have been given special names. Such a two-way system is also called a dyadic or sometimes a dual system, depending on subtle differences in implementation. Such a three-way system is also called a triadic system.

Note that this terminology is not always used consistently. Sometimes a central processor is just called a processor. Often any n-way machine is called a multiprocessor, since it contains multiple central processors. You have to judge the meaning of these terms by the context in which they appear.

The original question can be restated as: How can you determine if a given workload can make use of an n-way processor complex? We'll first discuss the principles involved, then describe techniques to determine the answer for any specific MVS system.

From an installation's point of view, work coming into the system appears as batch jobs, TSO/E users, or subsystems such as VTAM and CICS. However, MVS internally structures each such piece of work as one or more "tasks." Generally, a batch job or a TSO/E user can each be thought of as a single task, though that is a slight simplification.

A task is *ready* when it is ready to immediately execute instructions, or is *waiting* when it is waiting for some event, such as the completion of an I/O request, before it can execute instructions. In MVS, the dispatcher function controls which ready tasks are assigned to central processors in order to execute instructions.

At any time, a uniprocessor will be executing either zero tasks (meaning it is idle) or one task (meaning it is busy). At any time, an n-way machine will be executing anywhere from zero to n tasks on the set of n central processors; each central processor is either idle or busy. As workloads fluctuate over time, there may be more or less ready tasks than the number of central processors in the complex. If there is always a ready task for each central processor, the system would be 100 percent busy; if there is never a ready task, the system would be 0 percent busy.

In order to make effective use of an n-way processor complex, there must often be at least as many ready tasks as there are central processors, else one or more central processors might forever sit idle. For example, if a two-way system had at most only one ready task at any time, then only one of the two central processors could ever be busy, meaning you could never see better than 50 percent system utilization (100 percent busy on one central processor, and 0 percent busy on the other).

So it seems that workloads that create multiple MVS tasks are needed in order to be able to use an n-way system effectively. The more tasks in a system, the more likely there will be one or more ready tasks at any time. So, for example, systems with large TSO/E user populations and/or large numbers of batch jobs can generally make use of an additional engine when they outgrow the power of their current system.

If a system is primarily dedicated to a single job or subsystem, it is not immediately clear that there will be enough ready tasks to make effective use of an n-way system. Let's consider a system running just a single CICS subsystem (one CICS address space). This environment is essentially a single task from the point of view of MVS.[35] Some effort may be needed to ensure that a two-way system can be effectively used in this environment. For example, the CICS subsystem could be split into multiple CICS subsystems, or MRO (multiple region operation) could be used to create additional tasks that MVS could dispatch.

Let's consider how to answer the question more precisely in a given installation.

You can look at the RMF Monitor I CPU Activity Report. There are items called "IN READY," "OUT READY," and "LOGICAL OUT RDY" in

---

[35]Even though CICS supports many users, it does its own sub-dispatching under a single MVS task. Over time, CICS has been enhanced to offer additional use of MVS tasks, but most work generally continues to be done under a single MVS task in the CICS address space.

the System Address Space Analysis section. These items together indicate the number of (potentially) dispatchable tasks that exist at any instant. (Technically, only IN READY work is dispatchable. The OUT work is ready but is not swapped in at the moment; this should be considered latent demand that is being constrained and that could be dispatched if resources were available.) Minimum, average, maximum, and queue distribution values are given. If the average value is greater than one, there is work that could be dispatched on a second central processor if one were available on the current machine. If the number is greater than two, then a three-way system could be effectively used, and so on.

You can also gather useful information through RMF Monitor III. RMF Monitor III reports on processor delays, among many other things. By examining this information you can better understand the current use of the processor resource. For example, you could use the "System Information Report" to see the number of jobs delayed waiting for the processor, within the entire system and within application groups such as TSO/E. You might also examine the "Delay Report" and the "Processor Delays Report" to see which jobs by name are being delayed waiting for the processor and to see how the delays contribute to job elapsed time.

In reasonably busy commercial environments you should see multiple jobs being delayed waiting for the processor. In general, in such environments either a faster uniprocessor or additional engines are effective approaches to add processor capacity.

(References: 13, 94, 132.)

10

Performance and Capacity Management: Storage Devices

The dollar value of an installation's DASD and tape configuration can often far exceed the cost of a processor. Many data centers are experiencing significant increases in the amount of storage space required to support their data processing needs. Given this demand, plus the recognition that storage I/O generally has a major impact on performance, performance management and capacity planning for storage is receiving a major focus in MVS data centers.

QUESTION 69—DASD PERFORMANCE CONCEPTS

Question 61—Processor Performance Concepts described an executive concerned that his processor was only 80 percent utilized when he was told a more powerful processor was necessary. But what about DASD? At least, says the executive, a processor can be driven to 80 percent busy. Why does he usually need more DASD devices or channels when those resources are far less busy than that?

First, remember that DASD provides both space and speed; it may be that more space is needed for data, even though performance is otherwise satisfactory.

However, assume that space is not the issue, but rather that the disk volumes are being accessed by so many transactions at once that the delays due to sharing (contention) are causing response time to be unacceptable. The question remains: Why does disk volume utilization, in practice (ignoring cached subsystems for now), tend to peak at much lower levels than processor utilization (a common rule of thumb is 30 percent maximum average utilization for an uncached DASD volume)?

In commercial environments, delays in I/O processing are generally of more significance than delays waiting for the processor resource. This is because in these environments the amount of time a typical transaction spends doing I/O is usually far greater than the amount of time it spends executing instructions—disk speeds are vastly slower than processor speeds. So a doubling of I/O time will generally have a much greater impact on total response time than a doubling of processor time. Thus it is important to keep disk volume and path utilizations relatively low; disk volumes are relatively slow as it is, without compounding the problem by adding substantial wait times.

Like processors, sharing of DASD by multiple users causes response time to increase nonlinearly. But DASD subsystems are rather more complicated than processors in how contention causes the elongation; the way DASD works causes the elongation to increase at a faster rate than for processors.

Here's the main reason this is so. DASD response time is highly dependent not only on how busy the individual volumes are, but on how busy the paths are that connect the volumes to the processor. A path is a channel—storage control—head of string connection between a processor and a set of DASD volumes. Many disk volumes typically share a small number of paths; when these paths are busy, other volumes cannot transfer data to or from the processor and must go through a complete rotation to try again. That single extra rotation may more than double the total time it otherwise takes to process the I/O request, and more than one additional rotation may be needed![36]

Let's return to our analogy of highway traffic, described in Question 61—Processor Performance Concepts. As the number of cars on the highway increases, the speed of each car slows down. However, making

---

[36]The formal term for this is an "RPS miss." RPS stands for Rotational Positional Sensing. A disk device has circuitry that can sense when a location of interest is nearing the read/write heads and will only then attempt to connect to a path. If it can't connect (because other devices are using the paths), it tries again on the next revolution. Early disk devices didn't have the RPS feature and stayed connected to a path for an entire I/O operation, even though the path was used for only a short time during that operation. RPS improves system throughput by increasing the time during which paths can be shared.

the highway subject to the effects of path busy would be as if, in addition to the slowdown, stoplights were added that caused a total halt to traffic periodically—and the lights are wired so that the frequency and length of each halt would grow as the traffic load increased!

The point is that the mechanical nature of storage devices causes contention to have a more dramatic effect on delays than a similar amount of contention (percentage-wise) has for processors. There can be additional "chunks" of delay due to busy paths beyond the delays just due to busy devices. This is why DASD volumes are often "out of gas" at a lower utilization than processors.

When DASD performance is degraded due to contention, solutions include such things as spreading the I/O activity across additional devices or paths, faster DASD devices, cache storage to reduce mechanical delays including rotational delays, and others.

(Reference: 15.)

QUESTION 70—DASD CAPACITY PLANNING

An installation has traditionally done capacity planning for DASD space by periodically gathering users' estimated gigabyte requirements for the next year and translating them into requirements for DASD volumes. The installation is implementing DFSMShsm to provide automated DASD space management. Can you discuss the implications this has for DASD space-capacity planning?

Surveying users' projected DASD space requirements is a useful technique for long-range capacity planning. If, for example, an application is moving its data sets to another site in six months but not taking the currently used DASD with it, that's clearly valuable information. In addition to users' projections, however, DFSMShsm space-management techniques can optimize the use of DASD space and, as we will see, provide additional information useful for DASD capacity planning.

DFSMShsm space-management techniques provide value by ensuring there is sufficient free space available on DASD volumes for an organization to run its work without being impacted by out-of-space conditions. Additionally, efficient space management can lower the effective cost per gigabyte of DASD through reducing or eliminating wasted data space, such as space occupied by unreferenced data sets.[37]

---

[37] See Question 23—DFSMShsm Space Management.

DFSMShsm space management employs several techniques to provide free space on managed DASD volumes, including deletion of unneeded data sets and migration of unreferenced data sets to other devices in a compacted format.

Before DFSMShsm space management is "turned on", it is possible to estimate the potential "first day" increase in DASD space available for new data sets, an effective increase in capacity, by running a program that reports on the size of data sets that could be migrated or deleted immediately. That information is available in volume VTOCs and in records produced by the IDCAMS DCOLLECT utility.

The DASD space capacity increase consists of

- Space allocated to data sets that will be migrated or deleted.
- – Space required to hold data sets to be migrated to DASD.

Data sets migrated to DASD are usually moved to volumes dedicated to that purpose. Typically, DFSMShsm migration techniques result in over 50 percent space savings for migrated data sets. So, for example, migrated data sets with a combined premigrated capacity of two volumes might occupy less than one migration volume.

Once DFSMShsm is implemented, predicting the future impact DFSMShsm space management will have on capacity is not quite so simple. For example, the ongoing impact of migration depends on actual patterns of use, something that humans are not very good at predicting. So what do we do?

A good solution is to monitor the actions that DFSMShsm takes in order to provide sufficient DASD free space to meet installation objectives. The ability to meet quantified objectives is something that can be tracked. If objectives can be met with little effort on DFSMShsm's part, all is well. But if DFSMShsm must work hard to meet objectives or is getting close to the point where there are no more tricks up its sleeves, then it is time for additional DASD capacity.

During its primary space-management processing, DFSMShsm first attempts to provide free space by low-overhead actions that require no data set movement such as deleting unneeded data sets. Migration, DFSMShsm's most powerful technique, is employed after that, if necessary. It is certainly possible to migrate data sets based on age only but in practice that can be very inefficient. This is because DASD only comes in fixed chunks of capacity: volumes. If volumes currently have more free space than users actually need, then migrating data sets based on age just to provide even more is a lot of unnecessary work;

it adds to processor overhead, may cause tape mounts, and may slow things down due to later recalls that could have been prevented.

DFSMShsm avoids this inefficiency through allowing installations to specify free space objectives in the form of volume *thresholds* of allocated space (occupancy). The idea is to have DFSMShsm automatically ensure there is enough free space on DASD volumes to avoid out-of-space conditions, but no more than that. Two thresholds exist, a high and a low threshold, described below. In a DFSMS/MVS environment, the thresholds are specified in the storage group definition and apply to each volume in the storage group.

The low threshold is used by DFSMShsm during its primary space management process, normally occurring once a day. The low threshold indicates a desired maximum percentage of allocated space on volumes. If the allocated space on a given volume exceeds the low threshold, then, and only then, will DFSMShsm attempt to migrate data sets, selecting candidates for migration using an algorithm that considers data set size and days since last reference. Migration stops as soon as there is less allocated space remaining than specified by the low threshold (or there are no more candidates).

The high threshold is used by an optional DFSMShsm space-management function called *interval migration*. In this process, DFSMShsm looks at volumes hourly and compares their allocated space to the high-threshold value. Volumes that exceed the high threshold undergo migration until the remaining allocated space is below the low threshold (the use of two values avoids hourly thrashing around a single value). Interval migration can be thought of as an "emergency" safety valve to help meet unexpected, and hopefully rare, peak demands for storage.

The way the low threshold works provides a standard against which we can monitor DASD space capacity over time. The basic idea is to create graphs something like Figures 10.1 and 10.2.

Figure 10.1 shows available capacity for new data sets. Figure 10.2 displays how much cushion DFSMShsm has to work with in order to provide that capacity. The installation now has information to allow it to acquire additional capacity before the cushion is exhausted.

Larger installations in particular might find it helpful to monitor a single graph for each pool of volumes rather than for individual volumes, showing the average cushion for all volumes in the pool.

Consider an example. Assume an installation has a service objective that says that only data sets that have gone unreferenced for at least two weeks are eligible for migration, meaning no one will ever be delayed, and no system overhead will be exerted, waiting for the recall

I. Report for Volume 123456 - available space

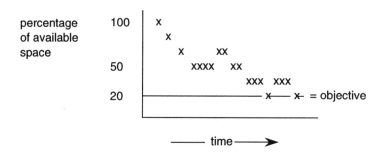

Figure 10.1.   Graph of available volume capacity.

of a data set referenced within the past 14 days. Further, assume that the installation has determined that as long as the volume pool of interest has at least 20 percent free space when the work day begins at 8:00 A.M., users won't experience out-of-space conditions. The low threshold would be set accordingly to 80 percent. When the policies are first implemented, the volumes may have only 50 percent allocated space, and migration will not be performed. Eventually, as data sets grow and

II. Report for Volume 123456 - data not migrated

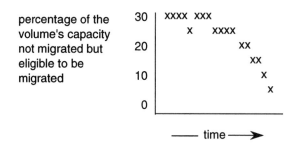

Figure 10.2.   Graph of quantity of migratable data.

new data sets are created, the allocated space on some volumes will grow beyond 80 percent. At that time, for each volume above the low threshold, DFSMShsm will migrate candidate data sets until there is at least 20 percent free space on the volume. If there are additional old data sets that did not need to be migrated to meet the threshold objective, they will be reflected as a value greater than zero in Figure 10.2. When it can be seen from the graph that DFSMShsm soon won't be able to find enough candidates to migrate to meet free space objectives, and the trend in Figure 10.1 is that available volume capacity continues to decrease, then additional capacity is required.

The information described by both figures is necessary to reveal the whole story. Figure 10.1 will usually show allocated space growing over time until it approaches and finally exceeds the low threshold, implying new capacity is needed. But it is only at that time that DFSMShsm migration kicks in, potentially allowing the volume to remain highly occupied for a long time, even as new data sets continue to be allocated. Figure 10.2 is needed to show how much reserve DFSMShsm has to work with to extend volume capacity—it could be that the volume's allocated space could stay near the low threshold for a long time, as DFSMShsm works to meet free space objectives. Similarly, Figure 10.2 by itself is not sufficient for capacity planning, since there may be no migration candidates (no cushion) on a volume that is only half full.

Note that in a DFSMS/MVS environment, MVS attempts to balance the allocated space across volumes in a pool by preferring to allocate new data sets on volumes with allocated space not exceeding the high-volume threshold. So it is possible that all volumes in a given pool may reach saturation at around the same time.

The data necessary to draw the above figures is available in "DASD Capacity Planning Records" produced by the DCOLLECT command in the IDCAMS utility. Some of the data is

DASD volume serial number

volume capacity

target occupancy of volume (the low threshold)

trigger occupancy of volume (the high threshold)

percentage occupancy before DFSMShsm space-management processing

percentage occupancy after DFSMShsm space-management processing

percentage of the volume's data not migrated but eligible to migrate.

The IBM Service Level Reporter licensed program can be used to produce graphs from DCOLLECT data.

(References: 19, 27.)

QUESTION 71—DASD RESERVE / RELEASE PERFORMANCE IMPACT

The hardware RESERVE/RELEASE function assists in preserving data set integrity in shared DASD configurations. However, this function is sometimes a source of performance bottlenecks. The MVS Global Resource Serialization (GRS) facility can reduce the potential for these bottlenecks. Can you describe the basic principle behind RESERVE/RELEASE and how GRS can improve performance?

When a job requests access to a data set, it specifies whether or not it can share access with other jobs. For example, to request exclusive control of a data set that it plans on updating, a job would specify "DISP=OLD" in the JCL DD statement for the data set. As part of the process of allocating the data set to the job, MVS processes the requested disposition by issuing an ENQ macro instruction in order to ensure that the job *can* get exclusive control, and that once it has it, other jobs cannot use the data set until a DEQ macro instruction is later issued when the data set is unallocated.

Normal ENQ processing only provides protection within a single system and does not protect a data set from access by another system. Programs that desire cross-system protection generally issue a RESERVE macro that names the data set to be protected.[38] This results in MVS issuing a RESERVE channel command to the DASD volume on which the data set resides. The data set and volume never actually "see" the RESERVE command—it is processed by the DASD control unit. The DASD control unit enforces the RESERVE by returning a "device busy" indication to any channel program issued by any other

---

[38]Strictly, data set protection is limited to a single system only in JES2 environments. JES3 can provide complex-wide protection for data sets through job scheduling techniques. However, even in a JES3 environment, the system will issue RESERVE requests for selected resources.

system to the reserved volume. Access continues to be denied to other systems until the reserved state is terminated by a RELEASE channel command from the reserving system.

In practice, most programs rely only on the ENQ provided automatically by MVS for data set sharing control. Only a few MVS functions take the additional step of using RESERVE/RELEASE—examples include VTOC processing and catalog processing. It is a common misconception that MVS automatically uses the RESERVE/RELEASE mechanism to protect any data set on a disk volume that is defined to MVS as being shared. See Question 16—Cross-System Data Set Sharing, for a discussion of data set sharing integrity considerations.

Here's the essence of the potential performance problem. Although MVS is just trying to restrict access to a single data set, RESERVE locks up an entire volume. Other systems are locked out of processing *any* data on the entire volume, even if that data has nothing to do with the data set being protected. This can cause queues of I/O requests to grow in the locked-out systems, leading to degraded performance. (In theory, DASD hardware could be designed to understand data set locations and provide a facility to lock at a data set level—but that's not the way things are.)

Other potential problems due to the way RESERVE works, such as the increased potential for interlock, are described in reference 89.

Installations that rely on RESERVE/RELEASE alone to provide data set integrity sometimes resort to ad hoc schemes to manage performance bottlenecks, such as scheduling all work against one volume from only one host.

GRS provides an alternative mechanism to RESERVE/RELEASE for data set protection. GRS allows an installation to serialize access to data sets on shared DASD volumes at the data set level rather than at the volume level. And this can be done within the system without any explicit action by jobs or programs. Thus two or more systems can both be accessing the same volume at the same time (in an interleaved fashion, as usual) without introducing integrity exposures. The way GRS does this is by communicating ENQ and RESERVE requests across multiple systems in the same complex that are connected in a "ring" via channel-to-channel communications.[39]

---

[39]Channel-to-channel communications can be provided through facilities ranging from ESCON channel-to-channel (CTC) adapters to 3088 Multisystem Channel Communication Units.

In a JES2 environment without GRS, for example, a job allocating a data set via

```
// DD ...DISP=OLD...
```

is only guaranteed exclusive control of the data set on the requesting system. Other systems are unaware of the request and could also use the data set. With GRS, the requesting system will notify other systems in the ring of the request; the other systems then either notify the originating system that they agree to honor the request, or that the requestor must wait since the data set is already in use.

GRS can also assist in recovery processing (which actually *is* a performance issue, since the faster you recover from a failure, the better the performance of the system from the viewpoint of the users). Without GRS, if a system abnormally terminates it may leave outstanding RESERVEs on DASD volumes it was accessing. This tends to rapidly degrade performance on the surviving systems as they queue up requests for the reserved volumes, waiting for RELEASES that will never come. The problem is resolved only when the MVS operator figures out what is going on and manually resets the RESERVES (e.g., via a command to the processor system console), allowing the nonfailing systems access to the volumes.

GRS, on the other hand, can automate the recovery process. In a GRS ring, the failing system is detected by GRS processing on the active systems. The ring can be automatically restarted minus the failing system, and global processing will be quickly resumed. The failing system can later automatically rejoin the ring when it is re-IPL'ed.

(References: 36, 89.)

QUESTION 72—ACCESS DENSITY

Installations are faced with many choices when planning DASD configurations. Variables include device capacity, string length, and cache size. What is the concept of "access density" and how can it aid in the process of DASD capacity planning?

The concept of access density is part of an approach to characterizing DASD capacity requirements so that the costs of alternative configurations that satisfy those requirements can be easily identified.

Sometimes, installations choose additional DASD devices to install by simply selecting more of the same models already installed. There may be little thought given to the possible advantages of alternative configurations, which could include cache or higher-capacity devices. Wouldn't it be preferable if DASD requirements were specified not in terms of n boxes of a given model, but in terms of the capabilities that the configuration must provide?

This might be called a "black box" approach in that you could say we want to configure a "nonvolatile, random access storage subsystem" to meet certain needs. If we can characterize our needs in terms of an amount of space, how often we will be accessing this space, and the required response time, then we can identify alternative configurations that will do the job and select the least-cost configuration from among them.

The concept of access density helps us do this. Access density means *the I/O rate per gigabyte of space*. Access density characterizes the intensity of I/O requests against some amount of data.

Applications that generate low-access densities can usually obtain adequate performance using high-capacity DASD devices, while applications that generate high-access densities often need low-capacity and/or cached devices for good performance.

Let's look at an example of how the concept of access density could be used to help determine the lowest-cost DASD configuration that will satisfy a particular need.

Assume you are given the following DASD capacity requirement. "We need 20 gigabytes of space for our new application. We will be accessing this data at 100 I/Os per second. And we require an average DASD response time of no more than 25 milliseconds per I/O in order to meet our end-user service level objectives. We want the lowest-cost configuration that will do all that for us." (The specific quantities may have come from detailed design work, or from just copying the numbers from an existing application whose performance is acceptable.)

This request, then, is for the lowest-cost configuration that consists of at least 20GB of space, can support an access density of at least $100/20 = 5$, and deliver average I/O response of no more than 25ms.

We can address this request in the following way. The given I/O rate of 100 requests/second can be applied, using modelling or benchmark techniques, against various configurations that provide the needed 20 gigabytes of space—notice that the access density remains constant across all cases. The configurations could range from many low-capacity volumes to a few high-capacity volumes under a cache;

each has its associated costs. The resulting DASD response times are recorded in a table or graph. The configuration that is able to deliver the desired response time (or better) at least cost can then be identified.

(Reference: none.)

QUESTION 73—PERFORMANCE OF HIGH-CAPACITY DASD

An installation is planning to acquire additional DASD capacity. The choice is between two units of single-capacity DASD and one unit of double-capacity DASD. The double-capacity unit is very attractive since it costs less and requires less floor space than two single-capacity units, while providing the same amount of space for data sets. However, the installation is concerned that placing data on double-capacity volumes will degrade performance, due to increased "arm stealing," and just the overall activity when there's "so much data on fewer volumes." How legitimate are these concerns?

It may be possible to achieve better performance by splitting work across two or more devices instead of just one—but not always, and not always significantly.

Installing fewer high-capacity volumes rather than a greater number of lower-capacity volumes offers the promise of savings in floor space, control units, maintenance, and so on.

"But what about performance?" was a common question during the 1980s when installations were selecting between single-, double-, and triple-capacity 3380 DASD volumes. The various capacity options available for 3390 DASD volumes has allowed the question to continue into the 1990s.

Experience has shown that the majority of DASD purchased in practice has often been the largest-capacity volumes available in the marketplace. However, the question of performance frequently surfaces and is worth exploring. The concerns are usually about elongated seek times due to "arm stealing" and elongated response times due to too many requests going to too few volumes.

Let's first address the arm-stealing concern. The fear is that if there are very many data sets on a large volume, there is increased probability that requests for different data sets will be interleaved, causing the access mechanism (read/write heads) to move frequently (seek) across the volume, lengthening the response time of I/O requests.

What exactly is seeking? Every I/O request begins with a seek command, even if to the same cylinder as the previous request. This way, the system does not need to track the arm position or worry about another system having moved the arm; there is no noticeable penalty if the arm is already correctly positioned.

In practice, most seeks turn out to be "zero seeks" with no arm movement at all, or minimal seeks to an adjacent cylinder (sequential processing clearly fits this description). That is, most seeking takes no or nearly no time at all on any size DASD device.

Keep in mind that seek times have been reduced over the years with ongoing improvements in DASD technology. Newer DASD generations generally offer faster seek times than previous generations; for example, 3390 DASD models have faster seek times than 3380 models. Moreover, seeking is arguably faster on the higher-capacity models of a given type of DASD (such as 3390-3 at 2.83GB vs. the 3390-2 at 1.89GB), since when the arm moves a given physical distance on the larger volumes, it is skipping over more megabytes (or cylinders) than it would on the smaller volume. In other words, seeking across the same number of cylinders takes less time on a higher-capacity volume since cylinders are closer together on those models than on the smaller-capacity models. So, in cases where both single- or multiple-capacity devices would seek, the multiple-capacity device may actually do so in the least time.

It's always possible to place two very busy data sets on opposite ends of a volume of any size and potentially create a seeking problem—but this situation is easily corrected by tuning and is not unique to high-capacity volumes. Studies have shown that, on real systems, arm stealing is generally not a significant performance factor—see reference 53.

Let's turn to the concern about placing "so much data" on one volume. First, the issue cannot be merely the number of megabytes of data on one volume—if the data is never accessed, performance can hardly be a problem. Of course, it is always possible to do yourself in by placing too many concurrently busy data sets on any one volume, regardless of size. The trick is to find the right data sets to place together on a volume, using the volume's capacity efficiently without creating contention problems.

On a single volume, at low utilizations there is a low I/O request rate. This means that there is a high probability that any particular I/O request will find the device free. In that case, there is at best a negligible performance advantage to splitting the data over multiple volumes since the I/O response time will be the same in each case.

It is only at higher utilizations that requests may begin to interfere significantly with each other (contention) so that new requests are more likely to have to wait for previous requests to complete. In this case, splitting data across two devices may increase the concurrency of processing requests—seek time and latency can be overlapped. It is not always easy to split activity evenly across two devices, however, and the less balanced the activity, the more performance reverts to that expected with a single device.

Graphically, the situation looks like Figure 10.3. Assume our data is either on one double-capacity device ("1"), or on two single-capacity devices ("2"), where other device characteristics are alike. Activity is balanced across the two single-capacity devices. At low utilizations, say to the left of "A" (in practice, A might represent the 20 percent or 25 percent mark), performance of one versus two devices is not significantly different. At higher utilizations, to the right of A, the difference becomes increasingly significant.

We can conclude that for data with relatively low usage, the double-capacity device offers cost savings with minimal impact on performance. Two single-capacity devices may be more appropriate where

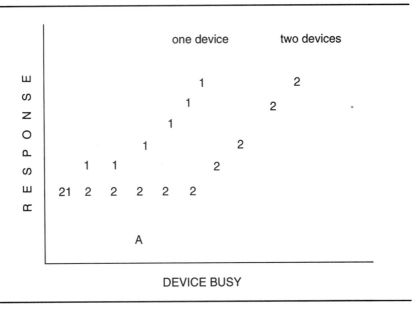

Figure 10.3. Performance of one device versus two devices.

smaller amounts of data are heavily accessed. Paging data sets are a good example of this since they are very small, possibly very active, and may have a major impact on system performance.

The Impact of Cache

The kind of analysis we went through above was common in the early and mid-1980s, when DASD capacities were increasing rapidly and cache subsystems were new and not as widely accepted as they are today. The technology of cached DASD control units goes hand in hand with the benefits of high-capacity DASD, while essentially eliminating the performance concerns. A high-capacity volume (or volume of any size, for that matter) might contain so much busy data in an uncached environment that it cannot perform acceptably. However, in a cached subsystem, the busiest data will tend to remain in the cache automatically, regardless of whether it came from one volume or was spread out across multiple volumes. The concern about too much busy data on one volume causing degraded performance largely vanishes. The need for manual tuning is lessened, and the cache will generally provide better performance than even finely tuned uncached DASD can possibly provide.

(References: 14, 53.)

QUESTION 74—MEASURING DASD CACHE PERFORMANCE

DASD cache subsystems offer significant performance improvements over uncached subsystems by allowing frequently referenced data to be accessed directly from an electronic cache storage rather than from the associated disk volumes with their relatively slow mechanical speeds. Cache has brought with it a unique set of terminology and measurements to assess its effectiveness. Describe the meaning of "read hit ratio," "fast write hit ratio," and "read-to-write ratio." How can installations estimate what cache storage size will be most effective for their data?

IBM offers cached versions of its large DASD subsystems. Cache has brought with it a few unique terms and measurements. The concept of "hit ratio" is central to understanding and measuring cache effectiveness.

- *Read hit ratio.* A read hit occurs when the processor retrieves a record that is already in the cache storage. A read hit bypasses the mechanical processes of seek, latency, and RPS disconnect time in retrieving the record. The read hit ratio is the ratio of the number of read hits to the total number of reads. The higher the read hit ratio, the greater the performance improvement will be.

For example, if 100 read requests are issued, and 60 are satisfied by data found in the cache while the other 40 requests require the data to be read from the backing DASD, then the read hit ratio is 60/100 = 60 percent.

- *Read-to-write ratio.* This is the ratio of read requests to write requests; it is independent of the number of read or write hits. This measure is most important for DASD cache where all performance benefits come only from read hits, and there is no performance advantage for write operations (the older 3880 cache models are examples of this). In those cases, it is desirable to have a high read hit ratio and a high read-to-write ratio. Data that is mostly written but rarely read, such as data base logs, would generally not benefit from being under such a cache.

- *Fast write hit ratio.* A fast write hit occurs when a write operation is able to write data to the cache and immediately notify the application that the I/O operation is complete without having to wait for the data to be destaged to disk. The fast write hit ratio is the ratio of the number of fast write hits to the number of total writes. The higher the fast write hit ratio, the greater the performance improvement will be. One reason all data cannot be written directly to the cache is that in certain cases the disk must be accessed for error checking purposes. In practice, IBM 3990 installations generally attain fast write hit ratios well above 90 percent.

For installed cache controllers, you can get a report of the actual read hit ratios, fast write hit ratios, and read-to-write ratios using the IBM Cache RMF Reporter program offering.

(References: 8, 38, 54, 102.)

QUESTION 75—EXPANDED STORAGE AND DASD CACHE

An installation is establishing improved response time objectives for a major online application in order to improve productivity of data entry personnel. The director of MIS has had some introduction to the ability of both expanded storage and DASD cache to reduce response time. However, the director is unclear about the relative merits of these resources and asks for your advice. How would you respond?

Actually, this is not an either/or issue. Both resources have their places in any system. Let's look at how cache and expanded storage work separately and together to improve service in a data processing environment.

- *Comparing the performance of 3990 cache and expanded storage*
  Both DASD cache and expanded storage (ES) can improve performance through different implementations of a common strategy: reducing the time to access data by keeping data in electronic storage rather than on mechanical devices.

  The 3990 implements the strategy by providing a front end to spinning DASD, keeping frequently referenced data in a cache under microprogram control, thus reducing the time it takes to perform a physical I/O request. Expanded storage implements the strategy by managing data in processor storage under control of MVS and applications, eliminating some physical I/O operations altogether.

  Reasonably tuned uncached 3390s might have average response times of perhaps 20–25 milliseconds (ms.). Cached 3390s might have average response times of perhaps 3–10 milliseconds. ES is much faster than outboard cache; movement of a 4K block of data to or from ES takes about 75 microseconds.[40] Comparing likely best times in this model:

	faster ⟵————————⟶ slower		
DEVICE:	ES	cached 3390	uncached 3390
AVERAGE RESPONSE:	.000075sec	.002sec	.020sec
RELATIVE SPEEDS:	1	27	267

  ES is clearly the best performance option.

---

[40]Actually, this understates ES efficiency. The ES time was originally published by IBM in reference 47, which reported the time for the original 3090 "base" models—subsequent models have improved times. Further, the time reported consists of both the physical transfer of data between ES and CS as well as the software time to manage that move, which can be significant at these speeds. Some types of data access use the MOVE PAGE instruction, eliminating the operating system software overhead altogether. For I/O, on the other hand, the times shown do not include software times, which are likely very small by comparison. In addition, ES is generally accessed synchronously whereas I/O devices are accessed asynchronously, meaning that an I/O causes (1) additional overhead in the operating system for dispatching another task, and (2) degraded performance due to the need to reestablish active instructions and data in the processor high-speed buffer after the task switch.

Some data, such as paging and swapping data, is made ineligible for caching by MVS. In this case, the only comparison is ES versus uncached DASD.

The dramatic performance improvements possible with ES offer more than just improved response time. For example, the use of ES can lower processor utilization and allow the processor to be driven to higher utilizations while meeting service level objectives. See Question 89—Data in Memory—Benefits of Exploiting Processor Storage, for a general discussion of data in memory benefits.

Given all this, then, why not acquire only ES and ignore DASD cache? It turns out there are several reasons why 3990 cache is still very desirable. The rest of this discussion will explore these reasons.

- *Picking up where ES leaves off*
  First, ES can improve performance for read requests but not for most write requests. This is because ES is volatile, meaning it requires constant electrical power to maintain data (this is also true of central storage). If you kept updates only in ES and didn't also write them to a nonvolatile medium, and if power were to fail, all changes to data would be lost. Therefore, changes to data must generally be written back to a nonvolatile medium such as DASD or tape in order to preserve data integrity.

  There is a case where not writing changes to a nonvolatile medium is acceptable: temporary data sets, such as "&&" data sets in JCL or DFSORT SORTWRK files in a hiperspace. Temporary data only exists for the life of a job or job step and can be read and written just to expanded storage. Since the data is temporary by definition, if it's lost, the job can simply be rerun. The risk of lost updates is not relevant.

  Can anything be done to improve performance for write I/O requests for nontemporary data? This is where the 3990 comes in, with its DASD Fast Write facility. DASD Fast Write processes write requests at cache speeds (e.g., 2ms), rather than disk speeds (e.g., 20ms); the data is "dropped off" in the cache, and the 3990 later writes the data to the spinning disks. Data integrity is not a problem because battery backup in the 3990 supplies emergency power even if standard power fails, and there are two copies of the data, one in cache and another in nonvolatile storage (NVM).

  Second, not all data can be kept in processor storage, let alone in ES. Today, some techniques such as VSAM buffers in hiperspace, VIO, and large DB2 buffer pools support maintaining data in processor storage; see Question 88—Data in Memory—Exploiting Processor Storage, for a discussion of these and other techniques.

There are some types of data, however, that do not take advantage of processor storage in this way. Examples include VTOCs, non-strategic access methods such as BDAM, and some non-IBM subsystems. In these cases, only outboard cache provides improved performance over uncached DASD.

- *Minimizing DASD subsystem costs*
  A DASD subsystem, sometimes called a Basic Configurable Unit (BCU), consists of a DASD control unit and its attached DASD—e.g., one 3990 supporting one or more strings of DASD. Many customers have historically configured only short DASD strings per BCU to lower contention for the paths supported by the BCU. The motivation was to lower the number of extra rotations (called RPS misses) that spinning DASD otherwise incurs when paths are busy; if paths are busy when a disk is in position to send or receive data, it must spin again to reposition itself at a cost of about 17 milliseconds per revolution on a 3380 or about 14 milliseconds on a 3390.

  DLSE mode is one way to alleviate this problem by increasing the number of paths from two to four; the probability that all four paths are busy at any one time is small for most workloads. DLSE mode is available on 3390 model DASD and the older 3380 J and K model DASD. Cache is another way to reduce delays due to RPS misses. When the 3990 contains cache, a high percentage of requests (hopefully) are satisfied from the cache, in which case delays due to RPS misses do not apply (they still apply, of course, to accessing data not in the cache). Optimally, cache and DLSE mode would both be configured.

  So cache and/or DLSE mode means that there is less worry about the penalty of RPS misses, making it more practical to configure full-length strings. This can lower DASD subsystem costs through maximizing the number of less expensive "B" units, minimizing the number of 3990s required and reducing floor space.

- *Exploiting large-capacity DASD*
  There is a clear trend towards higher-capacity DASD volumes. High-capacity DASD is desirable because it lowers overall DASD cost. For example, a high capacity 3390 model 3 unit has 50 percent more capacity than a 3390 model 2 unit at much less than 50 percent additional cost! But installations are sometimes concerned about potential response-time problems caused by placing too many data sets on a single high-capacity volume.

  This concern can usually be alleviated by modelling the proposed combinations of volumes. A simpler, though not foolproof, strategy might be to install the high-capacity volumes behind a high-speed cache, providing even better performance than trying to carefully place data sets on uncached volumes. When used in conjunction with data set level caching under DFSMS/MVS, you have control over which data sets get the best performance and which don't.

As an aside, there are obvious productivity benefits here for systems programmers. You might find it an interesting exercise to estimate how much time is spent in moving data sets and volumes around in the name of DASD tuning. And, of course, this movement generally occurs only after a performance problem has surfaced. Improved productivity and improved performance mean additional savings to an organization.

With cache, data centers and users can enjoy the benefits of both high-capacity DASD *and* improved performance. And, when the cost of an entire BCU (control unit plus disks) is considered, a cached configuration is generally not that much more costly than an uncached one.

- *Function*

The 3990 cached controller provides unique function as well as performance.

The 3990 *Dual copy* function provides the ability for installations to ensure the availability of data in the case of a single physical error in a DASD subsystem.[41]

Dual copy can be applied to one or more volumes in the subsystem. For each "primary" volume selected by the installation, a "secondary" volume is assigned. Data on this pair of volumes is automatically kept synchronized by the 3990 subsystem. Data is normally read from the primary volume and written to both volumes. If data is not available due to an error on the primary volume, then the 3990 automatically retrieves that data from the secondary volume. Installations would typically not protect all volumes in this way, which can be expensive, but could protect volumes containing critical data sets such as catalogs or key data bases. This is a tremendous advance in availability. And you get cache performance besides!

---

[41]The 3990 Storage Control can itself be configured without any single points of failure (e.g., multiple channel paths, dual power cord, etc.). The disk volumes containing the data, however, are historically single points of failure, and, being mechanical, are generally the DASD subsystem components most likely to fail. Note that dual copy protects against physical errors but not logical errors. For example, if a program writes invalid data to a file, the data would appear on both volumes in a dual copy pair.

From one point of view, why install ES to provide the ultimate in speed for important applications, yet suffer the exposure of taking the applications down because a critical DASD volume failed?

Another unique function available through 3990 cached controllers is *concurrent copy*. Concurrent Copy allows a point-in-time copy or dump to be made of selected data sets. Normal dump processing can sometimes be measured in hours, during which update activity against data being dumped must be quiesced to ensure the dump contents are consistent. In contrast, the time to make a concurrent copy is measured in seconds, so that update activity against the data only needs to be quiesced for a very small amount of time. Concurrent copy can be very helpful in improving data availability and in allowing increased flexibility in selecting the time of day and frequency at which dumps are taken.

- *Summary*

For best performance, a key technical strategy is to put as much Data as you can Into Memory, and retrieve the rest as fast as possible.

Expanded storage provides the best performance by far for reading data (and writing in some cases) and offers secondary benefits such as lower processor utilization. Providing the ability to manage more and more data in processor storage is clearly a major thrust of MVS/ESA.

3990 cache provides optimal performance for the large amounts of data that cannot be kept in processor storage. And the 3990 provides the only facility to improve the performance of write I/O requests. In addition, 3990 cache can reduce the overall cost of DASD subsystems. Through the dual copy function, DASD volumes can be eliminated as single points of failure. And through concurrent copy, data availability is increased.

Both ES and DASD cache have their place, offering unique and complementary facilities that add value to every system.

(References: 47, 54, 82, 122.)

QUESTION 76—DEVICE SPEED AND JOB PERFORMANCE

An installation is replacing older tape drives with new ones that are expected to handle I/O requests twice as fast as the older drives. A member of the production scheduling group tells you that they expect the elapsed execution time of jobs using the new devices to therefore be cut in half. Is that reasonable? Give an example to support your answer.

While it is reasonable to expect that, in general, faster tape drives will reduce job elapsed time, it is not reasonable to expect that elapsed run time will be reduced by the same fraction as tape I/O response time is reduced.

First, total job response time consists of time spent in several different ways, possibly including the following:

- Time spent by the processor executing instructions.
- Time spent doing I/O to DASD devices.
- Time spent doing I/O to tape devices.
- Time spent waiting for page-ins from DASD.
- Time spent waiting in queues for the above resources.

Reducing time spent using one of these resources will not generally reduce the time spent using the others.

Consider a simple example. Assume that a job runs in an elapsed time of 20 minutes:

```
   10 minutes using the processor
 + 10 minutes doing I/O to a tape device
   ___
   20 minutes job elapsed time
```

If the tape I/O response time is reduced by 50 percent, then the 10 minutes spent doing tape I/O is reduced to 5 minutes. The total job elapsed time would then be reduced to 15 minutes, a reduction of only 25 percent.

Note that some jobs are able to overlap time spent doing tape I/O with time spent doing other things, in which case a reduction in tape I/O response time due to faster devices would have an even smaller impact on job elapsed time than if there were no overlap.

The main point is that the impact of replacing a slower device by a faster device depends on the contribution of the slower device to a job's elapsed time. Does a job that takes one hour to complete do 10 minutes of tape processing, or 50? The larger the contribution of the slower device to job elapsed time, the more to be gained by replacing the slower device with a faster one; the less the contribution, the less to be gained. In practice, most commercial batch jobs are I/O bound, meaning that faster tape and/or DASD devices can make a significant contribution towards improved performance.

(Reference: 50.)

QUESTION 77—DETERMINING THE NUMBER OF TAPE DRIVES

As part of a plan to review an installation's total storage configuration, time has been set aside to study the tape configuration. You are asked to help determine what the "proper" number of tape drives is for the current workload—are there too many drives now or too few? What considerations can you bring to bear on this question?

This is not an easy question to answer. There is no simple formula that generates the optimal number of tape drives for a given workload. Most of the following discussion is based on experience to give you an idea of how you might approach an answer.

The number of tape volumes to be supported is usually not a good indicator of the appropriate number of tape drives. There are typically anywhere from a few hundred to a few thousand tape volumes in a tape library for every tape drive. There is no known way to predict what the ratio should be for a given installation—that is, the number of tape drives is rather independent of the number of tape volumes. It's more an issue of usage.

The number of tape drives installed will affect the timeliness of accessing tape volumes. If there were one drive for every tape volume, there would be no need to mount tapes at all, and tape processing would look a lot like DASD processing. But that's obviously not a practical way to go, for financial and physical space reasons among others.

In the real (reel?) world there will be delays as jobs wait for tape drives that are in use to be freed. Further, there will be delays as jobs wait for tapes to be located and mounted once drives are available. The amount of delay that is acceptable is a matter of installation policy and schedules. So we can say, at least, that the optimum number of drives is the minimum number that allows an installation to meet its data processing objectives. Let's see if we can refine that a bit more.

Evidence for Too Few Drives

Let's look at factors that indicate that additional tape drives would reduce delays due to tape processing.

When too few drives are available for the workload, jobs will wait for in-use drives to be freed. It is reasonable for this to happen occasionally—but if this occurs frequently enough to impact schedules, additional tape drives could improve job throughput.

A good place to begin is to determine how often all drives are in use. You might simply try talking to operators. You may also want to refer to the RMF Monitor I Magnetic Tape Device Activity Report. The "% ALLOC" field tells you the percent of time during the reporting interval each tape drive was allocated (to the reporting system only). You could look at reports for multiple intervals and get a feel for the average number of drives in use at the same time.

In JES2 systems, and JES3 systems using native MVS device allocation, MVS issues messages that will appear on the console log when jobs request tape drives and none are available (these messages are issued as part of a process called "allocation recovery"). When these messages appear frequently, that's a good sign that additional tape drives could reduce job delays significantly. You can use the IBM Service Level Reporter (SLR) program product to analyze SYSLOG message activity. In JES3 environments when JES3 allocation is being used, JES3 simply delays initiating jobs in the first place if tape drives are not available. In this case, if all drives are usually in use and it is frequently the case that additional jobs are waiting for initiation but held back due to lack of drives, then, again, additional tape drives could reduce job delays.

You must keep in mind that delays in tape processing can be due to factors other than having too few drives to meet the demand.

Time spent waiting for operators to find and mount tapes adds to delays. These delays can be reduced by methods such as additional personnel, better physical planning, improved use of JES2 or JES3 job setup, and tape cartridge subsystem features such as cartridge loaders and IBM's Improved Data Recording Capability (IDRC). In addition, frequently referenced tape data sets can be moved to DASD to eliminate mounts altogether. Refer to Question 28—Reducing Tape Processing for further discussion.

It takes time to read data from a tape. It might be that job elapsed time would be improved by faster tape drive speed. This conclusion could be supported by an analysis of SMF records showing that a large portion of elapsed time of delayed work consists of tape I/O time that is not overlapped with other I/O or processor time. Reference 50 discusses this technique.

The current drive configuration may benefit from tuning. For example, it may be that tape I/O performance would improve if tape activity was spread across more channels or better balanced across existing tape channels. This conclusion would be supported by indicators on RMF reports such as high or unbalanced channel utilizations, high tape I/O response times, and high queue lengths.

The installation may be creating delays through inefficient scheduling techniques. For example, there may be an unnecessary restriction on the number of jobs that need tape drives and can run concurrently.

Evidence for Too Many Drives

Let's now consider the opposite question: Might there be more tape drives configured than are needed to satisfy performance requirements? Perhaps jobs are finishing well within schedules. Or, perhaps there are now drives that sit idle, although they may have been necessary in the past. An easy and practical technique to determine if there are excess drives is to gradually vary drives offline. Start by varying one drive offline; the drive is easily varied back online if needed. If the drive is not needed after some agreed period of time, or is needed but the delays are few and acceptable, then vary an additional drive offline, and so on.

You might also want to refer to the RMF Monitor I Magnetic Tape Device Activity Report. The "% ALLOC" field tells you the percent of time during the reporting interval each tape drive was allocated (to the reporting system only). You could look at reports for multiple intervals, and get a feel for the largest number of drives in use at the same time.

In JES3 installations, keep in mind that use of JES3 "setup" causes JES3 to attempt to mount tapes on all available drives, even for jobs that may not be initiated for some time. Thus it may seem that all drives are in use, when in fact many are idle.

Finally, keep in mind that many installations want intentionally to install a small number of additional drives above the number strictly required. The purpose is to have extra drives available in case some drives need repair. This was more of a concern with the older 3420 type of technology than it is with today's improved tape cartridge subsystem technology, but still may provide a desired safety factor in installations with very heavy tape processing and tight schedules.

Closing Remarks

Determining the appropriate number of tape drives for a given installation is still more of an art than a science. Yet there are many situations where this needs to be done, such as when assessing requirements for new tape units to replace older ones, saving floor space to make room for other equipment, or analyzing the tape configuration as part of a total storage system study.

(References: 50, 94, 98, 117.)

11

Processor Storage, Virtual Storage, and Paging

A significant portion of MVS is devoted to managing processor storage through techniques such as paging. It is paging that makes large virtual storage possible. Because paging involves processor storage as well as the I/O subsystem and has a global impact on response time and throughput, it continues to receive the focus of performance analysts and capacity planners. Paging algorithms have been changed several times during the evolution of MVS to increase their efficiency.

Advances in technology are making large processor storage sizes a reality—and that has the potential for greatly improving performance by reducing page I/O and general I/O processing.

QUESTION 78—PAGING VOCABULARY

The management of real storage through paging has its own specialized vocabulary. Define the following terms:

1. *real storage*
2. *virtual storage*
3. *page*
4. *page frame*
5. *expanded storage*
6. *slot*
7. *page stealing*

8. *page fault*
9. *working set*
10. *swapping*

---

1. *Real storage* is a term that has been used for a number of years in order to contrast the physical storage in a computer from the virtual storage that programs can address. Other terms used include "memory," "main" storage (to contrast this storage with "auxiliary" or "secondary" DASD/tape storage), and sometimes "core" by those who have been around since the days when computer storage was made of small magnetized rings. Recently, the terms "processor storage," "central storage," and "expanded storage" have been introduced to better describe the advances in computer storage technology. Processor storage is all addressable electronic storage in the machine, both central and expanded. Central storage contains active programs and data and corresponds to the old "real" storage concept. Expanded storage, available on some machines, contains less active programs and data.

    Because of the architectural use of a 31-bit address, central storage is limited to 2(31) bytes = 2 gigabytes in size.

2. *Virtual storage* is the mechanism that makes it possible for a program to access the maximum amount of storage that can be addressed (in 31 bits as of MVS/XA) even though the system might contain much less central storage. Virtual storage works because MVS keeps active portions of each address space in central storage and less active portions in expanded storage or auxiliary storage.

    That virtual storage is a mechanism or technique means that it doesn't physically exist. There is an old joke about a systems engineer telling a marketing representative that the customer was almost out of virtual storage. The salesperson was unconcerned and simply suggested that they just sell them some more.

3. A *page* is a contiguous block of virtual storage, 4K bytes in MVS.

    A printed page, such as the one you are now reading, typically contains about 2000 to 3000 characters, hence the terminology.

4. A *page frame* is a block of central storage. A page frame may contain a page or may be on a queue of page frames that are available to contain pages.

5. *Expanded storage* is electronic storage that is physically installed inside a processor. While some central storage is always required on a system, it can optionally be augmented by expanded storage (ES) for improved system performance. Because ES is electronic, it

is much faster than mechanical DASD and is used by MVS as a very fast paging and swapping device, as well as an area in which to hold data for fast access. MVS reads and writes pages between central and expanded storage in 4K blocks. Given the importance of large processor storage sizes, note that expanded storage is architected to support up to 16 terabytes (trillions of bytes) of storage, compared to the two gigabyte limit of central storage.[42]

6. A *slot* is a 4K block of auxiliary storage used to contain an inactive page. MVS moves pages containing programs and data between page frames in central storage and slots on auxiliary storage.

7. *Page stealing* is the name of the technique MVS uses to remove from central storage pages that aren't being used frequently, in order to make frames available for pages that will be used in the immediate future. Stolen pages may be placed in expanded storage or auxiliary storage.

8. *Page fault.* When a program references a virtual storage address, the central processor executing the program attempts to translate the virtual address to an address in central storage. If the translation process indicates that the page associated with that virtual address is not in central storage, the central processor creates an interrupt called a page fault. The interrupt causes control to pass to a function within MVS that will bring the page into central storage.

It may happen that the desired page actually does happen to be in central storage because it was recently stolen (which made it unavailable to the application) but not yet moved out of central storage. In that case the page is *reclaimed* by MVS (just in the nick of time, you might say) and control is returned to the application. In general, however, the page must be brought in from expanded storage or from an external paging data set. In any case, handling of page faults is transparent to application programs.

Page faults that result in page-ins (rather than reclaims) are important in performance analysis. This is because applications generally can't continue processing until a page fault is resolved. Writing pages out of central storage does not delay applications in this way. A high rate of page-ins and/or long times to resolve individual page-ins can have a severe impact on application performance.

---

[42]Expanded storage is addressed by a 32-bit address, and each location is the beginning of a 4K block of storage. Therefore the architected maximum size of expanded storage is 2(32) * 4096 = 16 terabytes, otherwise known as "a lot."

9. The *working set* of a job is the number of pages that must be resident in processor storage for the job to run efficiently, that is, with paging I/O delays minimized so as not significantly to degrade performance. For example, a job may require a virtual storage area of two megabytes to contain all its programs and addressable data. Yet its actual use of those programs and data may be such that only one megabyte of processor storage is really needed to hold the most active pages at any time, while keeping paging I/O at a level acceptable for satisfactory performance. In this case, the job has a working set of one megabyte.

Generally speaking, processor storage should be configured at least large enough to support the sum of the working sets of all the jobs that could be running at the same time. That will minimize the impact of paging on performance during even the heaviest peak periods.

10. *Swapping* is a mechanism used to control access by jobs to system resources. You might think of swapping as a control over jobs that have already begun execution, the control being to make the jobs eligible or ineligible to compete with other jobs for use of the system from time to time. In contrast to a job's priority, which defines how an executing job competes with other jobs for processor cycles, swapping controls whether a job is allowed to compete for any additional resources at all. We say a job is "swapped in" when it is eligible to compete for resources and "swapped out" when it is not.

The term swapping comes from the original intent of this process, which was to move the pages used by an idle TSO user out of processor storage in one single operation; this would make room to bring in another user. This was especially important when TSO was first developed, because processor storage sizes were much smaller then compared to today. True, page stealing would have written unused pages to DASD over time, but stealing would not recover large amounts of unused storage very quickly. So the system was designed to detect that a TSO user was not going to be doing anything for a while, and would immediately write all of the user's pages out to DASD at once, freeing that storage for use by others. When the user eventually entered a command, the pages were brought back into processor storage—again, all at once instead of gradually being read in as each was referenced.

Swapping has evolved considerably since its earliest inception and now applies to nearly all jobs, not just TSO users (certain system address spaces that are key to system performance are always designated nonswappable). Yet the efficient management of processor storage generally remains the major benefit of this mechanism.

While nearly all jobs could be managed by swapping, in practice swapping is usually limited by installations to mainly batch jobs and TSO users. Installations generally set a few jobs, such as CICS, nonswappable. In the case of CICS, this is because many terminal users are being supported by one CICS address space—swapping this job out could affect the performance of all CICS users. Also, a CICS production system is usually so busy that it doesn't pay to swap it out since it would likely need to be immediately swapped back in. On the other hand, a lightly used CICS test system may be made swappable if it is not constantly used.

(References: 83, 113.)

QUESTION 79—BENEFITS AND DRAWBACKS OF PAGING

Sometimes it can seem that paging is little more than a cause of performance problems. Describe both positive and negative effects paging can have on performance.

To begin with, paging in itself isn't a problem. To have a performance problem you need a performance objective that isn't being met, and in data processing this usually means response time or turnaround time. If response time is not satisfactory, then it may be paging, and/or something else, that is a major contributor to the problem.

Paging has both positive and negative impacts on performance. Let's look at the positive first.

Paging is part of the mechanism that makes virtual storage work. Paging allows programs to be written as if a large, continuous addressable storage was available, even though much less central storage may in fact be installed on a given machine. This can simplify program design.

Paging allows more jobs to share processor storage at once than would otherwise be possible, by only keeping frequently referenced portions of programs and data in central storage and maintaining everything else in expanded storage or on DASD. Since more programs can then be in central storage at the same time, the multiprogramming level of the system can increase, improving throughput.

By breaking data and programs into 4K chunks that need not be contiguous in central storage (although they appear contiguous to the programmer), the problem of storage fragmentation is greatly reduced. In the days prior to paging, operators spent a good deal of time scheduling jobs so that gaps created in storage as jobs came and went were minimized.

These benefits are not without some costs. An individual job or transaction runs more slowly if it incurs page faults than if all its data and programs were resident in central storage. Also, the processor time spent handling page faults is time not spent executing applications; however, this is usually not a significant factor on today's large systems unless the paging rates are extremely high or storage is very underconfigured. Experience has shown that the benefits such as increased throughput generally far outweigh any performance loss as long as paging is kept in control.

(Reference: 100.)

QUESTION 80—BENEFITS OF REDUCING PAGING I/O

Paging I/O is implicit I/O (not requested by applications), and I/O processing is very slow compared to processor speeds. The delays caused by these I/Os can often add up to poor performance. The easiest way to reduce paging I/O delays is to provide additional processor storage. This hardware resource has an associated cost that is often justified just on the basis of the improved performance. However, can you identify additional benefits that can accrue by reducing paging I/O rates through installing additional processor storage?

Here is a list of some of the "side" benefits of installing additional processor storage to reduce paging I/O rates. Note that this discussion is actually a special case of the kinds of benefits to be derived by reducing I/Os of any type through the techniques of Data in Memory. See Question 88—Data in Memory—Exploiting Processor Storage and Question 89—Data in Memory—Benefits of Exploiting Processor Storage.

- *Improved performance.* Response time is improved because as paging delays are reduced, jobs and online transactions complete faster. Throughput is improved because new work can be started earlier and because processor time formerly used to manage paging is made available to applications.
- *Systems programmer productivity.* When performance is not ac-

ceptable, systems programmers often spend a significant amount of time trying to "tune" around the problem. If sufficient resources are provided for adequate performance, the time spent tuning can be used more productively.

- *I/O subsystem benefits*. I/O subsystem performance may generally improve. Additional processor storage will reduce the amount of I/O to the page data sets. This paging I/O load not only has an impact on the volumes containing page data sets, but also on the strings, control units, and channels which provide the paths to those data sets. Reducing paging I/O thus reduces the I/O load across these shared components, reducing contention and thus improving the performance of other work on the system using these components. Reducing the need for paging volumes and returning channel, control unit, and string capacity for use by other work can result in reduced I/O subsystem costs.

- *Reduced processor overhead*. MVS must execute some number of instructions (historically, in the thousands) to handle each page I/O request. Very high paging I/O rates can have a noticeable impact on processor utilization (what is "very high" varies with processor speed). Reducing paging I/O rates would make those processor cycles again available to applications.

(Reference: 100.)

QUESTION 81—EVALUATING PAGING I/O RATES

A technical support manager asks you if the paging I/O rate on the system is too high. How might you respond to such a question?

While the question is very short and is very common, the answer will take a bit of discussion. What the question is really asking is if paging is a major cause of performance problems. Paging can really only be too high if some objective is not being met and reducing paging would solve that problem.

Keep in mind that "paging rate" can be ambiguous. A system's total paging rate may include demand paging and swap paging, as well as VIO paging. Within demand paging, generally only the page-in rate is of interest since that's usually what impacts performance. For the remainder of this discussion, paging rate will generally mean demand page-in rate.

Let's discuss several approaches to assessing the impact of paging on performance. These techniques may be used individually or together.

Approach 1—Estimating Working Set Storage Requirements

An effective way to look at the issue is not to consider the system paging rate as a whole directly, but rather to estimate the processor storage required for satisfactory performance of individual workloads. In any given installation, TSO users, batch jobs, MVS itself, CICS, and so on each have desirable working set requirements. That is, each workload type needs a certain amount of processor storage to run with satisfactory performance. The sum of the individual storage requirements (of work that runs concurrently) is the total processor storage requirement.

MVS must share installed processor storage among competing jobs and must often assign working sets that are less than optimum, given total demand. Reference 113 shows how to use RMF reports to determine the working sets the system implements for existing workloads. You are shown how to create simple graphs to help identify desired working set sizes to minimize the impact of paging delays on performance. The combined desired working set sizes determine the desired processor storage size. The reference also explains how to use that information to estimate storage requirements for future workloads.

Approach 2—Reducing Paging to Negligible Rates

With the availability of large processor storage sizes, performance can be greatly improved through the use of Data in Memory (DIM) techniques.[43] For data on an external device to be brought into processor storage, it generally must first be brought into virtual storage. If there is insufficient processor storage (central plus expanded) to hold the data in virtual storage, it may be paged out to DASD. In that case, there is really no performance gain since the physical I/O to the data is replaced not by an access to memory, but by a paging I/O—and all I/Os are very slow compared to accessing data directly from processor storage.

Therefore, to gain the benefits of DIM, it is important to provide enough processor storage to minimize paging as well as to provide room for all the data to be kept in storage. Note that minimal does not necessarily mean zero but some value so close to zero as to make any delays due to paging negligible.

---

[43]See Question 88—Data in Memory—Exploiting Processor Storage for a discussion of DIM.

Reference 113 describes how to draw a simple graph called a "paging miss ratio curve" that shows the relationship between paging rates and storage sizes for an entire system. See Figure 11.1. The reference cleverly helps you draw this curve from just four easily determined values. Three points can be easily obtained from RMF reports: the paging rate between processor storage and DASD, the rate of page movement between central and expanded storage (assuming the processor under study has expanded storage), and zero for the paging rate for a processor storage size equal to current processor storage plus all auxiliary paging space (slots) used. To obtain a fourth point, the reference states that the paging rate that would exist if processor storage were halved can be estimated as four times the current paging rate. In all cases, use the total paging rate: page-ins and page-outs, including swap pages. These points provide the general shape of the curve. You can then estimate how much processor storage is required to make paging rates negligible for existing workloads.

Approach 3—Designing a Paging I/O Configuration

The idea here is to figure out how much time can be tolerated by the system (or by key applications) per page-in from an auxiliary storage device. Given that, you can then go about designing a paging I/O subsystem to deliver that performance. This approach is discussed in reference 100.

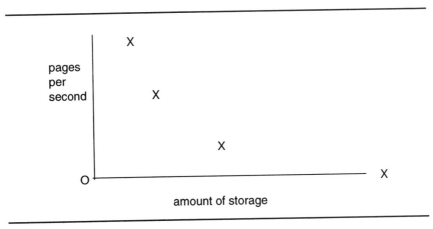

Figure 11.1.   General shape of a paging miss ratio curve.

Approach 4—Correlating Performance with Page-Fault Rates

An approach to evaluating the impact of paging on an existing system is to correlate the paging rate for a given workload to that workload's performance. That is, to see how the workload's performance varies with changes in working set size or paging rate. Using performance monitors such as RMF, it is possible to determine working sets, page-fault rates, and performance measures such as TSO response time, all occurring at the same time. These quantities can then be graphed together so you can see how they relate to each other. For example, you might create a graph that has TSO average response time on the vertical axis and page-fault rate on the horizontal axis. If variations in paging rates are the major cause of performance fluctuations, then you should see this in the graph. The lack of a clear correlation probably means that some other resources are causing the problem, perhaps along with paging rates.

Approach 5—Determining Total Paging Delay Time

This approach determines the total amount of time that an application is delayed due to paging. If that time is a significant portion of overall response time, you will know that it will pay to decrease the effect of paging on that application. The RMF Monitor III Delay Report identifies the amount of time a job or user is delayed by paging, as well as by other factors.

Approach 6—Estimating Effect on Processor Capacity

Excessively high paging rates can have a noticeable impact on processor utilization. Historically, an informal guideline has been that if more than 5 percent of processor time is used for paging, especially at high utilizations where there is little capacity to spare, the installation is probably incurring excessive overhead. This leaves the problem of determining the processor utilization caused by various paging rates.

A study conducted within IBM's Washington Systems Center in the early 1980s showed that the approximate processor utilizations caused by processing a swap and a nonswap page on a 3081KX processor under MVS/XA were .0086 percent and .0286 percent, respectively. Utilizations on other processors can be estimated based on their power relative to the 3081KX.

Suppose that in some installation the paging I/O rate on a particular processor is so high that it adds 10 percent to the total processor busy time. That's saying that 10 percent of the processor is unavailable to applications (not to mention the performance implications). Assuming that the purpose of the processor is to run applications rather than to stress test MVS paging capabilities, the cost of this paging can be translated to 10 percent of the processor value in dollars. Adding processor storage to reduce that paging and buy back that lost capacity will generally more than pay for itself.

Approach 7—Monitoring Page Fault Time

Some installations monitor the time it takes to resolve a page fault. The goal is to keep this time as small as possible, or at least be able to detect if it is increasing. Unfortunately, page-fault resolution time is not directly tracked by the system. There are several measures that are sometimes used to estimate page-fault resolution time, such as page-transfer time and page-delay time (also called MSPP or milliseconds per page), both reported by RMF. Because these measures are based only on paging to auxiliary storage, they do not account for the fast paging times to expanded storage. While once popular, this approach seems to be losing favor due to the development of the above approaches and advances in technology.

(References: 94, 100, 113.)

QUESTION 82—EFFECT OF PAGING ON TSO AND CICS

Different applications can tolerate different page-fault rates and still achieve acceptable performance. The tolerance of CICS is generally low (perhaps under five page I/Os per second) compared to other work, such as TSO. Why is this so?

When a page fault occurs and the page is on auxiliary storage, the associated MVS task is made nondispatchable until the page has been brought into central storage. A single CICS system executes most work under a single MVS task—it does its own sub-dispatching of transactions. Thus when CICS takes a page fault and the page is on a DASD device, all transaction processing stops—all CICS users are affected. (CICS actually may have separate MVS tasks for certain functions such as processing VSAM requests, and Multiple Region Operation can be used to create other MVS tasks—but the point being made is still basically correct.)

Consider an example. Assume a single page-in I/O takes 20 milliseconds, and CICS experiences 10 such page-ins each second. Then for 200 milliseconds out of each second, or 20 percent of the time, CICS would be waiting for page-ins and unable to execute instructions or dispatch transactions. CICS processor utilization could not rise above 80 percent (of a single engine) based on paging delays alone.

TSO users, on the other hand, are each structured as an individual job from MVS's point of view, and each user has a unique MVS task under which the user's commands are executed. Thus a page-fault only affects the user incurring the fault, and other users are unaffected.

(Reference: 100.)

QUESTION 83—CONTROLLING PAGING

An installation has determined, for its important applications, maximum paging rates that will not impact performance objectives. What controls are available in MVS to manage paging performance and make use of this hard-won knowledge?

The following basic techniques can be used to control paging rates or reduce the effects of paging.

• *Storage isolation.* Once performance has been correlated with page-in rate and/or working set size, the MVS System Resource Manager's (SRM) storage isolation parameters can be used to protect a job against page stealing. Low and high thresholds can be specified for paging rate and/or working set size. Given sufficient processor storage, this is an effective mechanism to protect important work against any fluctuations in overall storage demand that could adversely affect performance.

Here's a good strategy for using these controls for online systems such as CICS. A page fault in CICS can affect all terminal users, since CICS generally runs transactions under a single MVS task. Storage isolation controls can be used to set a desired maximum page-in rate for CICS. SRM will attempt to maintain a working set size that in turn maintains the desired page-in rate. It could happen, however, that through normal fluctuations in workload CICS sometimes has little or no work to do or incurs a longer than usual delay for some resource. Since while its idle CICS' page-in rate is zero, the SRM can reduce CICS' working set while still meeting the maximum page-in rate objective. When CICS activity again resumes, there will be a flurry of page-in activity, perceived by users as degraded performance, as CICS references data and programs it needs but that were paged out. To avoid this situation, in addition to a desired maximum page-in rate, a desired minimal working set size can be set by the installation so that SRM won't steal too much CICS storage.

Of course, it will take some analysis by the installation to determine the values to which the controls should be set.

- *Multiprogramming level*. The SRM indirectly controls paging rates by adjusting the system multiprogramming level (MPL). SRM periodically examines several indicators of system performance, including paging activity. When any indicator is higher than an associated threshold, SRM will lower the target system MPL; a lower MPL will mean a lowered demand for all resources, including processor storage. Conversely, when all indicators are below associated thresholds, SRM will raise the target system MPL, which will allow more jobs to run concurrently, increasing the demand for all resources, including processor storage. The thresholds can be modified by an installation; further, the installation can set minimum and maximum MPLs for workload categories (e.g., TSO) through SRM "domain" definitions.

- *Scheduling practices*. The installation may effectively be able to reduce paging by rescheduling some of the work that normally runs during the time performance is degraded. Often, batch work can be moved from prime shift to second or third shift. This lowers the total demand for storage, making more processor storage available for the remaining work.

- *Reduced page-fault resolution time*. A higher page rate can be tolerated if the page-fault resolution time is reduced. This can be achieved most easily through additional central storage ("no paging is faster than fast paging"), expanded storage, or, to a far lesser extent, through a faster paging I/O subsystem.

(References: 83, 100.)

QUESTION 84—SWAPPING PERFORMANCE

An installation is interested in improving TSO response time in order to increase user satisfaction and productivity. A performance analyst has shown that TSO swap-in time is the major contributor to unsatisfactory response time at this location and that the problem cannot be solved by simply tuning existing resources. The analyst therefore recommends that hardware resources be acquired to improve swapping performance. How does swapping use system hardware resources? What resources could be installed to improve swapping performance?

Let's look at a simplified example of how swapping works, focusing on the use of hardware resources.

The most common reason the system will swap out a TSO user is that the system is waiting for the user to enter a command; this wait usually lasts for seconds or even minutes. This wait could be very short if, for example, the user is quickly browsing through a data set. Or, this wait might be very long if the user has gone off on a coffee break.

TSO, at least given the current state of the art, doesn't know and can't predict how long the wait might be, which poses a dilemma. It would be inefficient to allow the user's address space to continue to occupy processor storage that might be better used by more active work, but it would also be inefficient to swap the user's pages out to DASD only to have to swap them back in quickly. To handle this dilemma, MVS proceeds as follows:

1. If the current use of central storage by all jobs is low enough, the user will be "logically swapped." This means the user's pages will remain in central storage—at least for the time being. If the user quickly enters the next command (generally within a few seconds), then the user will be able to resume processing quickly. System overhead is minimal in this case since pages never had to be moved out of and back into central storage.

2. If, in MVS's judgment, the use of central storage by other jobs is high, or the user takes too long to enter the next command, MVS will write the user's pages to expanded storage, if available. If the user enters the next command while swapped to expanded storage, the swap-in process just moves the pages back to central storage; this time is relatively short since no I/O is required.

3. If expanded storage is not installed or is needed for other work, MVS will issue I/O requests to write the user's pages to auxiliary storage.[44]

Swapping I/O is designed to perform best when there are multiple page or swap data sets available on unique I/O paths. This is because the number of pages to be swapped is generally so large—often on the order of 100 or more—that MVS tries to reduce the time a swap-in or swap-out could take by writing groups of pages in parallel to the data sets.[45]

When swap data sets are available, MVS breaks down a swap request into groups of 12 pages called swap sets and attempts to concurrently read or write each swap set to a different data set. Since there may be about 10 or more swap sets per swap, at least 10 swap data sets on 10 different paths would be required for optimal performance. If only local page data sets are used for swapping, up to 30 pages can be read/written to each data set at once.[46]

If insufficient page/swap data sets are available to support the system's attempt to perform parallel I/O, or if the data sets happen to be on the same paths, the effect is to defeat MVS's attempt at optimization and to elongate swap I/O time.

While parallel swap I/O requests will shorten swap-out time, the real benefit is during swap-in, since that occurs when the user has actually entered a command and is expecting a response. When a command is entered, MVS issues the necessary I/Os to bring the pages into central storage from auxiliary storage and the user can continue processing.

Most installations will not find it practical to support the optimum number of paths for swapping, further supporting the argument for providing sufficient processor storage to minimize if not eliminate swap I/O.

---

[44]I/O operations cannot occur directly into or out of expanded storage, so MVS must in fact first move the pages from expanded storage back to central storage in order to write them to auxiliary storage. This clearly adds to system overhead.

[45]100 pages amounts to 4 megabytes of data. It is interesting to observe that this is in line with the memory sizes of single-user personal computers in commercial environments. The actual average number of pages per swap in a given system is reported in the RMF Paging Activity Report.

[46]This is documented in *MVS Paging Considerations with an Emphasis on 3090 Environments*, a paper by Thomas Beretvas of IBM presented at GUIDE 72.

Summary

To provide optimal performance for TSO users and minimize system overhead, installations should configure enough processor storage to minimize swapping I/O to auxiliary storage. Minimizing I/O is the most important issue; it is much less important to replace swaps to expanded storage with logical swaps, unless page movement to expanded storage is so high as significantly to reduce remaining processor capacity. For swapping I/O that does occur, performance can be improved by providing multiple swap data sets (or page data sets if swap data sets aren't defined) on different I/O paths.

(Reference: 83.)

QUESTION 85—ALL-LOCAL PAGING CONFIGURATIONS

MVS uses both paging and swapping as techniques to manage processor storage. Installations may see acceptable or improved performance if there are no swap data sets defined, in which case all paging and swapping I/O is performed against local page data sets. What considerations can make this true?

The trend is toward minimizing paging and swapping I/O through large processor storage, so that the effect of paging and swapping on performance is decreasing. Correspondingly, the number of page and swap data sets is generally decreasing compared to what was required in the past; one or two local page data sets may effectively handle the page/swap I/O load for an entire system with sufficient processor storage configured. However, while this is the trend, not all installations are there yet. Let's pursue the answer assuming there is significant paging and swapping I/O activity.

While paging can occur only to page data sets, swapping can occur to either swap or page data sets. Swap data sets are optional; the purpose of using swap data sets is to have MVS separate swap requests (each of which involves large numbers of pages) from individual page I/O requests. This can improve the performance of page data sets. If there are no swap data sets, MVS will use the local page data sets for swapping as well as for paging.

Swapping is designed to perform best when there are multiple page or swap data sets available on unique I/O paths. Question 84—Swapping Performance includes a discussion of how this parallelism works.

In most installations, it will not be practical to provide sufficient paths for optimal swapping—the system may be too small, or other work may not tolerate the I/O path usage that swap requests can generate. But the efficiency can be maximized by using all local data sets rather than a combination of swap and local data sets. For example, assume an installation can only "afford" ten volumes for paging/swapping. Some number of local page data sets are always required by MVS, and swap data sets are always optional. So a configuration of five swap and five paging volumes is one possibility. But configuring the ten volumes as all local paging volumes would allow for maximum parallelism.

An all-local configuration has generally proven to be the better performer on a TSO or TSO/batch machine. But what if other major subsystems such as CICS or IMS are also running? Historically, the performance of these applications is very sensitive to paging rates and how fast page-in requests can be completed. Performance could degrade significantly if page-in requests from these applications were delayed behind lengthy swap requests for the same page data set. Defining swap data sets to separate swapping activity from paging activity is one solution to this problem. However, even in this case an all-local configuration could still be acceptable if swapping is minimal such as in a small TSO population, or paging is minimal for those applications most sensitive to paging rates, such as CICS.

Ultimately, the best way to find the best configuration for a given installation may be to experiment. Use of the PAGEADD operator command makes it easy to undo any unforeseen negative impact on performance if the experiment goes awry.

(Reference: 83.)

QUESTION 86—DEDICATING VOLUMES TO PAGING

A well-known recommendation for configuring page data sets is to dedicate each disk volume that supports paging to just a single page data set, even if most of the disk space goes unused. What is the basis for this recommendation?

Dedicating entire DASD volumes to single page data sets has been a recommendation since the early days of virtual storage. The recommendation is not a requirement, but if followed can improve the performance of paging I/O activity. This will be important in environments with applications that are sensitive to the response time of paging I/O.

Typically, such environments are characterized by relatively high paging I/O rates. Since there are no external controls over which data sets a given application's pages go to, providing good performance for every page data set is essential in such environments.

Keep in mind that the trend in large systems is toward minimizing page (and swap) I/O rates through using large processor storage. This decreases the impact of page I/O on performance, so that the need to dedicate DASD volumes to page data sets for optimal performance decreases. This will allow installations to use DASD volume space more efficiently, rather than dedicate an entire volume to each relatively small page data set. For installations where paging I/O performance is still critical, dedicating volumes to page data sets can reduce time to access those data sets. Let's discuss the reasons for this.

Minimizing nonpaging activity on a device with a page data set will avoid having page I/O requests waiting behind unrelated requests. Some installations have sufficient resources and performance requirements that not merely devices, but entire paths are dedicated to just paging data sets. Also, if other data sets reside on a single volume in addition to a page data set, seeking between the data sets could add a performance penalty to accessing the page data set.

A final reason is based on the use by MVS of Suspend/Resume channel commands. The MVS Auxiliary Storage Manager (ASM), which manages the transfer of pages between central storage and DASD, will always try to append ("tack on") new page I/O requests to the end of an existing, active channel program. This saves instructions compared to what ASM must do to start a brand new channel program. But it will sometimes be the case that there is no I/O request currently in progress to the target page data set, and so no CCW (channel command word) to tack on to. Suspend/Resume helps address this case.

Basically, what Suspend/Resume does is try to ensure that there will always be an outstanding CCW present to tack on to. It does this by "suspending" a channel program when it finishes. To allow a channel program to be suspended, ASM always sets a special bit in the last CCW in the channel program. This causes the channel to suspend the channel program rather than terminate it after that CCW is executed. In this way there is always a CCW available for tacking on to, even if a channel program is not active in the usual sense. When ASM receives a new request for a page, it tacks on new CCWs to the suspended CCW and then issues a Resume Subchannel instruction to resume execution of the suspended I/O request.

The suspended channel program remains associated with the I/O device for which it was started. If another I/O request is made to the same device (through the standard Start Subchannel instruction), then MVS ends the suspended channel program in order to issue the new request. Thus Suspend/Resume can be defeated unless a single page data set is the only data set on the volume. Note that this is true only for the suspended system—other systems could access the volume without breaking the suspended channel program, but that would have the performance implications discussed earlier in this answer.

(Reference: 83.)

QUESTION 87—SOLID STATE DEVICES AS PAGING DEVICES

An installation is experiencing unacceptable delays due to paging, and one solution being considered is a solid-state device (SSD). An SSD contains solid-state storage, attaches to processors via channels, and emulates an IBM DASD device. What considerations can you offer the installation as to how best to handle their paging performance concerns? What drawbacks might an SSD have?

The following are steps you might take in looking at solving a performance problem due to paging, contrasting various IBM solutions to an SSD solution.

- *Widen the focus*
  First, you should always ensure that the performance problem really is mainly due to paging delays and not something else. Examining the output of system performance monitors can usually reveal this kind of information.

  Once you have determined that paging is truly the problem to be solved, there is no need to keep the focus narrowed only to hardware alternatives. The goal is to solve the problem in the most effective way, not just compare the speeds of external paging devices. The problem should be broadened to: What are all the solutions available to help reduce paging delays?
- *Look at tuning as the low-cost solution*
  There may be a tuning solution to the problem, which would be the least cost solution of all. For example, MVS storage isolation techniques might be used to reduce paging delays for critical applications. Or, some work (such as batch) could be moved off-shift,

lowering demand for storage. Or, maybe adding another page data set to the system would help.

- *The fastest paging device is processor storage*
  The price for an SSD is generally lower than for processor storage, though both are fast electronic storage. Sounds good, until you realize that the storage in the SSD is constrained by channel speed. Access times are therefore actually much slower than for processor storage. For example, the relative times to access data from 3090 central storage or expanded storage or an SSD are approximately

  `CS:1 ES:150 SSD:6000`

  The SSD is about 6000 times slower than central storage and 40 times slower than expanded storage. It is unlikely that the price differential is anywhere near the same ratios. The price of the SSD would have to be 1/40 the price of expanded storage just to break even on price/performance.

  Moreover, this simple analysis tends to underestimate SSD response time, since in environments with enough paging I/O to warrant considering an SSD there would almost certainly be some queueing for the device; the requests sitting in line for the SSD are delayed for longer times than the minimal SSD time to service a request. With sufficient processor storage, you can greatly reduce or even *eliminate* the paging that is causing delays. "No paging is faster than fast paging."

- *Any paging I/O reduces processor capacity*
  The time MVS spends managing paging I/O takes processor cycles, as does the time spent managing any type of I/O. High paging I/O rates can add significantly to processor utilization, decreasing the capacity available to an installation's applications. Recovering that capacity certainly has the value of that fraction of the processor cost. An SSD may reduce paging I/O time, but that does nothing to recover the lost processor capacity since it does not change the overhead MVS must go through to manage paging I/O requests. On the other hand, processor storage not only provides the fastest solution, but its cost is at least partially offset by the value of the recovered capacity.

- *Other advantages of processor storage*
  There is another reason why processor storage is highly desirable. The technology capability/trend is to provide optimum performance through keeping data in memory (DIM), thus eliminating many physical I/Os. To eliminate I/Os in this way requires that there be processor storage to hold the data. If a system has high paging I/O

now, that's just saying there isn't enough processor storage to even hold the current pages. What will happen when you attempt to bring MORE data into processor storage through the new techniques of large buffer pools, data spaces, and so on? The data won't fit and so will be paged out. There will be no DIM benefit, since you've exchanged a normal I/O for a paging I/O. Investment in an SSD, then, amounts to prolonging the inability to take advantage of DIM technology.

- *Inherent inefficiencies of SSDs in a paging environment*
  An SSD as such is not a device type recognized by IBM operating systems, so SSDs are designed to act like supported devices such as 3380 DASD. Operating systems know how 3380s look and how large tracks are, and the SSD must emulate that geometry. A 3380 track is 47,476 bytes in size. In MVS the size of a page is 4096 bytes. On a 3380 only 10 pages totaling 40,960 bytes fit on one track, leaving about 14 percent of the track unused (gaps and control information take up the "unused" space). This means that installing a 64MB SSD, for example, results in only about 55MB usable for pages. The number is actually even lower, since volume labels and VTOCs add additional overhead. This also means that the cost per (usable) megabyte on an SSD is higher than it may initially appear. Looked at another way, an installation might be forced to buy more SSD capacity than technically needed, just to get a sufficient amount of usable storage.

  The process of swapping reads and writes groups of related pages with a single I/O. Since swapping is dominated by nonmechanical data transfer time, and since this time tends to be similar for both disks and SSDs, the SSD may provide only minimal improvements in swapping performance.

  The price of SSDs is usually high enough so that most customers are not willing to pay for enough SSD storage to handle all paging I/O, meaning disks would still share a portion of the load. This has a few consequences.

  Some paging would occur to SSDs, some to normal DASD. This means that while the speed of the SSD may help reduce the time for some paging I/O requests, other paging I/O still occurs at mechanical speeds. There is no way to dedicate the SSD to just "important" applications. The average page I/O time goes down, but not as low as the speed of the SSD itself.

  Once a page is placed on a paging device, it stays there until read in by the operating system. As pages are written to an SSD and not referenced for a long time, the SSD becomes less effective. This phenomenon is sometimes called "pollution."

A paging configuration with an SSD may have less paths than an all-disk configuration (e.g., an installation might want to attach an SSD to two channels, replacing several page/swap data sets on multiple channels). This defeats the MVS swapping algorithm, which optimizes performance by spreading swap requests across multiple paths. Thus an SSD configuration could potentially degrade TSO performance.

• *SSDs are not strategic*
Given the advances in chip technology, a key IBM technical strategy is to exploit large processor storage. Processors and operating systems, especially MVS, are continually being enhanced to take greater advantage of large processor storage sizes. There is no support in MVS for SSDs (which is why they have to emulate a supported IBM device such as a 3380).

Given all of the above, is an SSD ever justified? The one case that may be justifiable is when an installation has a severe paging constraint on an older generation processor, will not be able to replace that machine with newer technology in time to solve the problem, and does not want to invest more dollars in the older machine. In this case, short-term acquisition of an SSD may be a solution. Even then, be sure to consider tuning solutions first.

Summary of the Above Points

SSDs are not the only solution to application delays caused by excessive paging I/O activity. Tuning is the best solution if it can be done. If tuning is not possible, processor storage offers much better performance and price/performance than any external paging device. And processor storage is a requirement to reap the benefits of DIM techniques.

(Reference: 83.)

QUESTION 88—DATA IN MEMORY—EXPLOITING PROCESSOR STORAGE

Advances in storage technology have been leading to increased processor storage sizes at decreased cost per megabyte. This offers the potential for improved performance by replacing relatively slow physical I/O with fast access to data in processor storage. The exploitation of large processor storage in this way is sometimes called "data in memory," or DIM. Give examples of how installations can exploit the presence of large central and expanded storage sizes by using facilities provided by MVS and major subsystems.

Below is a list of some of the facilities provided by MVS and major subsystems that can help installations take advantage of large processor storage (both central and expanded) to provide improved performance. Some opening comments are appropriate before we look at the list to provide some background for what's going on.

The trend in technology is toward managing more and more data in processor storage. This can provide dramatically improved performance by replacing relatively slow I/O operations by fast, simple addressing of data in processor storage.

Processor storage is currently measured in megabytes or a small number of gigabytes, yet the full external storage on a computer system is often measured in the hundreds of gigabytes, or more. Since it is not feasible to keep all data resident in processor storage, the system is designed to keep the most frequently referenced data in processor storage. This has been true since the inception of MVS (that's how a large virtual storage can be implemented on processors with smaller "real" storage). The system is evolving over time to support ever-increasing amounts of data in processor storage through advances in processor storage technology and implementation of sophisticated storage management techniques.

Keep in mind, however, that processor storage is volatile, meaning that its contents are preserved only while power is available. Data that has a requirement for permanence must be kept on a nonvolatile medium such as disk or tape. The time it takes to read such permanent data can be greatly reduced by reading a copy of the data that has been placed in processor storage; changes to such data still require an I/O operation to record the change on a nonvolatile medium. Since data is typically read more often than it is written, the potential for improved performance exists even for permanent data. Further, there are some types of data without the requirement for permanence; such data can be both read and written within processor storage. If the system fails, this temporary data is recovered naturally just by rerunning the job.

As you review the list below, notice how these considerations come into play and how many ways there are to benefit from large processor storage.

System Use for Paging/Swapping

- *Paging.* Paging delays have traditionally been a major focus of performance analysts. With large central storage sizes, paging and its associated delays can be reduced as applications' working sets (i.e., resident pages) are increased in size. With large expanded storage sizes, the paging that does occur can be handled at speeds near that of central storage at a lower cost. All workloads can benefit by reduced paging delays.
- *TSO swapping.* When the system detects that a TSO user is inactive, it attempts to keep the user's pages in central storage. If central storage is being heavily used or the user remains inactive for a relatively long time, the pages will be moved as a group to expanded storage, if available. The time to swap in (reactivate) the user is minimal when pages are in either central or expanded storage. However, if demand for processor storage is high (meaning there isn't enough processor storage to readily support the current workload) and the user remains inactive for too long, MVS will issue I/O requests to swap the user's pages to auxiliary storage. That adds to system overhead and lengthens the time it takes to bring the user's pages back to central storage when the user is ready to run.
- *Virtual I/O.* VIO is a facility that uses the paging subsystem to support temporary data sets. VIO data sets can reside in expanded storage, which can improve performance by reducing or eliminating physical I/O to VIO data sets.

Indirect Use by Applications

The following DIM techniques are implemented primarily through hardware, operating system, and subsystem facilities, without any changes required to applications—and, with one exception, without even changes to JCL. This means DIM benefits can be accrued quickly by many installations.

- *Sequential batch processing.* Through an MVS facility called *Hiperbatch*, the elapsed time for many batch jobs can often be significantly reduced. Hiperbatch allows batch jobs to access QSAM and sequentially accessed VSAM DASD data sets from a hiperspace, which is backed by expanded storage, rather than from DASD. The first time a record in one of these data sets is read by a program, MVS issues a physical I/O to retrieve it and places a copy of the record in expanded storage. It is that copy that MVS will return to other jobs reading the same data set. The installation can control which jobs and data sets are eligible to use hiperbatch.
- *Sorting.* For many installations, sorting comprises a significant amount of batch processing. The DFSORT program product offers techniques called *Hipersorting* and *dataspace sorting* that use processor storage in place of or along with DASD for temporary work space, reducing physical I/O operations and thus improving the elapsed time of sort jobs.
- *Program library access.* The MVS/ESA Library Lookaside facility (LLA) is an enhancement of the Linklist Lookaside facility introduced in MVS/XA. LLA maintains the directories of selected PDSs (libraries) in the LLA address space, and frequently referenced load modules in a data space managed by the MVS Virtual Lookaside Facility (VLF). TSO, batch, CICS/ESA, and IMS can all use LLA/VLF to maintain frequently referenced program load modules in virtual storage. When sufficient processor storage is available to avoid paging these objects, performance is improved by eliminating the I/Os that would normally be needed to search directories and to read frequently referenced programs into central storage.
- *DB2 buffer pools.* DB2 supports the specification of a large number of buffers. Large buffer pools, backed by sufficient processor storage, can reduce the number of physical I/O requests to DB2 tables. DB2 can also make good use of the buffers to speed up the numerous internal sorts that occur in a relational environment.

    Originally, DB2 buffers could only be in the DB2 address space; based on usage, these buffers are paged between central and expanded storage (or even to DASD, defeating the DIM intent) transparent to DB2. In DB2 Version 3, address space buffer pools were augmented by a function called *hiperpools*. Hiperpools are DB2 buffer pools explicitly placed in expanded storage. This allows larger buffer pool sizes than can be contained within an address space, and also provides additional efficiencies since DB2 directly controls movement of data between hiperpool buffers and address space buffers. Hiperpools are supported on ES/9000 processors that include the Asynchronous Data Mover Facility which provides efficient movement of data between central and expanded storage.

- *VSAM buffer pools.* VSAM supports large pools of buffers in an address space or in both an address space and hiperspace. By allowing VSAM to maintain frequently referenced records in virtual storage, these large buffer pools can reduce the time for random accesses to VSAM files. This requires using the Local Shared Resources (LSR) buffering option of VSAM, which is optimized for random rather than sequential processing. The CICS and IMS transaction managers support LSR, so that transaction programs accessing data bases through CICS or IMS implicitly use that buffering option. However, consider a batch job accessing VSAM files directly through a high-level language such as COBOL. Unfortunately, highlevel languages generally do not support VSAM LSR (they use VSAM Non-Shared Resources, NSR, which is optimized for sequential, not random, access). The good news is that the MVS/ESA *batch LSR* facility allows batch programs written in high-level languages to use VSAM LSR through a JCL change and so gain the performance benefits of large buffer pools for random processing.
- *CICS data tables.* CICS data tables are intended to contain frequently accessed records in the CICS address space, reducing disk read I/Os and lowering processor overhead. While similar in principle to large VSAM buffer pools, data tables offer additional savings in processor utilization and are not restricted only to VSAM records.
- *Catalog requests.* In MVS/ESA, the catalog address space (CAS) maintains catalog information in a data space. When sufficient processor storage is available to avoid paging this information, performance is improved by eliminating I/Os that would otherwise be required to read some catalog entries. This is of most benefit in batch and TSO environments.
- *TSO/E CLIST and REXX procedures.* TSO/E can maintain CLIST and REXX procedures in a data space. When sufficient processor storage is available to avoid paging these objects, TSO performance is improved by eliminating I/Os that would otherwise be required to access these objects from DASD.
- *Partitioned data set extended (PDSE).* PDSE can replace the older PDS organization for managing a data set that consists of a library of members (program load modules will be supported in the future). PDSE uses data spaces and hiperspaces to hold directories and members, offering improved performance.

Direct Use by Applications

It may sometimes be the case that an application can benefit from Data in Memory only by a change to its design. Let's discuss some of the data in memory facilities in MVS that are available for applications to use directly.

- *Data in virtual (DIV)*. Many applications have been designed to run within the pre-MVS/XA restriction of a 16 megabyte address space (actually, only about half that amount was generally available to applications). An example is engineering/scientific applications with very large arrays. These arrays are often kept on DASD, with the application managing the movement of parts of the arrays between DASD and virtual storage.

    With the large virtual storage available in MVS/ESA for applications, it may be possible to address large arrays directly by copying them in their entirety into virtual storage. It might seem that this would just trade off standard access method I/Os for paging I/Os. However, MVS will manage the hierarchy of central and expanded storage so that the most active pages will remain in central storage, and the less active pages will be maintained in expanded storage with performance near that of central storage. Only the least frequently referenced pages will be placed on DASD. Thus the array is managed efficiently by MVS based on frequency of use; real I/O is minimized.

    Direct use of virtual storage in this way may allow some programs to be recoded to simplify the addressing of large arrays. However, in many cases there are other management issues to consider. For example, should the entire array be read in, or only the portion needed today? If the array is updated, should the entire array be written back to DASD, or should the program track and write only changed information?

    To assist applications with these issues, MVS provides a facility called *Data-in-Virtual (DIV)*. DIV supports the mapping of arrays and certain other large files directly to virtual storage. A DIV file is implemented on DASD as a VSAM linear data set, which is a string of 4K blocks (the same size as pages in MVS). DIV works by allowing a program to set aside a "window" of virtual storage, and to be coded as if a portion of the linear data set was resident in that window. In fact, DIV only reads into the window the blocks that are referenced by the program (just as normal page faults are processed by MVS). If the data is updated, DIV ensures that only changed data is written back out to the linear data set, or can even throw away all changes if the program so requests.

DIV provides an easy-to-use yet powerful interface that simplifies the logic needed by programs to manage large arrays and tables. DIV can be used by assembler language programs and by high-level language programs through a facility in MVS/ESA called "data windowing services."

- *Data spaces.* MVS/ESA allows the creation of data-only spaces called data spaces. Each data space can provide up to two gigabytes of virtual storage. While an address space contains programs and data, a data space contains only data (possibly including programs stored as data). Data spaces allow programs to address vast amounts of data directly, possibly simplifying application design. If sufficient processor storage is installed, the contents of data spaces can be accessed with minimal paging delays, offering high performance.

- *Hiperspaces.* In MVS/ESA, a *high per*formance space, or hiperspace, is designed to provide high performance storage and retrieval of data. Special services in MVS are used to transfer data between an address space, where it is backed by central storage, and a hiperspace, where it is backed by expanded storage and, possibly, disk storage. The data is accessed and transferred in 4K blocks on 4K boundaries.

An MVS facility called "data windowing services" allows high-level language applications to use hiperspaces. Data windowing services support a standard CALL interface.

Architecturally, the amount of expanded storage available to back hiperspaces is 16 terabytes (trillions of bytes). Current implementations support quantities of expanded storage that can be measured in gigabytes on the largest IBM mainframe systems.

Prior to hiperspaces, expanded storage was limited to being used as a very fast paging and swapping device. With hiperspaces, the system allows data to reside in expanded storage under user control. If data can be accessed from a hiperspace, the vastly slower I/O request that would otherwise have been issued is eliminated, offering significant performance improvements.

- *Virtual Lookaside Facility (VLF).* VLF is a generalized object manager that maintains named objects in data spaces. Several MVS facilities use VLF, including Catalog Address Space (CAS), LLA, and TSO/E. VLF interfaces are documented and so are usable by user-written applications.

Here's a brief description of how VLF can be used. A program asks VLF for an object by name. If VLF has it, VLF returns the object. If not, the program is so informed and must retrieve the object itself (usually from DASD). It may then choose to give the object to VLF to maintain for future retrieval, so that the next time the object is requested VLF has it and can return it. If there is sufficient processor storage to maintain VLF objects without requiring paging I/O to access them, performance may be improved by eliminating I/O requests that would otherwise be needed to access the objects.

(References: 3, 24, 33, 75, 76, 77, 78, 79, 81, 82.)

QUESTION 89—DATA IN MEMORY—BENEFITS OF EXPLOITING PROCESSOR STORAGE

Question 88—Data in Memory—Exploiting Processor Storage identified many ways that data can be moved into processor storage, reducing time to access the data. It turns out, however, that there are additional benefits DIM provides beyond just improved performance. Identify as many benefits as you can that may accrue by moving data into processor storage.

The following list identifies benefits that can accrue by implementing "data in memory" (DIM) techniques.

1. *Faster response time.* Analysis of commercial workloads generally shows that I/O activity accounts for the largest portion of interactive response time and batch job run time. Therefore, reducing the number of relatively slow physical I/O accesses by replacing them with relatively fast accesses to data in processor storage can significantly reduce this time. This means increased productivity and satisfaction for online users, and reduced batch job time.

   Further, removing some portion of I/O activity may benefit the performance of the remaining activity, since contention for resources is reduced. This can indirectly improve the performance of all work on the system.

   In the case of batch jobs, DIM can help reduce elapsed run time, leading to a reduction in the overall batch window and allowing more time for online systems to remain active.

2. *Lower processor utilization.* When an application requests data that is located on an external device (e.g., tape or DASD), MVS must execute a large number of instructions to satisfy the request. Some of this is in the access method (e.g., VSAM) that receives the request and must build channel programs to access the data, some is in the MVS supervisor that manages the execution of the channel program, and some is in the MVS dispatcher that must schedule new work while the requesting job waits for the I/O to complete. If an application accesses data directly in processor storage without all of this overhead, or an access method can retrieve data in buffers without requesting MVS to manage a physical I/O request, then the number of instructions executed may fall significantly. This means lower processor utilization. This in turn means more work can run on the same processor after DIM techniques are implemented. Processor capacity is effectively increased, so the processor has a longer life on the data center floor.

Some simple arithmetic shows the principle involved. Assume a transaction takes .1 second of processor time and that 8 such transactions execute every second. Then processor utilization is 80 percent. Assume that implementing DIM techniques reduces processor time per transaction to .09 seconds. Then the processor utilization would drop to 72 percent. The interesting thing is that the increase in processor capacity is achieved through adding processor storage, not through upgrading the processor to a faster model.

While DIM techniques such as CICS data tables, and VSAM and DB2 buffer pools have been shown to reduce processor utilization, replacing physical I/O requests with accesses to processor storage might not reduce processor utilization in all cases. Some techniques used to manage data in memory may consume enough processor time to offset the savings of eliminating the instructions that supported the I/O process. But note that the benefits of improved response time are still accrued—the primary strategy of DIM is to replace slow I/O times by fast memory accesses. Any reduction in processor utilization that also occurs can be viewed simply as a bonus.

3. *Ability to run online subsystems at higher processor utilization.* Many installations have established a maximum processor utilization under 100 percent for their online systems. Either through detailed analysis or just based on past experience, they have found that, beyond some "bar," transactions spend so much time waiting for the processor that response time becomes unacceptable.

As discussed above, response time decreases when I/Os are eliminated through implementing DIM techniques. This means that after response time is improved, it is possible to let the time spent waiting for the processor resource to elongate. As the workload grows, response time will still be less until at some point waiting for the processor increases response time to an unacceptable value.

The principle is illustrated in Figure 11.2. A transaction consists of PROCessor time and I/O time. Processor time itself consists of time executing instructions, shown as a string of "e"s, and time waiting to get control of the processor, shown as a string of "w"s.

So, if an installation now has a guideline that says online systems must run at no higher than 80 percent utilization in order for response time to be acceptable, DIM may allow this bar to be relaxed, so that 90 percent, say, becomes the new bar. While not discussed here, a simple queueing theory formula could be used to estimate how much processor utilization could be increased while

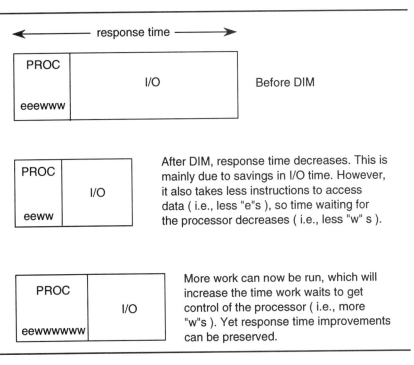

Figure 11.2.   DIM techniques can increase processor capacity.

still maintaining equal or better response time compared to response time before DIM techniques were implemented.

Sometimes the remaining processor capacity beyond the "bar" is filled with batch jobs. However, it's usually online growth and service, not batch, that drives processor decisions. So, if an installation sees that the bar COULD be raised and performance maintained or improved, it might choose to reschedule some batch work to another shift in order to postpone a processor upgrade.

Just as lower processor utilization due to DIM effectively increases processor capacity, raising the utilization bar has a similar benefit. Drawing from the example above, assume the utilization bar is 80 percent, and transactions each take .1 second of processor time before DIM techniques are implemented. Thus 8 transactions can run in 1 second before the installation considers capacity exhausted. If DIM techniques lower processor time per transaction by 10 percent to .09 seconds, then .8 / .09 = 8.9 transactions can run at the 80 percent bar. If the bar can be raised to 90 percent, because slow I/Os were replaced by fast accesses to data in memory, then .9 / .09 = 10 transactions can be run in 1 second.

4. *Less physical I/O.* An immediate effect of DIM techniques is to lower the amount of physical I/O activity. This in turn can provide several benefits:

- Reduced need for channels and controllers.
- Reduced need for DASD volumes only to spread the workload.
- Increased exploitation of large capacity DASD.
- Reduced tuning effort.

The main reason DIM may decrease the need for I/O resources is that I/O resources provide both capacity and performance, and often installations find they need to add superfluous capacity in order to obtain acceptable performance. For example, a 3390-2 volume has a capacity of 1.89 gigabytes. However, it may be the case that an installation intentionally does not use all this capacity so that the I/O load can be spread across multiple volumes, allowing more concurrent accesses and thus improving performance. If DIM lowers the I/O load, then the capacity that was given up may again be usable. The same principle applies to channels and control units.

Finally, since I/O is relatively slow, it has traditionally been a major focus of performance tuning. If the I/O activity on a system is lowered through DIM techniques and performance is thereby improved, the need for tuning the I/O subsystem to meet performance objectives may lessen. This is even more true when you consider that removing some I/O activity reduces contention, thus improving the performance of the remaining activity.

(Reference: 82.)

QUESTION 90—VIRTUAL STORAGE TUNING

When the requirement for virtual storage exceeds the amount available, we say that there is a virtual storage constraint. This situation is more serious than it may sound since it can prevent work from running altogether, unlike shortages of other resources that may just slow things down.

MVS/370 provided a 16-megabyte virtual storage address space per job. However, MVS/370 often allocated half or more of that to system areas so that less than an 8-megabyte space was actually available to most jobs. While MVS/ESA provides an address space of 2 gigabytes, there are still many IBM programs, and many user programs, that must continue to run below the so-called 16-megabyte line because of their sensitivity to 24-bit addresses. If an installation is projecting a virtual storage constraint below the 16-megabyte line and asks where they should initially focus for virtual storage tuning, what would you recommend?

Tuning virtual storage in the Pageable Link Pack Area (PLPA) is likely to buy back the most space with the least effort. One reason is because the PLPA is usually the single largest system area, thus offering the best chance for a significant payback.

PLPA is a part of common storage, meaning it is part of every address space. PLPA contains system programs that are part of MVS but that are pageable, unlike system programs in the nucleus. Installations may also place frequently used programs such as TSO commands into PLPA in order to improve performance by avoiding I/O to load the programs, and in order to reduce paging by having one shared copy of a program in processor storage rather than a copy in the private area of each job using the program.

Tuning the PLPA to reduce its use of virtual storage can include the following:

* *Reviewing the PAKLST specification.* The original intent of the IEAPAKnn SYS1.PARMLIB member was to allow an installation

to control the placement of programs in PLPA so as to minimize paging by placing related programs on the same set of pages. However, a poorly maintained PAKLST can result in inefficient use of virtual storage. It has been found that in most cases IEAPAKnn can be eliminated with no measurable impact on performance and as much as a 500K savings in virtual storage.

- *Deleting obsolete modules.* Sometimes installations have kept unneeded programs in SYS1.LPALIB over the years due to inefficient procedures or failure to run cleanup programs as new products were installed. Reference 67 discusses how to identify such obsolete programs.

- *Relocating programs not required in PLPA.* Sometimes the decision to place a program in PLPA was made a long time ago, and program use has changed over time. Or, given a virtual storage shortage, trading off some performance in order to stay in business might seem like a good idea. It may be possible to buy back some virtual storage by removing some programs from PLPA and placing them in the LNKLST libraries. This is especially reasonable if concurrent use is rare; the additional I/Os to load the program are offset by the page-ins that probably occur when the program is in PLPA. If sufficient processor storage is available, maintaining multiple copies of programs may not noticeably degrade performance.

In MVS/ESA, the Library Lookaside (LLA) facility can maintain frequently referenced program load modules in a data space managed by the Virtual Lookaside Facility (VLF). This can eliminate I/O to fetch these programs if sufficient processor storage is available, as well as reduce the virtual storage requirement for PLPA. Be aware that, when needed, modules are copied from the VLF data space to the requestor's private address space, which can increase processor storage requirements compared to having a single copy of a shared program in PLPA.

While PLPA is usually the most fruitful area of virtual storage to attack, tuning other areas may also prove beneficial. The Resource Measurement Facility (RMF) program produces reports describing private area and common area virtual storage usage.

(References: 67, 94.)

12

Hardware Configurations

The traditional data center goes back to the days when data processing equipment was covered with blinking lights (that few people understood) and was an organization's pride and joy that was shown to every visitor. Even today, many data centers can still be found enclosed in rooms of glass. The selection and management of data processing hardware continues to be a major focus of any I/S organization.

Large system hardware configurations basically consist of Central Processor Complexes, DASD, tape, and other auxiliary equipment. The process of configuring these machines is the process of selecting machine models, the number of machines, and any associated features that meet the needs of a particular installation.

QUESTION 91—CHOOSING BETWEEN ONE PROCESSOR COMPLEX OR TWO

An installation that has always been a single-processor shop is now weighing the alternatives of upgrading the existing system or installing a second, additional system. What general considerations should be addressed in making the decision? Put your answer in the form of two lists: possible benefits and possible drawbacks of adding a second processor complex.

Below is a list of items that should be considered when deciding whether to upgrade an existing central processor complex (CPC) or to install a second CPC. Additional issues not listed may apply in specific situations. No relative importance is assigned to the items identified—every installation will have its own set of priorities.

Possible Benefits of Adding a Second CPC

1. The ability to provide more processing power than can be provided by a single system.
2. The ability of each CPC to act as a backup for the other. This is a very common justification for installing a second machine. For example, if one CPC becomes unavailable, critical work could be moved to the other CPC. In particular, the Extended Recovery Facility (XRF) of MVS that is used by IMS/TM and CICS can exploit this configuration by dynamically switching networks between two CPCs for recovery purposes.
3. The ability to separate workloads that might require superior service but that would compete on a single system in such a way that satisfactory performance may not be obtainable.
4. The ability to run separate "test" and "production" machines. For example, new releases of the operating system, new or changed user programs, and maintenance could be first installed on the test system. Only after the changes are considered stable would they be placed on the production system. This could increase availability for users on the production system.
5. The ability to add a more granular increment of processing power to an installation. For example, if an installation is operating an ES/9000-821 (2-way) class machine, the next upgrade is to a three-way model, an increase in processing power of almost 50 percent. If only 10 percent more capacity is needed over some period of time, then acquiring a second, less powerful system may seem an attractive alternative.
6. The ability to increase available virtual storage by splitting workloads across two systems. If there is a virtual storage constraint on the current system, or one is projected in the future, moving some of the work to a second system may buy back some virtual storage. For example, common area storage usage could be lowered by isolating appropriate applications. This is an expensive solution if it is intended only to solve this one problem, and other solutions should also be considered.
7. The ability to isolate workloads that require a very high degree of

security. Given the sophistication of current security hardware and software technology, workload isolation in this way for security reasons is not warranted in most installations.

Possible Drawbacks of Adding a Second CPC:

1. The additional cost of a second system might be significantly greater than the cost of upgrading the capacity of the existing system, especially considering

   Additional technical support personnel (e.g., systems programmers, operators)

   Additional software licenses (this doesn't apply in the case of two images on the same physically or logically partitioned CPC)

   Additional hardware for operating system needs (e.g., consoles, DASD for SYSRES and paging, etc.)

   Additional floor space, power, and cooling requirements

   Additional switching capability to allow sharing of devices between systems. In systems supporting ESCON architecture, such switching can often be handled through an ESCON director. In non-ESCON systems, shareable devices such as disks can be configured with additional channel adapters, and nonshareable devices such as printers may be attached to a standalone switch such as an IBM 3814.

   More total processing power may be required than for a single system. This is because each system must supply sufficient capacity for its workload, but each may reach its peak utilization at a different time. A single system only needs to support the highest utilization of the combined workload.

2. There's more to running a multiple CPC installation than just putting in the physical connections to support shared devices. The management of shared devices can add operating complexity above that required in a single-image environment. For example, the use of shared DASD requires consideration of data integrity issues that can't arise in a single-image complex; Global Resource Serialization, JES3, or non-IBM programs are often used to provide this integrity and may require supporting hardware such as channel-to-channel adapters.[47]

---

[47]See Question 16—Cross-System Data Set Sharing.

Similarly, because tape drives are inherently unshareable (that is, unlike disk volumes, only one system can be allocated to any one tape drive at any time), JES3 or non-IBM programs that manage tape drive allocation across multiple systems are common in large installations.

3. Workload management. A decision must be made about how the current workload can best be broken up into two separate workloads to run on the two systems. For example, should the TSO workload be split? On which systems should batch jobs be run?

Note that some of these benefits and drawbacks also apply to the more general question of one *system image* or two for which there are more solutions than just separate CPCs. That takes us to our next question.

(Reference: 108.)

QUESTION 92—COMPARING MULTI-IMAGE IMPLEMENTATIONS

A large corporation is acquiring a smaller company. To reduce costs, the two data centers will be consolidated by moving the data processing work from the acquired company into the corporation's existing MVS-based data center. However, the operating system in use by the smaller company is VSE. Plans include eventual conversion to MVS, but even then the corporation wants to keep the workloads separated for management purposes. What alternatives are available to support the concurrent operation of these two systems in one data center?

There are several alternative strategies to support two separate operating systems (two system images) in the same data center.

As you review the strategies, you may find it helpful to compare them from the following points of view:

- Availability. Are there single points of failure that could bring down all images at once? Is that an important consideration?
- Hardware resource sharing, that is, sharing of central processors, processor storage, channels, control units, and devices. At one extreme, you can configure a solution so that no resources are shared, as if the two images have a wall between them. Unshared resources may offer availability and perhaps security benefits. At the other

extreme, it is generally possible to share almost all resources by multiple images. Shared resources may allow greater efficiencies than unshared resources, such as a lower requirement for the total amount of resource. Each strategy discussed below offers differing degrees of resource sharing; the amount of sharing possible can even vary within a given strategy.

- Ease of operations. The technical skills required to support multiple images vary across the different strategies.
- Performance. Strategies that allow an operating system to run in "native" mode may seem, at least at first glance, to offer better performance than strategies that try to manage resource sharing between images, because such management adds processor overhead at a minimum. Current technology has minimized that overhead, often to well under 10 percent, so that in practice this tends not to be the deciding factor. In fact, efficient resource sharing may more than make up for this. For example, the ability in some strategies to share central processors across images may result in improved response times compared to strategies where central processors are dedicated to images.

Let's look at the strategies that support multiple images.

1. *Multiple processors.* One simple solution is to run each operating system natively on a physically independent central processor complex (CPC). This maintains the maximum independence of the two systems.

   An advantage of this solution is that no single failure within a CPC can bring down both images. Also, it would be possible to upgrade or replace each processor independently of the other.

   A disadvantage is that sharing of processor resources (e.g., channels, processor storage, engines) is not possible between images. Some I/O devices such as DASD can be shared. This issue is addressed more fully in the discussion below on physical partitioning.

   Another potential disadvantage is the possibility of higher software licensing costs, given that there are multiple processor serial numbers.

2. *Physical partitioning.* Physical partitioning is the capability of certain processor models to be partitioned into two processors ("sides"), each capable of running its own operating system. This partitioning is controlled through the system console. IBM calls machines with this capability "multiprocessors." The assignment of processor resources to each partition is fixed in that the assignment is deter-

mined by the physical resources "hard-wired" into each side of the machine. In some multiprocessor models, each resource must be installed in a symmetrical fashion—e.g., the same amount of central storage and the same number of channels must be configured on each side. Some processor models offer a degree of asymmetry.

An advantage of physical partitioning (just as for the two processor strategy) is isolation of each partition from both logical (software) and physical (hardware) failures in the other partition. Physical partitioning may offer software license cost savings since the two sides of a multiprocessor share a single serial number.

The main disadvantage of physical partitioning is the fixed resource assignment in each partition. This assignment may not necessarily match workload requirements. For example, assume that configuration options only support central storage increments of 64 megabytes on a side. Further assume that one partition runs a workload needing 80 megabytes while the other partition needs 48 megabytes. Then there is no way to configure the total 128 megabyte requirement as 64 megabytes installed on each side and allocate this storage to meet the individual workload requirements. To solve this problem it would be necessary to configure 64 megabytes on one side and 128 megabytes on the other side (or 128 megabytes on each side if asymmetry is not allowed), which is more total storage than is strictly necessary to meet workload requirements. Similarly, central processors cannot be shared across physical partitions; an idle engine in one partition cannot be used to run work in the other partition.

There are other considerations. Only some processor models support physical partitioning. Also, the backup capabilities in some processor controllers such as the IBM 3092 are not available when a machine is physically partitioned. You must also keep in mind that the two sides are truly independent—sharing of I/O resources such as DASD requires the same support that would be necessary if the two operating systems were running on physically separated machines. Lastly, given our original question, it must be noted that VSE is not supported natively on all processor models that support MVS; in some cases, PR/SM LPAR mode or VM, discussed below, would be required to support the VSE image within a physical partition.

3. *Software partitioning.* The VM operating system has been the traditional means to run multiple guest operating systems on one physical machine. Advantages of VM in this context include the ability to support a large number of guest operating systems, the ability to use "minidisks" to simulate a large DASD environment

and the ability to share processor resources such as central processor cycles, channels, and storage among the guests. DASD sharing is facilitated through virtual channel-to-channel adapters. If VM is also required for other reasons, such as for support of VM-based applications, then this solution may work well.

A disadvantage of a VM solution is the additional technical support requirement, such as systems programmer skills.

In a VM environment it is possible for a single failure in the processor or in VM itself to bring down all guests.

4. *Logical partitioning.* PR/SM (Processor Resource/Systems Manager) is a feature available on some S/370 IBM processors, and standard on all S/390 IBM processors. One function of PR/SM enables the processor to run in *LPAR* (logical partition) mode. In LPAR mode the installation can define and allocate computer resources to multiple logical partitions within a single processor; each partition supports a single operating system image. The maximum number of partitions varies with processor model. For example, certain IBM processors support up to 10 partitions, or even up to 20 in a physically-partitioned system.

Sharing of processor resources in logical partitioning is not as flexible as in software partitioning. In PR/SM logical partitioning, central processors can always be dynamically shared across partitions, and ESCON channels can be dynamically shared across partitions on selected ES/9000 processors. Parallel channels, ESCON channels on some processors, and processor storage must be pre-assigned to partitions (though processor storage can be reconfigured later by operators or by MVS in response to certain events).

Physical partitioning is more restrictive than logical partitioning. This is because logical partitioning does not require resources to be allocated according to the way they are physically configured on each side of the machine. For example, referring to the earlier discussion on physical partitioning, assume a physically partitionable processor is configured with 128 megabytes of central storage, 64 megabytes on each side. In LPAR mode one logical partition could be assigned 80 megabytes of central storage while the other is assigned 48 megabytes.[48]

Central processors may be shared across all logical partitions.

---

[48]This is a slight simplification since LPAR mode itself takes away a few megabytes of central storage for management purposes.

Work in logical partitions is dispatched using an event-driven scheduler. This is more efficient than the time-slicing schemes that are sometimes used to provide facilities similar to LPAR on non-IBM processors.

The issues relating to resource sharing come into play under logical partitioning just as with physical partitioning. For example, shared DASD requires special considerations for integrity control. As in a VM system, a single hardware failure may terminate all logical partitions.

Making a Choice

There may not be a "right" answer, but usually there is a "best" answer for a given situation.

Separate CPCs is the most restrictive solution as far as sharing resources, but it certainly offers maximum isolation.

Physical partitioning is also restrictive but may offer savings in software license costs. Given our problem statement, and the availability of physical partitioning generally only on processors that do not support VSE natively, physical partitioning is only an option after the VSE system is converted to MVS or if the installation is willing to run VSE under VM or under PR/SM LPAR mode.

Today's processors are highly reliable. However, if there is an availability requirement that at least one processor always be running (perhaps as in an online Extended Recovery Facility (XRF) environment), then physically separated machines or physically partitioned machines may be appropriate. Even in that case, keep in mind that the machines could still support logical or software partitioning within physical partitions.

VM is the most flexible solution in terms of resource sharing but adds operational complexity. While generally an excellent solution to the problem in the past, given LPAR mode, VM is probably now most appropriate when the installation requires software that only runs in the VM environment or requires more guests than LPAR can support. Additionally, for some CMS workloads, VM may sustain higher throughput rates on a given machine than MVS can for similar workloads, allowing for other cost savings.

Logical partitioning is more flexible than physical partitioning, though not as flexible as VM; for example, unlike LPAR mode, VM can dynamically allocate processor storage to each guest based on demand. But LPAR mode is much less complex to operate than VM, which may be an important consideration to many installations. Overall, logical partitioning may be the most practical solution to the problem of supporting the dual MVS-VSE configuration given in the original question.

(References: 42, 108.)

QUESTION 93—BENEFITS OF ESCON ARCHITECTURE

Channels are the facilities, generally inside processor frames, that provide for communication with external devices. In 1990, IBM announced System/390, including Enterprise System Connection (ESCON) Architecture, a new channel architecture that replaced the S/360 and S/370 channel architectures in use since the 1960s. A data center needs to replace an older S/370 processor and is deciding if it should invest in a processor that supports ESCON channels. What are some of the major benefits of ESCON channel architecture, and how do these compare to the limitations of the prior IBM channel architectures?

The following list identifies some of the major benefits of ESCON channel architecture, and discusses limitations of the older channel architectures replaced by ESCON.

* *Reduced cable bulk weight*
  Most large data centers are constructed on artificially raised floors constructed about 12 to 24 inches above the actual floor. In the space between the actual floor and the raised floor often lies an incredible mass of bulky cables that connect devices to processors with parallel channels.[49]

  The mass of cables is often best described as spaghetti. The cables are often so hard to move about that rather than move or remove cables when equipment is moved or removed, some data centers just lay new cables on top of old ones; over the years this has sometimes created a need for a raised floor to be raised even further.

---

[49]Actually, channels are not always connected directly to devices. In the case of DASD such as 3990/3390, for example, channels are connected to a control unit and that control unit is connected via another set of cables to the disk drives that may be located some distance from the control unit. However, for convenience we will talk as if the channels were directly attached to devices. The term "control unit" will be used occasionally for clarity.

Parallel channels attach to I/O devices through pairs of cables called "bus and tag" cables, or sometimes "copper" cables because the cables contain copper wires that conduct electrical signals. Basically, the bus cable carries data and the tag cable carries signals identifying the type of data (for example, the bus might indicate that the data on the tag cable is the address of an I/O device, or that the data is a record). Parallel cables are relatively bulky and heavy, weighing about 1488 grams per meter (one pound per foot) for a bus and tag pair, with each cable almost an inch in diameter.

Cabling technology is greatly improved by ESCON architecture through its support for fiber optic cables. A device is attached to a channel through a single fiber optic cable that uses pulses of light waves rather than electricity to transmit data. Fiber optic cables are much thinner and lighter in weight than copper cables. A fiber cable weighs only about 20 grams per meter (.013 pounds per foot) and has a diameter of 4.8 millimeters (.019 inches).

One cable contains two thin glass filaments, each comparable in diameter to a human hair. Each filament is used to transmit data in one direction only. The information that was formerly sent separately down bus and tag cables is now sent down a single fiber in a format that distinguishes data from control information.

- *Increased speed*

In parallel channel technology, the multiple bits that make up a single character or byte are sent down the cable concurrently via individual copper wires. While this parallelism was designed to improve performance, it eventually turned into a limitation as technology improvements supported higher channel speeds over the years. The bits would all begin their journeys at the same time, but due to the varying electrical properties of each wire, they generally didn't arrive at their destination at the same time, a phenomenon called *skew*. Skew tends to increase as speed and distance increase. Channels and devices were designed to tolerate some amount of skew, but that tolerance was limited. Therefore, to contain skew on parallel channels, channel speeds were limited to 4.5 megabytes per second, and the maximum distance between a channel and control unit was limited to about 400 feet.

ESCON technology transmits data serially, that is, one bit at a time, down a single fiber. While in data processing serial processes are generally slower than parallel processes, that isn't true here. The elimination of skew allowed the data rate of ESCON channels to be up to 10 megabytes per second the day ESCON was announced, and increased to 17 megabytes per second a year later.[50]

ESCON channel speed is either 10 or 17 megabytes per second, depending on the processor model. While these speeds are significantly greater than the 4.5-megabyte-per-second maximum speed of parallel channels, that doesn't mean that I/O response time is reduced proportionally. For one, the time to transmit data over a channel is only one component of I/O response time; DASD response time, for example, also includes mechanical motion to position disks for reading or writing. Further, ESCON uses new communication protocols appropriate to a fiber optics environment, and these protocols reduce the performance gain somewhat. As announced, ESCON generally was expected to provide performance comparable to parallel channels (while providing many other benefits). In the case of selected models of the 3490 Tape Subsystem, however, performance on ESCON channels is significantly better than on parallel channels, a trend that will likely continue as channel technology evolves over time and devices evolve to take advantage of the higher channel speeds.

• *Increased distance*
Just as eliminating skew allowed the data rate to increase, it also allowed the maximum distance between a channel and attached devices to increase. As mentioned above, the maximum distance between a channel and device connected by copper cabling is 400 feet—less for some devices. This limited data centers, in effect, to 400-foot spheres.

There are two types of ESCON channels, each of which supports increased distances: standard ESCON channels and Extended Distance Feature (XDF) ESCON channels.

Let's discuss standard ESCON channels first; we'll refer to these simply as ESCON channels, and explicitly refer to XDF channels when necessary. ESCON channels are the channels appropriate for most data center and campus environments. ESCON XDF channels are appropriate mainly when distances greater than those supported by standard ESCON channels are required, or if

---

[50]It is important to note that both ESCON channels and parallel channels only provide a capacity—a maximum supported speed. The effective speed of any given transmission is determined by the device as well as by protocols ("handshaking") that manage the transmission.

the fiber cable being used must conform to XDF standards (XDF uses a smaller fiber than standard ESCON).

In ESCON channels the fiber media is driven by LED (light emitting diode) technology. Devices connected to ESCON channels can be up to 9 kilometers (5.6 miles) from the processor. This distance is achieved in the following manner. If the device is cabled directly to the channel via an ESCON fiber optic cable, the maximum distance is 3 kilometers. A special ESCON device called an *ESCON Director* (ESCD) can be used to redrive the signal for up to another 3 kilometers. And this can be done twice, so that the maximum distance of 9 kilometers is achieved by connecting the channel to an ESCON Director, connecting that Director to a second Director, and finally connecting that second Director to the device. See Figure 12.1.

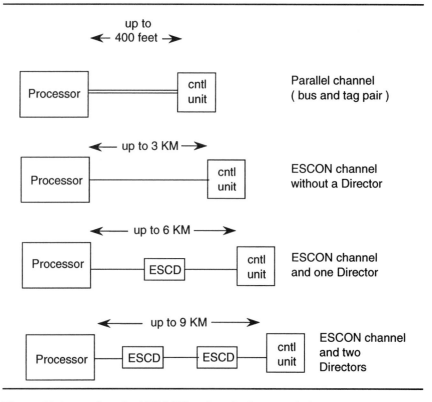

Figure 12.1.   Standard ESCON options for increased channel-to-control unit distances.

This flexibility provides new options for configuring data centers. Devices that in the past were configured to be relatively near to the attached processor can now be placed in other rooms, on other floors, or even in other buildings. This can reduce the need for growing data centers to move to new locations or undergo reconstruction. Devices that might otherwise require attachment via networking facilities (such as terminal cluster controllers) can now be channel attached, offering potential performance improvements.

Let's move from the discussion of standard ESCON channel distances to the benefits of XDF (extended distance feature) ESCON channels.

In contrast to standard ESCON channels that are driven by LED technology, XDF channels are driven by lasers, allowing for increased distances. XDF channels can also reduce the number of ESCON directors required to reach a given distance since a director is only needed to redrive the laser signal after a distance of 20KM, versus 3KM for LED-driven channels. As stated above, standard ESCON channels are the appropriate choice for most environments. XDF is available if needed but comes at a higher price than standard ESCON channels.

With ESCON XDF channels, the maximum channel-to-control unit distances vary by device type. For example, 3990-3 DASD control units can be located up to 15KM from the channel; the 3990-6 controller extends this distance to 20KM. 3490 tape subsystems may be up to 23KM from the processor, and cluster controllers such as the 3174 can be up to 43KM from the processor. Processors connected by XDF ESCON channel-to-channel communications can be up to 60KM apart.

There is some logic to some of these numbers. Unlike standard ESCON, XDF channels *require* the use of one or two directors (except for direct channel-to-channel communications within 20KM). This is because IBM control units that support ESCON only attach to LED-driven fiber. The director closest to the control unit will have a laser-driven fiber coming in, but an LED-driven fiber going out to the control unit. So, for example, an XDF fiber can go out of the processor channel for up to 20KM and then be plugged into a director. An LED-driven fiber will exit the director and attach to the control unit, which can be up to 3KM from the director. See Figure 12.2.

- *Reduced number of channels*
  ESCON can help reduce the number of channels needed on a processor in two ways: enhanced multidropping and sharing of channels by PR/SM logical partitions.

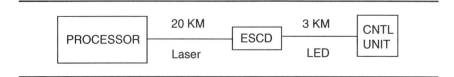

Figure 12.2. An example of an ESCON XDF configuration.

Let's first look at multidropping. Multidropping is the ability of multiple control units to share a single channel. In parallel channel architecture, the maximum number of control units that could be placed on a single channel was eight. Cables would go from a channel into the first control unit, then another set of cables would go out from that control unit and into the next control unit, and so on; this is sometimes called daisy chaining. The limit of eight was generally more than sufficient for DASD and tape control units, since they can generate such heavy activity that it was usually impractical to put more than one or two such units on the same channel. However, some devices, such as communication controllers, often only use a small fraction of a channel's capacity, so that more than eight such devices could theoretically share one channel. The limit of eight meant that additional channels were required in some installations for connectivity reasons rather than for performance reasons.

An ESCON cable by itself can connect a single channel to a single control unit; unlike parallel channel architecture, another cable cannot attach that control unit to a second control unit on the same channel. This is called a point-to-point design. However, an ESCON Director can be used to allow multiple control units to share a single channel, even increasing connectivity beyond the limits imposed by parallel channels. Instead of being directly cabled to each other, cables from multiple channels and cables from multiple control units can be connected to ports in an ESCON Director. These channels and control units communicate through a switching facility within the Director, providing multidropping through a switched-point-to-point design. Figure 12.3 shows an example of two control units sharing a single ESCON channel through using an ESCON Director.

The installation defines the switching that is allowed (that is, which channels can talk to which control units), and that switching is managed by ESCON protocols. In the extreme case, a single channel could be connected to one Director port and control units

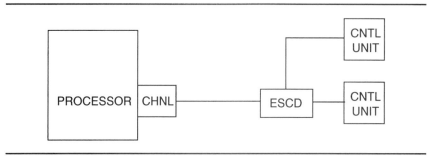

Figure 12.3.   Control units share an ESCON channel via an ESCON Director.

connected to all other Director ports; the ESCON Director model 9032 has 60 ports that could be configured to allow one channel to attach to 59 control units. A more likely configuration in practice is multiple channels connecting to a Director with each channel supporting a subset of the control units connected to the same Director.

So far, we've seen how an ESCON Director can be used to reduce the numbers of processor channels through enhanced multi-dropping. Another powerful technique for reducing the number of processor channels applies to PR/SM LPAR environments and is called EMIF: ESCON Multiple Image Facility. EMIF is available on selected ES/9000 processor models.

Prior to EMIF, every PR/SM logical partition had its own dedicated channels. Control units could be shared among LPAR images only in the same way that they could be shared among physically separate systems: by configuring dedicated channels. EMIF allows channels to be shared among the LPARs within a given processor, thus eliminating the need for dedicated channels. For example, consider a 3990 Storage Control being shared by three LPARS in a processor. Prior to EMIF, providing 4-path connectivity to the 3990 from each of the three LPARs would require 12 channels. With EMIF, however, 4 channels are sufficient to provide 4-path connectivity to each LPAR. There are physically only 4 paths—4 channel-to-control unit connections, but each LPAR "believes" that it has its own set of 4 paths. In other words, there are 12 "logical" paths sharing four physical paths. In this example, 8 channels are saved. Figure 12.4 illustrates this example.

Note that the benefits of EMIF apply to a given system in PR/SM

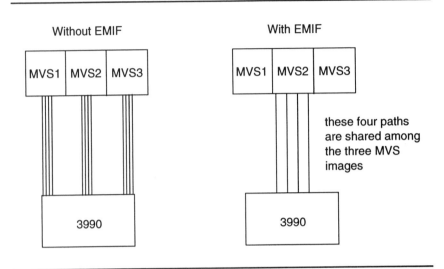

Figure 12.4. EMIF can reduce the channels needed in an LPAR environment.

LPAR mode, and require native ESCON connections.[51] Two MVS images on two separate processors would not benefit from EMIF. However, if either or both of the separate processors was in LPAR mode and running multiple copies of MVS, EMIF would apply to the channels on that processor.

- *Reduced number of channel adapters*

Some control units, such as an IBM 3990 Storage Control for DASD, support the ability to be attached to multiple channels. The attachment ports are called channel adapters. The reasons for attaching a single control unit to multiple channels include performance (to support concurrent data transfers) and connectivity (to allow multiple processors or system images to share the control unit). As can be seen in Figure 12.4, in reducing the number of channels required, EMIF also reduces the number of control unit channel adapters required.

Another technique to reduce channel adapter requirements is available for processors that support ESCON but not EMIF, and in

---

[51]A "native" ESCON connection has no ESCON converters. ESCON converters were designed to help installations migrate from parallel to ESCON environments. For example, one type of converter allows ESCON channels to be connected to control unit channel adapter ports that accept parallel channel cables.

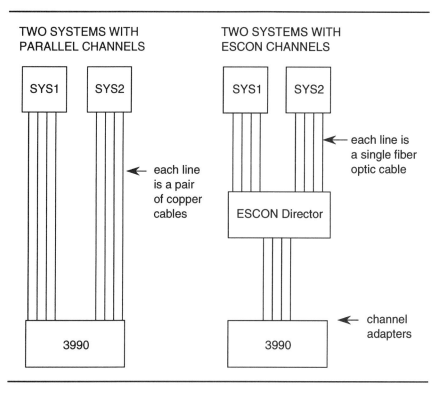

Figure 12.5. The ESCON Director can reduce cabling and channel adapters.

environments with separate physical processors. An ESCON Director can be used to connect a number of channels to a fewer number of control unit channel adapters. This means that adding channel adapters to control units just for connectivity reasons is not required if the ESCON Director is used to provide that function. For example, in a parallel channel environment, sharing a 3990 Storage Control among two physically separate system images in four-path mode (for maximum performance) would require four channels from each image to be cabled into eight channel adapters on the control unit. The 3990, however, can only use four channels at a time—the additional four channel adapters are for connectivity purposes only.

Let's look at how this configuration could differ in an ESCON environment. Four ESCON channels are still required from each of the two system images. These eight channels can be shared by just four channel adapters on the control unit by using an ESCON Director. Eight cables come into the Director from the two images, and four cables come into the Director from the control unit. Routing is managed through ESCON protocols. This is shown in Figure 12.5.

*   *Improved reliability / availability / serviceability*
    Parallel channels use electricity to transmit data. When a control unit is to be connected to (or disconnected from) a parallel channel via a copper cable, the customer engineer will generally require that the control unit and channel be powered off to avoid unexpected electrical discharge. In the case where multiple control units share the same parallel channels in what is called a daisy chain arrangement, all devices in the chain could be temporarily unavailable.

    ESCON channels use fiber optic cables. Using light rather than electricity, ESCON cables can be plugged into channels and control units at any time—there is no requirement to power down equipment. Further, the switched-point-to-point ESCON design means that unplugging one control unit cannot affect the ability to access other control units.

    ESCON architecture calls for light signals to be constantly transmitted down ESCON cables. If a cable is not plugged correctly or is unplugged, the loss of light is immediately detected and the operator is informed. In contrast, a similar problem with a copper cable can go undetected until an attempt is made to communicate using the cable.

(Reference: 55.)

QUESTION 94—3814 SWITCHING MANAGEMENT SYSTEM

ESCON channel technology is replacing parallel channel technology. In an ESCON environment, the ESCON Director provides the capability to switch control units among channels to enhance application availability, especially in installations with multiple processors. Installations that have not yet converted to ESCON channels often use IBM 3814 switches or similar devices to provide the switching function. Describe the basic function of a 3814 Switching Management System. What happens if power is unavailable to a 3814?

Control units are sometimes standalone boxes (e.g., a 3990 Storage Control for DASD) and are sometimes integrated into the same box as the supported device (e.g., 4245 printer). In any case, one function of a control unit is to provide the attachment interface between a device and a channel (cable). Some control units, such as those for DASD and tape, can be connected to multiple channels at the same time. Other devices, such as printers, can often be connected to only a single channel; in that case, if the channel fails or the system owning the channel fails, access to the device is lost.

This is where the 3814 comes in. A 3814 can be used to switch devices manually between channels on the same system or on different systems, in effect improving device availability. The 3814 makes it appear that the control unit attaches to multiple channels, though only one at a time.

Refer to Figure 12.6. Channel A and channel B are connected to a 3814. A single printer is also attached to the 3814. If the printer is initially switched to channel A, and System 1 fails, then an operator can issue a command to the 3814 to cause it to switch the printer to channel B on System 2. Thus the printer need not sit idle.

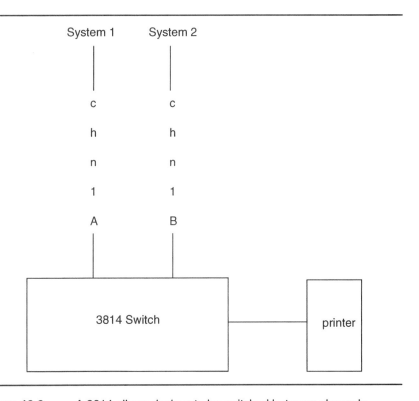

Figure 12.6.   A 3814 allows devices to be switched between channels.

The notation n x m means that n channel interfaces can be switched among m control unit interfaces. A common 3814 configuration is 4 x 8; other sizes are also available.

What happens if a 3814 fails by dropping power? In that case, all the connections through the 3814 fail since the 3814 uses power to redrive incoming and outgoing signals (the same is true of the ESCON Director as well). It is possible to configure additional 3814 units that back each other up dynamically to avoid this exposure.

Note that the ESCON Director and the ESCON Multiple Image Facility (EMIF) provide the switching capability in an ESCON environment. The ESCON Director in particular provides other functions as well, such as supporting increased distances between channels and control units, making it the logical replacement for 3814s and similar devices as installations move to advanced channel technologies.

(References: 52, 55.)

QUESTION 95—CONFIGURING I/O SUBSYSTEMS FOR MAXIMUM AVAILABILITY

Advances in technology have improved the reliability of I/O subsystems over the years. Nevertheless, equipment can fail. How can tape and DASD subsystems be configured to maximize availability?

The main principle to follow is to eliminate single points of failure. That is, to configure I/O subsystems so that the failure of any one component does not inhibit access to devices. Then the impact of a component failure is usually no worse than degraded performance, and this can be handled either by tolerating it or by rescheduling some jobs to temporarily reduce the workload. At least those applications the installation deems most important can continue to run.

From reference 93:

Before placing a system into operation, an installation should plan the input/output (I/O) device configuration for maximum availability and to provide the maximum capability for reconfiguration. I/O configuration planning concerns the number of paths to each device and the hardware elements in each path.

MULTIPLE PATHS TO A DEVICE SHOULD IN-
CLUDE AS FEW COMMON HARDWARE ELEMENTS AS
POSSIBLE TO MINIMIZE THE EFFECT OF A MAL-
FUNCTION, THAT IS, TO PREVENT A SINGLE MAL-
FUNCTION FROM DISABLING ALL THE PATHS TO A
DEVICE.

Consistent with this recommendation, it has been standard policy in most MVS installations for years to provide at least two paths (channels / storage directors) to tape and DASD units. Current DASD devices can run in four-path mode, further increasing availability and performance by minimizing the impact of loss of a single path.

Even when multiple paths are configured, however, devices themselves can remain single points of failure. For some devices, such as tape/cartridge drives and printers, installations can configure multiple devices so that if one is unavailable, the remaining devices can handle the workload. However, in the case of DASD, the device itself, including the associated media, has historically been a single point of failure, unless applications were specifically designed to manage duplicate copies of data.

But this has now changed. The 3990-3 Storage Control offers a capability called *dual copy* that maintains a duplicate copy of the data on one volume on a different volume in the same subsystem. New and changed records are written to both volumes, while records are read just from one volume called the "primary" volume. If the primary volume becomes unavailable, the "secondary" volume is used—all of which happens transparent to applications. This feature makes it possible to completely eliminate all single points of failure in IBM DASD subsystems.

(References: 54, 93.)

QUESTION 96—LENGTH OF DASD STRINGS

A given installation has for years configured their DASD into short strings in order to improve performance. As they now plan for additional DASD they want to continue that configuration philosophy, even though you point out there are significantly lower costs for full strings. What are the reasons behind the preference for short strings, and are short strings still a meaningful strategy given advances in DASD technology?

Put simply, the reason installations have often configured short DASD strings—strings containing less volumes than the maximum possible—is to improve performance by spreading the I/O load across a greater number of paths. For example, rather than one long string of 16 DASD volumes trying to handle 100 I/O requests per second down one path, an installation could configure two short strings of 8 volumes each on separate paths, each string handling 50 I/Os per second. Less contention means less delays.

Today, technology offers DASD cache control units, four-way DASD pathing, and high-speed data transfer, all of which generally make long strings very practical. However, the history of how things were done in the past often seems to carry some weight in future decisions—not everyone has the experience to know the full capabilities of current technology. Therefore, the rest of this answer will be a discussion of the short string philosophy, helping uncover the problems it has solved in the past and how those problems are now solved by advanced technology.

In the Best of All Possible Worlds . . .

In the best of all possible worlds, every DASD volume would have a dedicated I/O path (or two, for availability's sake) to every attached processor. This would mean that any or all volumes could be actively connected to paths at the same time; maximum concurrency of path-related operations, such as data transfer, would be possible. Unfortunately, this ideal is not feasible with current costs and product offerings, so we have to manage sharing a small number of paths by a larger number of volumes which are configured into strings of different possible lengths.

Installations have often configured DASD into short strings in order to improve the concurrency of path-related operations. There are two different situations where this can be done. The first is when DASD strings are broken up into shorter strings and spread across a greater number of paths. The second is where DASD strings are broken up into shorter strings on the same paths.

1. *Spreading strings across multiple paths*
   Taking DASD volumes that are sharing or could share the same I/O paths and configuring them on different paths can improve performance by spreading the I/O load across all the paths. See Figure 12.7 for an example.

   Spreading activity across more paths has been and continues to be a legitimate way to minimize DASD path contention problems. This strategy is actually not so much concerned with string length, but rather with spreading control units across multiple paths. A given control unit only supports at most a fixed number of volumes (e.g., 64)—the cost of channels is low enough that most installations generally place only one or two DASD control units on a given set of channels.

   Spreading activity across as many paths as possible lowers individual path utilizations. This means a path will more likely be available when a new I/O request needs it. More important, how-

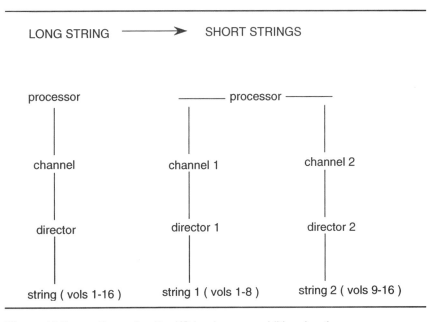

LONG STRING ⟶ SHORT STRINGS

processor	processor	
channel	channel 1	channel 2
director	director 1	director 2
string (vols 1-16)	string 1 (vols 1-8)	string 2 (vols 9-16)

Figure 12.7. Spreading the I/O load across additional paths.

ever, is the lessened probability of RPS misses. An RPS miss is an additional rotation that is required if paths are busy when a disk is in position to read or write data.

2. *Breaking long strings into short strings on the same paths*
    This is the less obvious strategy. In the past, there has sometimes been reason to break up long strings into short strings on the *same* paths. To understand why, it will help to review some history to explain the thinking that went into the short string strategy. We will then be able to assess whether this strategy is still valid with current technology. After all, short strings have a higher cost than long strings (more costly head-of-string units, possibly additional control units, usually more floor space), so they should only be implemented if and when there is a payoff.

History of Short Strings on the Same Paths

The historical reason for reconfiguring a long string into two or more short strings on the same path was to increase the amount of concurrency possible during disk I/O operations, thus improving DASD response time and throughput.

Within a string, any and all volumes can be concurrently seeking, or rotating to wait for the location of interest to come under the read/write heads. However, the number of volumes in a string that can be concurrently connected to I/O paths (transferring data, for example) is less than the number of volumes on a full string. 3350s, prevalent in the late 1970s and still found in some data centers, have only a single path per string, so that only one volume within a string of up to eight volumes can be actively connected to a host at any one time. If one volume is so connected, any of the other volumes on the 3350 string needing to connect to an I/O path have to wait for the first volume to disconnect. This means delays, and so degraded performance. And the problem is compounded if additional strings are sharing the same path.

Let's examine specific configurations to see when and how short strings can improve performance. Think of this as a leisurely stroll through recent DASD history.

*   *Case A—short 3350 strings on a single path*
    In this case, there is no benefit to short strings since only one volume can ever be connected to the path. See Figure 12.8.
*   *Case B—short strings on two (shared) string-switched paths*
    In this case, a long string is string-switched between two paths for availability. This is a very common 3350 configuration. However,

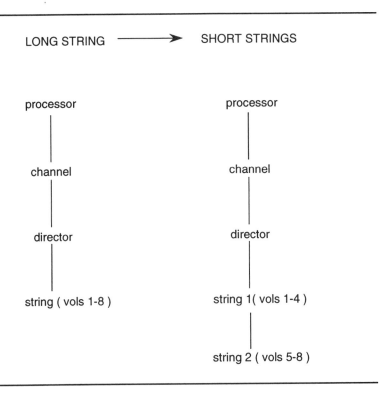

LONG STRING ⟶ SHORT STRINGS

processor

channel

director

string (vols 1-8)

processor

channel

director

string 1(vols 1-4)

string 2 (vols 5-8)

Figure 12.8. No performance gain for short 3350 strings on a single path.

still only one path-related operation can occur at one time for the one string (think of all the volumes in the string sharing the same wire). To achieve concurrency of up to two path-related operations, the long string can be reconfigured into two short strings on the same two paths. This allows two path-related operations to overlap, one from one string and a second from the other string. See Figure 12.9.

Note that the switch is connected (physically cabled) to both storage directors at all times, but the way it works is that only one volume within a given string can use one of the switch's paths at a time. Two volumes, one each from two strings, however, can use the paths concurrently.

So, unlike Case A, we now have a legitimate performance reason to replace a long string by two short strings on the same paths. It may even be desirable to place more than two short strings on the two paths. True, only a maximum of two concurrent data transfer

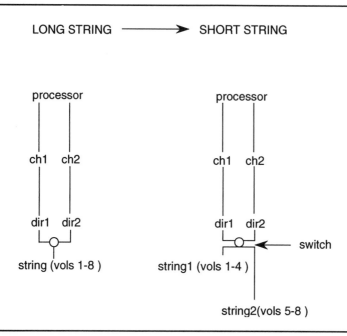

LONG STRING ⟶ SHORT STRING

Figure 12.9. Advantage of short strings when 3350s are string switched.

operations could still occur, but throughput is potentially increased since the possible combinations of volumes that can use the paths concurrently is greater. In other words, the greater the number of strings sharing the two paths, the more possible combinations of pairs of volumes that could be using paths at the same time.

Now, just because performance *could* be improved is not necessarily sufficient justification for short strings. The amount of improvement possible depends on the amount of path-related activity. And the amount of improvement needed depends on application service level requirements.

- *Case C—3380 standard models*
Standard 3380 models (AA4, B04) were the first 3380 models introduced by IBM. 3380s offered the Dynamic Path Selection (DPS) feature, which was similar to 3350 string switching in offering connections to two paths from one string but with the advantage that both paths could be used concurrently by two volumes in the *same* string.

However, internal paths within these units (still) posed restrictions on *which* pairs of volumes could be actively connected to paths at the same time. The longer the 3380 standard string, the greater the sharing of an internal path. So, as was done for 3350s, short strings of 3380 standard models were sometimes implemented on the same pair of channels to allow increased concurrency.

Even though 3380 standard models had internal paths, this was often offset by the fast data transfer speed relative to 3350s (3MB/second versus about 1.2MB/second). This lowered path utilization significantly over 3350s, which in itself helped make longer strings more feasible. Likewise, the Dynamic Path Reconnect (DPR) facility, new with 3380s when attached to processors in 370-Extended Architecture mode, reduced the effect of path utilization on RPS misses. Nevertheless, I/O workload growth and the goal of configuring for optimal performance still led many data centers to install short strings.

- *Case D—3380 D/E models*
  3380 extended capability models (AD4, AE4, BD4, and BE4) introduced a new feature called Device Level Selection (DLS). In contrast to 3350s and 3380 standard models, with DLS, any two volumes in the same string can be connected to the two associated I/O paths at the same time.

  With DLS, if 3380 long strings were reconfigured into short strings on the same two paths, there would be no performance benefit, because in each case there is no restriction over which two volumes can be concurrently transferring data. Thus 3380 D and E models offer the ability to configure maximum length strings without impacting performance. See Figure 12.10.

- *Case E—3390 and 3380 J/K models*
  3380 enhanced subsystem models (AJ4, AK4, BJ4, and BK4) can run in DLS or Device Level Selection Enhanced (DLSE) mode. 3390 DASD always runs in DLSE mode. In DLSE mode, up to four concurrent path-related activities are supported—twice that supported by DLS. This not only continues to make full length strings practical, but offers improved performance over DLS mode due to the increased number of paths available to each string. In fact, by placing a set of strings under a pool of four paths, significantly better performance is possible compared to having separate subsets of strings each accessing only two paths.

  Again, there is no advantage to multiple short strings versus one long string on the same set of channel paths.

- *Case F—implications of DASD cache*
  The electronic storage in a DASD cached control unit offers perfor-

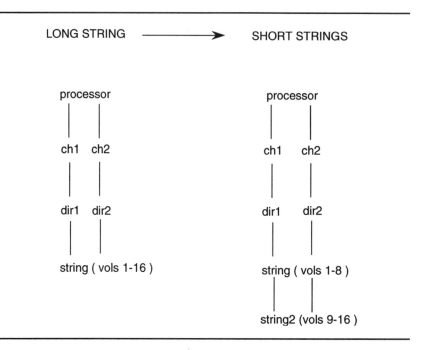

LONG STRING ⟶ SHORT STRINGS

processor

ch1   ch2

dir1   dir2

string (vols 1-16)

processor

ch1   ch2

dir1   dir2

string (vols 1-8)

string2 (vols 9-16)

Figure 12.10. No advantage to short 3380 D/E strings on the same paths.

mance far superior to that possible with uncached DASD by keeping frequently referenced data in the cache. References from the cache are thus very fast since mechanical delays are bypassed. In addition, the 3990 cache control unit can also take advantage of DLSE. These characteristics build upon the preceding arguments so that cache can almost always be backed by full strings of high-capacity devices while still delivering high performance.

Summary

The principle behind improving DASD performance by configuring short strings can be summarized as increasing the number of volumes that could potentially be doing path-related operations (mainly data transfer) at the same time. Two strategies have been employed. First, DASD volumes were spread across a greater number of paths; second, short strings were configured on the same shared paths.

Today's advanced DASD technology essentially eliminates the need for short strings to provide acceptable performance. Practical restrictions on concurrency have been all but eliminated; the DLSE feature (four-pathing) allows up to four concurrent data transfers from any four volumes in a string. Cache control units can offer improved performance compared to any short string configuration.

(References: 14, 15, 34, 53.)

QUESTION 97—TAPE CARTRIDGE LOADERS

IBM 3480 and 3490 cartridge tape subsystems support a cartridge loader facility to improve performance and operator productivity. How does MVS use the cartridge loader to advantage?

Cartridge loaders (ACLs)[52] may improve operator productivity by allowing the operator to premount up to five cartridges per drive in addition to a cartridge already mounted in the drive. This can improve performance by decreasing the amount of time jobs wait for tapes to be mounted.

The basic idea is to have the operator load up ACLs with empty tapes that MVS will select for creating new data sets. As an example, this could greatly speed up DASD dump processing since it may take multiple cartridges to hold the data on a single DASD volume. The operator could place all the empty cartridges needed in the ACL in one step, rather than responding to each message to mount an empty cartridge when the previous cartridge becomes full.[53]

The ACL can run in one of three modes, controlled by a switch on the ACL.

1. *Manual mode.* This mode allows either operator mounting of individual cartridges or operator-initiated automatic mounting of a premounted cartridge.
2. *Automatic mode.* This mode supports automatic mounting of cartridges under control of the ACL.

---

[52]We'll use the acronym ACL, for automated cartridge loader, for brevity, though the term is sometimes associated more with 3480 tape subsystems than with 3490 tape subsystems. The facility functions the same way in each case.

[53]The reason the ACL is designed to be used for stacking empty cartridges and not cartridges that are part of a multivolume data set is that in the latter case an error could occur such that the system would write over the data on the cartridges. See reference 37 for a discussion of this problem.

3. *System mode.* In this mode, automatic mounting of cartridges is under control of the host operating system. That is, the operating system can select the next volume from the ACL, or can request that a volume be mounted by the operator even though the selected drive has an active ACL ("active" means MVS is aware that the ACL contains cartridges in the input stack).

IBM recommends that MVS installations run in system mode. To understand how MVS supports system mode, we need to know that MVS distinguishes between three types of tape requests:

"specific," for tapes with specific volume serial numbers; usually, these are requests for tapes containing existing data sets, (e.g., DISP=OLD in JCL).

"PRIVAT," for nonspecific tapes on which nontemporary data sets will be placed (e.g., DISP=(NEW,KEEP) in JCL; the next request for this tape would often be a "specific" request).

"SCRTCH," for nonspecific tapes on which temporary data sets will be placed (e.g., DISP=(NEW,DELETE) in JCL; such tapes may remain mounted and be reused for other SCRTCH requests).

The terms PRIVAT and SCRTCH appear just that way in messages asking the operator to mount tapes. For specific mount requests, MVS places the desired volume serial in the message.

Here's how MVS supports the ACL in system mode in a JES2 environment, and in a JES3 environment when device allocation is not controlled by JES3.[54] For a (nonspecific) PRIVAT request, MVS will allocate

1. An active ACL drive, if available, else
2. An inactive ACL drive, if available, else
3. Any cartridge drive that is available.

For a (nonspecific) SCRTCH request or a specific request, MVS will allocate

1. A non-ACL cartridge drive, if available, else
2. An inactive ACL drive, if available, else
3. Any cartridge drive that is available.

(Reference: 37.)

---

[54] In a JES3 environment when JES3 controls device allocation, it is possible to achieve effects similar to those in a JES2 environment. See reference 37.

QUESTION 98—REDUCING MACHINE ROOM FLOOR SPACE REQUIREMENTS

A data center needs to install additional I/O equipment to support new applications. However, initial planning indicates that there is just not enough floor space in the current machine room for the new devices. In what ways might the data center address this problem?

The problem of insufficient floor space for data processor hardware is becoming increasingly common as needs for data processing capacity continue to grow. While building a new, larger machine room is always the ultimate solution, that option is not always available at lowest cost.

There are two basic approaches to dealing with this problem: (1) using existing floor space more efficiently, and (2) placing selected equipment in locations outside of the machine room.

Using Existing Floor Space More Efficiently

- One tactic is to reexamine the current configuration to see if room for new devices could be created by repositioning installed equipment. Perhaps some equipment could be moved closer together while still observing service clearances.
- Some installations save space by stacking 3X74 terminal control units on specially constructed racks.
- Replacing older or lower-capacity equipment with newer technology can often buy back significant floor space. For example, you might consider

  Replacing multiple slow-speed printers with fewer high-speed printers.

  Using four-path (DLSE) DASD such as the 3390 and/or cached DASD control units such as the 3990. Four-path DASD and cache not only provide superior performance, but also make it practical to configure full-length, high-capacity DASD strings rather than short strings, which may reduce the number of control units required.

  Replacing installed DASD with high-capacity models such as the 3390 or the 9340. In particular, IBM's 3390-9 DASD offers a capacity of 8.5GB per volume, and up to over half a terabyte(!) of capacity in a single 3990/3390-9 subsystem. While the technology needed to deliver this capacity results in slower performance compared to other 3390 models, the 3390-9 is very suitable for applications such as DFSMShsm migration, image processing, and others that do not need the highest possible performance.

Using the 3995 Models 151 or 153 Optical Library Dataservers. These devices use high-capacity optical disks to store data in a 3390-compatible format. Hundreds of gigabytes of capacity are provided in a relatively small floor space. This solution has a low cost per megabyte compared to standard DASD, but also has slower performance characteristics and so is mainly suitable for applications that can tolerate this slower performance.

Replacing older reel-to-reel tape drives by tape cartridge subsystems, especially the 3490, which can reduce the space required for both the drives and the supporting library.

Employing capabilities on 3480/3490 cartridge drives to increase cartridge capacity. This may reduce the number of cartridges needed in a library, thus reducing library floor space. This technique is useful when a library contains many multivolume data sets, often the case for DASD volume dumps and other large data sets.

1. The 3480/3490 Improved Data Recording Capability (IDRC) can improve cartridge capacity typically by three to five times or more.

2. The 3490 Enhanced Capability models (3490E) use high-density recording techniques that double the amount of data on a cartridge.

3. Finally, the 3490E models support an Enhanced Capacity Cartridge System Tape that further doubles the capacity on a cartridge through use of a longer tape.

These techniques can be employed together for maximum benefit.

- Less obvious than new hardware technology, software techniques to manage existing DASD and tape capacity more efficiently can save floor space. Managing DASD space through DFSMS/MVS with techniques such as migration of unreferenced data sets can reduce overall DASD capacity requirements. Moving small data sets from tape to DASD can reduce tape library size (see Question 28—Reducing Tape Processing).

Techniques to Locate Equipment Remotely

- Users may do enough printing to warrant their own remote printers managed through JES RJE techniques, perhaps reducing the number of printers needed in a central machine room.

- Newer technology can be used to extend the maximum distance between channels and control units that is supported through the older bus-and-tag copper cabling technology that was originally introduced in the 1960s; this distance has never been greater than 400 feet and is less in some cases. Extended distances offer great flexibility in placing equipment.

The strategic solution to extend this distance is Enterprise Systems Connection (ESCON) technology. With ESCON, bulky and heavy copper cabling is replaced by thin, lightweight fiber optic cables. Control units that support standard ESCON attachment may be placed up to 3 kilometers (about 1.9 miles) from the channel in the mainframe; this can be extended to 9 kilometers (about 5.6 miles) using intermediate ESCON Directors that redrive the signal to achieve the greater distance. Converters exist that can attach control units that don't support ESCON cabling to processors with ESCON channels; that lowers the maximum distance supported but does offer considerable relief from the 400-foot limit imposed by copper bus and tag cabling.

The ESCON Extended Distance Feature (XDF) can be used to extend channel-to-control unit distances beyond 9 kilometers. The maximum distance varies by control unit type. For example, an IBM 3490 tape subsystem can be located up to 23 kilometers from a channel using XDF.

ESCON technology offers other advantages besides distance, such as improved device switching capabilities and improved performance, making it the technology of choice for channel-to-control unit connections.

See Question 93—Benefits of ESCON Architecture for more information about ESCON.

(References: 48, 49, 51, 55, 102.)

13

Reliability, Availability, Serviceability

The system attributes of reliability, availability, and serviceability are often referred to by the acronym RAS. Simply put, in what can be called the ABCs of RAS: reliability is Avoiding failures, availability is Bypassing failures, and serviceability is Correcting failures.

In other words, by design, system components should rarely break. When they do, the effect on the overall system from the point of view of users should be minimal. And problems should be easy to diagnose and repair. Stated yet another way, RAS means fault avoidance, fault tolerance, and fault correction.

RAS has been an important principle in large systems design for many years, and is a significant attribute of IBM systems. RAS will continue to be key as more and more installations strive for increased, even continuous, system availability.

Availability in particular has received increasing focus in recent years. In the early days of data processing prior to online systems, work was run as batch jobs, and data processing was mainly confined to workers within a data center and periodic printed reports sent to management. With the advent of online systems, data processing has proliferated throughout an enterprise. Consider, for example, how many businesses have roomfuls of employees entering product orders into terminals, or executives entering data base queries into terminals on their desks in order to display current sales information in graphic form.

And awareness of an enterprise's data processing system has not been limited to workers within the enterprise. Customers use systems indirectly when placing product orders through the telephone, or more directly when using automated teller machines.

This increasing role of data processing in daily business operations—this visibility of data processing beyond the traditional data center—has put the requirement on systems to approach what is called "continuous availability," minimizing any time that the system is perceived to be unavailable. From this point of view, improving reliability and serviceability can be seen as means to help achieve the real objective: continuous availability.

QUESTION 99—DEVICE INSTALLATION AND SYSTEM AVAILABILITY

Installations add or replace devices in their I/O configurations for reasons such as increased capacity and performance, and improved availability and environmental characteristics. Changing I/O configurations is not a trivial process. One problem in particular that installations have traditionally had to manage is the impact such changes have on system availability. With the growing requirement for near continuous system availability, installations are looking for ways to minimize down time. Describe the various steps involved in adding a new DASD subsystem (a control unit and disk drives) to the system—from physical installation through first use by an application—and identify existing hardware and software technologies that minimize any negative impact on system or application availability.

Here are steps that almost any installation has to follow in order to add a new DASD device to an I/O configuration. Of course, any particular installation will have additional steps and procedures to be followed that are tailored to the specific environment.

1. The DASD control unit must be connected to a processor channel. For control units and processors that support Enterprise Systems Connection (ESCON) cabling technology, this connection can be made while the system is active.

2. The DASD must be added to the control unit. For 3380J and 3380K DASD devices attached to a 3990 DASD Storage Control in DLSE (four-path) mode, once the first pair of "A" units is installed, additional units can be added at any time, nondisruptively. For 3390

DASD, once the first "A" unit is installed, additional units, or additional pairs of head disk assemblies (HDAs) within installed units can be added nondisruptively.

3. The DASD must be defined to both the processor channel subsystem and to the MVS operating system. This can be done dynamically, without impacting system availability, by using the Hardware Configuration Definition (HCD) facility in MVS. HCD provides an interactive interface under TSO/ISPF that is much easier to use than the batch-like facility it replaced (sometimes called an I/O gen). HCD can be used to define and test the consistency of a changed configuration definition. On command, HCD will invoke MVS services to update the software I/O configuration definition (i.e., control blocks), and HCD will invoke hardware facilities called *dynamic reconfiguration management* to update the hardware's representation of the I/O configuration as well. Dynamic reconfiguration management is supported on selected ES/9000 processor models.

4. The DASD must be initialized, that is, formatted—for example, the VTOC must be built on each volume. This is done using the ICKDSF utility.

5. Once the DASD is initialized, the installation specifies to MVS how the DASD will be used. The installation can (preferably) allow data sets to be allocated on the new DASD in a device-independent manner (that is, without users having to specify a device type, volume serial number, or other device-dependent attributes) through having data set allocation managed by DFSMS/MVS, the Data Facility Storage Management Subsystem/MVS. In this case, the storage administrator uses ISMF, the Interactive Storage Management Facility, to dynamically add each new DASD volume to a list of volumes eligible for data set allocation. Such a list of volumes is called a storage group; new storage groups can themselves be created on the fly if need be.

    When a new data set is created, it is assigned to one or more storage groups, and the system will allocate the data set on selected volumes within those groups based on criteria such as performance and available space. The rules that assign new data sets to storage groups are specified by the installation in automatic class selection (ACS) routines. The rules within these ACS routines can be changed dynamically.

6. At this point, the new DASD is ready for data set allocations. However, that doesn't necessarily mean that work in the system can immediately use it (no one said this was going to be trivial).

The typical batch job allocates new and existing data sets via JCL when the job is initialized and does not deallocate those data sets until the job is terminated. Such jobs cannot take advantage of DASD volumes that become available while the job is running.

Long-running subsystems have to be analyzed individually. As one example, TSO users frequently allocate data sets during their sessions and can use a new volume as soon as it is available. As another example, as of JES2 Version 4 Release 2, JES2 allows spool volumes to be added dynamically; on the other hand, dynamic allocation of JCL procedure libraries is not supported.

7. If existing data sets are to be moved to the new device, that can be done only when those data sets are not allocated to any jobs. Whether or not jobs using the data sets support dynamic allocation and deallocation depends on the job. Again, typical batch jobs do not support dynamic allocation in this way; however, some major subsystems do offer this kind of support. For example, CICS and IMS offer commands to deallocate a data base, then reallocate it (after it has been moved). Of course, between the time the data set or data base is deallocated and reallocated, users may not be able to submit related work, and that is definitely an availability impact.

(References: 88, 95, 131.)

QUESTION 100—HOT I/O AND MISSING INTERRUPTS

MVS can recognize and handle two unusual I/O subsystem conditions: hot I/O and missing interrupts. Before MVS handled these conditions, they were often responsible for causing the system to terminate abnormally. What are hot I/O and missing interrupts, and how are they related?

Hot I/O and missing interrupts are basically opposite, abnormal conditions.

Hot I/O is a hardware malfunction that causes repeated, unsolicited I/O interrupts. Undetected, such hot I/O interrupts can cause the system to loop or to exhaust the system queue area (SQA), which is part of MVS common storage.

A missing interrupt is the condition where an I/O interrupt is anticipated by MVS due to an outstanding I/O request, but the interrupt doesn't occur, generally due to a device malfunction. If such a condition were to remain undetected, the system or dependent applications could "hang," that is, wait indefinitely for an event that won't happen.

The IECIOSxx SYS1.PARMLIB member contains parameters that allow an installation to control how MVS handles hot I/O and missing interrupt conditions. The installation may choose between having the system automatically attempt recovery, or having the operator prompted to select a recovery action.

(References: 40, 84, 93.)

QUESTION 101—AUTOMATING AVAILABILITY MANAGEMENT

The Information/Management product provides support for managing problem and change management functions. Information on system availability generally has to be entered manually. For example, if MVS should abnormally terminate, a person would have to enter that information manually into Information/Management. However, there is a way to have availability information automatically communicated to Information/Management. How is that done?

The Resource Measurement Facility (RMF) includes a function called System Availability Management (SAM). SAM provides the means to record, track, and report software and hardware availability.

SAM has a "collector" that gathers data for both hardware and software problems. The collector can detect IPLs, stalls (e.g., hangs, waits, loops), and abnormal terminations of selected job names. The collector transfers the information to the Information/Management data base. For incidents the SAM collector does not detect, the user must manually enter problem records.

It is still the installation's responsibility to ensure that problems are opened manually when necessary and that problems are investigated, updated, and closed. (I suppose that if the system could automatically figure out the causes of problems, it could probably fix them, too.)

RMF's support of Information/Management via SAM is an example of how the MVS system and its related products continue to become increasingly integrated—what we mean by providing a "system solution."

(Reference: 94.)

QUESTION 102—MANAGING DASD TEMPORARY ERRORS

*An installation informs you that one of their DASD volumes is expe-
riencing repeatable, correctable data checks on a particular track.
There is concern that the error may become uncorrectable, and that
preventive action should be taken before that happens. Should the
IBM service representative be called?*

The installation can likely handle this problem itself by running the
Device Support Facilities program (ICKDSF). Details about hardware
error conditions are recorded in the SYS1.LOGREC data set and reported by the Environmental Record Editing and Printing (EREP) program. For many DASD models, reference 64 discusses appropriate
actions to take for different types of errors. It may be necessary for the
installation to reinitialize the entire volume or just to set "skip displace-
ment" control information on the one track to cause it to skip over a defect
in the media. In either case, the installation can perform this level of
maintenance without IBM assistance by running the ICKDSF program.

For 3380 and older DASD, the installation would identify the occurrence of repeated temporary errors by manually examining EREP reports. However, this procedure can be simplified and even automated
with 3390 DASD. 3390 DASD incorporates a self-diagnosis capability
that will issue a message to the system operator indicating that track
maintenance is needed.[55] The installation can then run ICKDSF manually or could automate the process by having NetView respond to the
message and invoke ICKDSF dynamically.

For both 3380 and 3390 DASD under a 3990 Storage Control, track
maintenance through ICKDSF can be done without disrupting availability of the data to applications. This works because the contents of
the track being maintained will be moved temporarily to a spare, "alternate" track on the volume, and accesses will be automatically redi-
rected to that location until maintenance is complete and the track
contents are restored. This allows maintenance to be scheduled by an
installation as soon as it is needed, rather than having to be postponed
until a time when applications will not need access to the data.

If the recommended recovery actions do not correct the problem, or

---

[55]The message is called a Service Information Message, or SIM. SIM messages
are also placed in SYS1.LOGREC for later reporting by EREP.

the recommended action itself is to call for service, then an IBM service representative should be contacted.

(References: 25, 64, 134.)

QUESTION 103—EXTENDED RECOVERY FACILITY (XRF)

Availability has become an increasingly important concern in managing online systems. System availability may directly impact business operations, with users including customers, suppliers, agents and distributors, as well as employees. Time for planned system outages may be difficult to schedule. Can you describe how the Extended Recovery Facility (XRF) in MVS can help increase the availability of online systems?

Extended Recovery Facility is a related set of programs that allow an installation to improve data availability for selected endusers running in CICS or IMS transaction subsystems. The related set of IBM software products that work together to make up XRF are MVS, VTAM and NCP, and either IMS or CICS. The basic principle behind XRF is the ability to duplex major hardware and software resources. Let's look at a typical XRF configuration and describe how availability is enhanced. See Figure 13.1.

Initially, IMS1 in CPC1 (central processor complex one) is "active," and all terminals are communicating with that IMS. IMS2 in CPC2 is called the "alternate." Through the shared log data set, IMS2 tracks the active IMS1. IMS2 also opens backup sessions for XRF terminals that log onto the active IMS. To maintain an environment identical to that in the active, IMS2 updates many control blocks in the alternate to reflect those in the active.

Assume IMS1 abnormally terminates (ABENDs). IMS2 detects this through lack of log activity and begins the "takeover." IMS2 then tells the NCP to switch the XRF network (i.e., the remote terminals in session with IMS1) to IMS2. The takeover is complete when all the users at XRF terminals are communicating with IMS2 and can enter transactions and receive replies from their IMS applications.

Essentially the same scenario would occur if MVS or VTAM in CPC1 had terminated abnormally, or even if CPC1 itself failed.

While configuring the active and alternative subsystems to run in

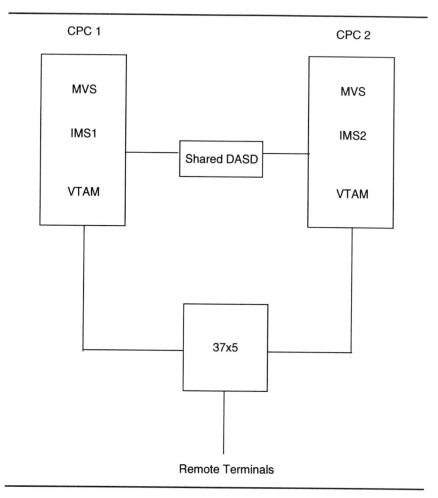

Figure 13.1. Example of an XRF configuration.

physically distinct processors maximizes availability, that is not a requirement. The two subsystems could reside in different PR/SM LPAR partitions on the same processor, or even within the same MVS image (which might be useful for testing).

The two images in an XRF configuration must share DASD so both can access the log and the data bases. Also, since the NCP participates in the takeover of the network, channel-attached cluster control units (e.g., local 3174s) are not included in the "XRF network." The system operator can initiate an XRF takeover at any time; this may be useful in providing continuous availability during a planned outage of one system.

When the alternate subsystem is running in a PR/SM logical partition, processor storage can be reconfigured from a neighboring partition to the alternate's partition, reducing the amount of processor storage required until a takeover occurs.

In closing, while XRF may not perform problem determination for an installation, it does reduce the pressure that exists in a non-XRF installation while the terminal users are without service during dumping and restarting.

(Reference: 99.)

QUESTION 104—QUANTIFYING THE ECONOMIC VALUE OF AVAILABILITY

An installation is evaluating alternative devices to support a major new application. The choice is now between device X and device Y. Availability ranks near the top of the installation's list of decision criteria since the devices would be shared by multiple users. The installation believes that device X has an average failure rate of .01 per year, and device Y a failure rate of .02 per year (in other words, on average, 1 out of every 100 X devices fails once a year). The installation is planning on installing 100 devices, either all X or all Y. Making reasonable assumptions, can you demonstrate a fairly simple method for quantifying the economic value of the lower failure rate of device X (or the "cost" to the installation of the higher failure rate of device Y)?

Here is one method of quantifying the benefits of higher availability or the costs of lower availability. The approach is to quantify the cost to the business of the lost productivity of users who are affected by the outage.

We are given 100 devices, either all type X or all type Y. X has a failure rate of .01 per year, and Y has a failure rate of .02 per year. Thus, on average, the number of failures of device type X that occur in one year for every 100 devices is 100 x .01 = 1. For Y, this is 100 x .02 = 2.

Assume that

- 500 users are affected by the outage of any one device.
- Each user is valued at $20/hour.
- The length of an outage is 2 hours.

Different numbers will likely apply in any particular situation.
Then the cost of a single outage of one device is:

```
500 users x ($20/user)/hour x 2 hours = $20,000.
```

Therefore the cost to the installation in terms of lost productivity is $20,000 per year if device X is installed, and $40,000 per year if device Y is installed (because Y will experience an average of two outages in one year). Device Y has a $20,000 per year greater cost with respect to availability than device X; or, in other words, device X may save the installation $20,000 year over device Y due to higher availability.

Some comments are in order. The fact that device Y has a $20,000 per year greater cost than device X relative to availability is a "hidden" cost—it is not part of the usual list price and so must be calculated using values appropriate to the installation. The analysis should be tailored to your particular needs. For example, it may be the case that different groups of users must be considered, perhaps because some can do other tasks during an outage, or because salary rates differ. These kinds of considerations should be incorporated if necessary but do not affect the basic technique.

(Reference: none.)

Program Product Version/Release Levels

The following list identifies major programs and the associated versions and/or release levels used in developing this guide. This list is not complete in that many other IBM program products are also referenced in this guide as well as many hardware products—but the following identifies the major products referenced here.

- Data Facility Sort (DFSORT) Release 12
- Data Facility Storage Management Subsystem/MVS Version 1 Release 1
- ICKDSF (Device Support Facilities) Release 14
- Integrated Catalog Forward Recovery Utility (ICFRU) Release 1
- ISPF/PDF Version 3 Release 5
- JES/328X Print Facility Version 2
- MVS/ESA System Product (MVS/ESA SP) Version 4 Release 3
- NetView File Transfer Program for MVS (NetView/FTP) Version 2
- Report Management and Distribution System (RMDS) Release 4
- Resource Access Control Facility (RACF) Version 1 Release 9
- Resource Measurement Facility (RMF) Version 4 Release 2
- Service Level Reporter (SLR) Version 3 Release 3
- System Display and Search Facility (SDSF) Release 3
- Target System Control Facility (TSCF) Release 1
- TSO Extensions (TSO/E) Version 2 Release 4

References

This section lists the publications that are referenced by the questions and answers in this guide.

Publications, unless otherwise noted, are available from the IBM Corporation.

1. *A Guide to the IBM 4381 Processor*, GC20-2021.
2. *Advanced Function Printing Software General Information*, G544-3415.
3. *An Introduction to Data-in-Virtual*, GG66-0259.
4. *Automated Console Operations for MVS/XA Systems*, GGG24-3142.
5. *Automated Operations Control/MVS General Information*, GC28-1080.
6. *Automated Systems Operations for High Availability: Concepts and Examples*, GG66-0260.
7. *Balanced Systems and Capacity Planning*, GG22-9299..
8. *Cache RMF Reporter Program Description Operations Manual*, SH20-6395.
9. *Capacity Planning and Performance Management Methodology*, GG22-9288.
10. *Capacity Planning Basic Hand Analysis*, GG22-9344.
11. *Capacity Planning Overview*, GG66-0254.
12. *Console Automation Using NetView*, SC31-6058.

13. *Customer Information Control System General Information,* GC33-0155.

14. *DASD Expectations,* GG22-9363. (Be sure to reference at least the "03" version of this manual.)

15. *DASD path and DDDEVICE Contention Considerations,* GG22-9217.

16. *Data Extract Version 2 General Information,* GC26-4241.

17. *Data Facility Data Set Services: User's Guide,* SC26-4388.

18. *Data Facility Hierarchical Storage Manager General Information,* GH35-0092.

19. *Data Facility Hierarchical Storage Manager Installation and Customization Guide,* SH35-0084.

20. *Data Facility Hierarchical Storage Manager System Programmer's Guide,* SH35-0085.

21. *Data Facility Hierarchical Storage Manager: User's Guide,* SH35-0093.

22. *Data Facility Sort Presentation Guide,* G360-2686.

23. *Data Facility Storage Management Subsystem,* G520-6624.

24. *Data Tables General Information,* GC33-0684.

25. *Device Support Facilities Primer for the User of IBM 3380 Direct Access Storage,* GC26-4498.

26. *DFDSM Presentation Guide,* GG24-3913.

27. *DFSMS Planning and Reporting with DCOLLECT,* GG24-3540.

28. *DFSMS Value Guide,* GG24-3311.

29. *DFSMS a World of Difference,* GG24-3598.

30. *DFSORT Benchmark Guide,* GG24-3019.

31. *The Economic Value of Rapid Response Time,* GE20-0752.

32. *Enterprise System/9000 Models 820 and 900 Functional Characteristics and Configuration Guide.* GA22-7139.

33. *ESA Exploitation by NIC Applications,* GG24-3539.

34. *Evolution of the DASD Storage Control,* G321-5355. (Reprint from the IBM Systems Journal Vol. 28, No, 2, 1989.)

35. *File Transfer Program Version 2 General Information,* GH12-5141.

36. *GRS Primer — MVS/ESA SSP Version 4,* GG66-3187.

37. *Guide to the IBM 3480 Automatic Cartridge Loader,* GG24-3094.

38. *Guide to the 3880 Storage Control Model 23,* GG24-1642.

39. *How JES2 uses SNA for RJE and NJE,* GG22-9378.

40. *IBM ES/3090 Complex Systems Recovery and Availability,* GG24-3343.

41. *IBM ES/3090 Complex Systems Recovery and Availability Configuration Considerations,* GG24-3340.

42. *IBM ES/3090 Models J and JH PR/SM Feature Presentation Guide*, GG24-3537.
43. *IBM Report Management and Distribution System: General Information Manual*, GC30-31191.
44. *IBM Systems Journal, Volume 29, No, 3, 1990.*, G321-0100. (This issue is devoted to image processing technology.)
45. *IBM 3090 Performance: A balanced system approach*, G321-52259. (Reprint from the IBM Systems Journal Vol. 25, No. 1, 1986.)
46. *IBM 3090 Processor Complex: Planning and Installation Reference*, GG66-3090.
47. *The IBM 3090 System: An overview*, G321-5258. (Reprint from the IBM Systems Journal Vol. 25, No. 1, 1986.)
48. *IBM 3390 Direct Access Storage Introduction*, GCC26-4573.
49. *IBM 3480 Magnetic Tape Subsystem Introduction*, GA32-0041.
50. *IBM 3480 Tape Subsystem: Performance Considerations*, GG22-9335.
51. *IBM 3490 Magnetic Tape Subsystem Models A01, A02, A10, A20, B02, B04, B20, and B40 Introduction*, GA32-0125.
52. *IBM 3814 Switching Management System Product Description*, GA22-7075.
53. *IBM 3990 Storage Control and DASD Performance and Configuration Guidelines*, GG24-3361.
54. *IBM 3990 Storage Control Introduction*, GA32-0098.
55. *Introducing Enterprise Systems Connection*, GA23-0383.
56. *Introducing the IBM 9370 Information Systems*, GA24-4030.
57. *Introduction to Large Processor Capacity and Performance Evaluation*, GG66-0232.
58. *ISPF/PDF General Information*, GC34-4250.
59. *ISPF/PDF Guide,* SC34-41135.
60. *ISPF/PDF Software Configuration and Library Manager (SCLM) Guide and Reference*, SC34-42254.
61. *JES/328X Print Facility Version 2*, G320-9500.
62. *Job Networking Facilities*, GG22-9042.
63. *LANRES/MVS General Information*, GC24-5625.
64. *Maintaining IBM Storage Subsystem Media*, GC26-4495.
65. *Managing Data Availability in an Integrated Catalog Facility Environment*, GG66-02112.
66. *Multiple Operating Systems on One Processor Complex*, G321-55350. (Reprint from the IBM Systems Journal Vol. 28, No 1., 1989.)
67. *Multiple Virtual Storage (MVS) Virtual Storage Turning Cookbook*, G320-0597.

68. *MVS/Bulk Data Transfer Facility Version 2 General Information*, GC23-0223.
69. *MVS/Data Interfile Transfer, Testing, and Operations Utility User's Guide and Reference*, SH19-6112.
70. *MVS/DFFP Interactive Storage Management Facility User's Guide*, SC26-4563.
71. *MVS/DFP Managing Catalogs*, SC26-4555.
72. *MVS/DFP Managing VSAM Data Sets*, SC26-4568.
73. *MVS/DFP Storage Administration Reference*, SCC26-4566.
74. *MVS/ESA and RACF Version 1 Release 9 Security Implementation Guide*, GG24-3585.
75. *MVS/ESA Application Development Guide: Assembler Language Programs*, GC28-1644.
76. *MVS/ESA Application Development Guide: Batch Local Shared Resources Subsystem*, GC28-1672.
77. *MVS/ESA Application Development Guide: Extended Addressability*, GC28-1652.
78. *MVS/ESA Application Development Guide: Hiperbatch*, GC28-1843.
79. *MVS/ESA Callable Services for High Level Languages*, GC28-1843.
80. *MVS/ESA Data Administration Guide*, SC26-4505.
81. *MVS/ESA Data in Memory Concepts and Facilities*, GG24-3404.
82. *MVS/ESA and Data in Memory Performance Studies*, GG24-3698.
83. *MVS/ESA Initialization and Turning Guide*, GC28-1634.
84. *MVS/ESA Initialization and Turning Reference*, GC28-1635.
85. *MVS/ESA JES2 Commands*, GC23-0084.
86. *MVS/ESA JES2 Introduction*, GC23-0080.
87. *MVS/ESA JES3 Introduction*, GC23-0077.
88. *MVS/ESA Planning: Dynamic I/O Configuration*, GC28-1674.
89. *MVS/ESA Planning: Global Resource Serialization*, GC28-1621.
90. *MVS/ESA Planning: Operations*, GC28-1625.
91. *MVS/ESA Planning: Security*, GC28-1604.
92. *MVS/ESA Planning: Sysplex Management*, GC28-1620.
93. *MVS/ESA Recovery and Reconfiguration Guide*, GC28-1624.
94. *MVS/ESA Resource Measurement Facility Version 4 General Information*, GC28-1028.
95. *MVS/ESA SP Version 4 Technical Presentation Guide*, GG24-3594.
96. *MVS/ESA System Management Facilities (SMF)*, GC28-1628.

97. *MVS/ESA System Programming Library: JES2 Initialization and Turning Guide*, SC23-0082.

98. *MVS/ESA System Programming Library: JES3 Initialization and Turning*, SC23-0073.

99. *MVS/Extended Architecture Planning: Extended Recovery Facility (XRF)*, GC28-1139.

100. *MVS Paging Performance Considerations*, GG22-9264.

101. *MVS Performance Management*, GG22-9351.

102. *MVS Storage Management Library*, SBOF-3126. This is a collection of related publications discussing how people, procedures, and IBM products can be used to implement a system-managed storage (SMS) environment effectively. Ordering by the Bill-of-Forms number includes all manuals plus a binder. Members of this library include:

    MVS Storage Management Library: Focus on Storage Management, GC26-4655.

    MVS Storage Management Library: Lending an Effective Storage Administration Group, SC26-4658

    MVS Storage Management Library: Managing Storage Pools, SC26-4656

    MVS Storage Management Library: Managing Data Sets and Objects, SC25-46577

    MVS Storage Management Library: Project Planning for Storage Management, GV26-1022

    MVS Storage Management Library: Storage Management Reader's Guide, GC26-4654

    MVS Storage Management Library: Storage Management Subsystem Migration Planning Guide, SC26-4659

103. *MVS/TSO Dynamic STEPLIB Facility*, G320-9522.

104. *NetView File Transfer Program General Information*, GH12-5480.

105. *Netview Performance Monitor at a Glance*, GH20-6359.

106. *Network Job Entry Concepts and Protocols Overview*, GG66-0224.

107. *NJE with JES2 and Other Systems (JES3, RSCS, VSE/POWER, and OS/400)*, GG22-9339.

108. *Operating MVS/XA in Multi-image Environments*, GG24-3274.

109. *Operations Planning and Control/ESA General Information*, GH19-6715.

110. *OS/VS VSAM Data Set Sharing*, GG22-9043.

111. *Preparing for System Managed Storage*, GG24-1724.

112. *Presentation Guide for Integrated Catalog Forward Recovery Utility Program Number: 5798-DXQ*, GG66-0249.

113. *Processor Storage Estimation*. (A document by Gary M. King of IBM Enterprise Systems, first presented as "Processor Storage Estimation" at Guide 70 session SY-7708B.)

114. *Resource Access Control Facility (RACF) General Information Manual*, GC28-0722.

115. *Resource Access Control Facility (RACF) Security Administrator's Guide*, SC28-1340.

116. *Response Time Data Gathering*, GG24-32112.

117. *Service Level Reporter Version 3 General Information*, GH19-6529.

118. *Service Level Reporter Version 3 User's Guide: Performance Management*, SH19-6442. (In addition to information about SLR, there is an interesting discussion on how to approach performance management as a discipline.)

119. *Service Levels: A Concept for the User and the Computer Center*, G321-5040. (Reprint from IBM Systems Journal Vol. 15, No. 4, 1976.)

120. *The Small-Data-Set-Packing Data Set Primer*, GG66-0295.

121. *SNAP/SHOT An Executive Perspective of Capacity Planning*, G520-0083.

122. *Storage Hierarchies*, G321-5348. (Reprint from IBM Systems Journal Vol. 28, No. 1, 1989.)

123. *System Display and Search Facility General Information*, GC23-0406.

124. *System-Managed Storage Technical Overview Presentation Guide*, GG24-3201.

125. *Systems and Network Operation Automation Using NetView Release 3*, GG22-9112.

126. *Systems and Products Guide*, G320-6300.

127. *Target System Control Facility Announcement Presentation*, GG24-3608.

128. *Target System Control Facility General Information*, GC28-1063.

129. *TSO/E Version 2 Command Reference*, SC28-1881.

130. *TSO/E Version 2 General Information*, GC28-1869.

131. *Using IBM 3390 Direct Access Storage in an MVS Environment*, GC26-4574.

132. *Using RMF Version 3 Release 5 Monitor III*, GG24-1674.

133. *3270 Information Display System 3174 Subsystem Control Unit*, GA23-0218.

134. *3990/3390 Storage Subsystem Service Information Messages & Concurrent Media Maintenance*, GG66-3198.
135. *7171 ASCII Device Attachment Control Unit Description and Planning Guide*, GA24-4019.

Index